ILLINOIS

By
WILLIAM A. L. BEYER, A.M.
Head of Department of Social Science
Illinois State Normal University
Normal, Illinois

LAIDLAW BROTHERS
Publishers

Chicago   San Francisco   New York

OUR DEVELOPING CIVILIZATION

A Textbook in Civics

FUNDAMENTALS OF CITIZENSHIP

G. L. BLOUGH, M.A.
Instructor in the Social Sciences
Joliet Township High School and
Junior College
Joliet, Illinois

C. H. McCLURE, PH.D.
Formerly Head of the Department
of Social Sciences
State Teachers College
Kirksville, Missouri

LAIDLAW BROTHERS
Publishers
CHICAGO NEW YORK SAN FRANCISCO
DALLAS   ATLANTA

The National Capitol, Washington, D. C.

TEACHER PREFACE

The *Fundamentals of Citizenship* is part of the series
OUR DEVELOPING CIVILIZATION—a series designed to stimulate the pupil's interest in the social studies, to develop in
him an appreciation of how the world in which he lives has
grown out of the past, and to aid him in adapting himself
to the complexities of modern society. *Fundamentals of
Citizenship* is planned particularly to give the pupil an
understanding of his relationship to his ever expanding
circle of interests—including himself, his family, his other
social groups, his community, and finally his various governmental units, local, state, and national.

OBJECTIVES. The purpose of teaching Civics is to make
worthy citizens. Such teaching should *inform, inspire,* and
challenge pupils to their sense of duty and responsibility
to themselves and to their fellowmen. The objectives of
teaching Citizenship are: (1) to inform the individual
about his social environment, whose rules and laws guide
and protect him for his own good; (2) to inspire him to
realize that he is an important member of his community
and of society at large, and that as he grows older, his
help is awaited; and (3) to challenge him to do his part
sincerely and courageously. The result of such teaching
will cause young citizens to recognize the fact that although
they have privileges, they also have duties and responsibilities.

Because the way civic institutions function is more important than the mere organization of the institution, the
teaching of citizenship must be made purposeful, practical,
and real. The relationship of the individual to the family,
school, community, and government is emphasized. It is

5

natural for the individual to desire to express himself and to want to have an active part in the affairs about him. With these objectives in mind this textbook has been written. Self-expression and self-activity form the keynote of the book.

ORGANIZATION. *Fundamentals of Citizenship* consists of four parts. The theme in Part One is the individual's responsibility to himself; in Part Two it is the individual's relationships as a member of different groups, such as the family, school, and community; in Part Three it is the community working through the individual citizens; in Part Four it is the individual's responsibility to his government.

The book attains its aims by the following definite procedures:

1. *The individual pupil* becomes the center of discussion. Facts are stated in his own language and practical references are made to his own level of experiences.

2. *Practical ideals* are held up constantly for the pupil's assimilation. Open-mindedness, critical-mindedness, and social-mindedness are recognized as the keynote of his education. He is challenged to do his own thinking at all times and to evaluate his personal development as a growing citizen.

3. *Individual differences* constitute a major problem of class instruction. They are constantly kept in mind and definitely shape the exercises at the end of each chapter. The *Test Exercises* of each chapter are based almost entirely on that chapter and so should be the minimum requirement for all pupils. The *Suggested Activities* contain items which may tax the ability of the more capable pupils. However, they are all within the interest range of normal pupils. The more resourceful pupils should do the investigating and report their findings to the class. They should do more outside reading from the suggested books.

They may keep individual notebooks. The less resource-ful pupils may omit some of the *Suggested Activities*. A class scrapbook may be more suitable for their talents than the individual notebook.

4. Various *pupil helps* are found in each chapter. The *Preparatory Notes* contain a summary of those points in the chapter which a teacher would call to the attention of pupils for their study guidance. The *Aids to Learning* are a statement of the essentials of each chapter. The *Test Exercises* are in the form of completion, matching, multiple choice, or question exercises and are graded to the ability of the normal pupil. The *Suggested Activities* are prob-lems for either individual or group consideration. They cover many fields of interest associated with different fields of study, especially history, literature, and the other social studies.

5. The *vocabulary* is carefully chosen so as to be well within the understanding of the average pupil. The less common words, which are nevertheless necessary for the adequate expression of the ideas, are either explained in the context or defined in footnotes. The *Explanation of Terms,* added to the text material, gives more detailed explanation to less common or technical terms. The sen-tence structure is carefully adapted to the age level so as not to occasion difficulty in understanding.

6. *Many interesting facts* are added to the text which will contribute to the pupil's interest. Here is a *Compen-dium of Civic Information* containing hundreds of up-to-date civic facts on the state and nation, including detailed state qualifications for voting. There is also a valuable section on the use of the *Flag.*

7. *Illustrations* of various kinds are used. A number of pictographs and other charts and graphs vividly illustrate the text. Pertinent photographs and original drawings also add to the pupil's interest and understanding.

TEACHING AIDS. The following suggested aids will stimulate interest and activity in the classwork.

1. *Class organization.* A class may be organized with its officers and committees for the purpose of developing parliamentary practice and the spirit of co-operation.

2. *Class scrapbook or notebook.* A large book may be maintained to which any pupil may contribute according to his talents and interests.

3. *Occasional debates.* Current topics or issues debated in class instruct, inspire, and challenge pupils to further study.

4. *Bulletin board.* A bulletin board in the classroom for notices of civic occurrences has many advantages.

5. *Elections.* On election day sample ballots may be obtained and an election can be conducted in the classroom.

6. *Court trials.* To conduct a mock trial in the classroom, with a jury and necessary officers, is instructive and interesting.

7. *Field trips.* In a city many institutions can be visited with great advantage.

8. *Officers' day.* Many cities set aside a civic day for pupils to conduct the duties of regular city officers for an hour that day.

THE AUTHORS.

CONTENTS

PART I

The Citizen as an Individual

PART II

The Citizen as a Member of a Group

PART III

The Community Working Through Its Citizens

9

PART IV

Your Government and Its Citizens

PART I

THE CITIZEN AS AN INDIVIDUAL

Every boy or girl born in the United States and every man or woman born here or naturalized here is a citizen of this country unless, for some reason or other, he or she has given up that citizenship. Citizenship is a possession which people have worked hard for and waited long to secure. You have it as a priceless gift if you were born in this country or if your parents are naturalized citizens here. There are certain qualities which you, as a citizen, should possess if you are to get the most out of your life. These qualities will be discussed in the first part of this study of citizenship.

Determination stands first among the qualities that count most in life. This will-to-do has been the driving force behind many of the poor immigrants who have overcome obstacles in their path, and who, in this way, have proved that even poverty may be no barrier to progress. But determination alone is not sufficient. It must be properly directed.

11

The desire to render a real service to others must accompany this determination if you are to have a well-rounded life. Edward Bok is a splendid example of the proper combination of these qualities. As a youth he came to this country from Holland almost penniless, but with an eagerness for an education which made him continue to learn, even after he had begun his business career. Success came to him because of his determination to make the most of his life. As an editor and publisher he reached a position of great influence. After nearly half a century of active business he began spending his fortune in the service of his fellow men.

Faith in yourself should also be added to determination and the desire to render service to others, as an important quality for your success. Belief in the value of his product is necessary for the successful salesman. Belief in yourself is even more necessary. If you possess this kind of faith in yourself you will exert a strong influence on all whom you meet. These three qualities play an important part in developing the type of citizenship needed in our country.

The success you have in gaining these qualities will depend to a great extent upon your *physical, mental,* and *moral fitness,* and also your *economic* and *civic efficiency.* So first of all, you should consider how you may secure the highest degree of satisfaction as well as success in life, through the development of these stepping stones.

CHAPTER I

PHYSICAL FITNESS

Preparatory Note: As you read this chapter you will realize that you cannot put too high a value on good health no matter what you do in life. But good health consists of more than bodily strength. It includes physical health, mental health, and also emotional health. As a rule, no one of these comes merely by chance. They all are the results of careful efforts on your part, formed by right habits of living.

Value and Importance of Health. A great physician defined health as "the quality of life that renders the individual fit to live most and to serve best." You are a healthy person if you have a sound mind in a sound body. If you have no disease or physical defects, you should have an abundance of energy. Health is the condition of living physically and mentally at the highest level of which you are capable.

Health is the first objective because all else depends on it. Good health means an active, joyous life. It includes emotional fitness or self-control as well as mental and physical fitness. Your success in school and on the athletic field depends on your good health. It enables you to work better and to enjoy life more and to live longer.

Physical Health. To keep physically fit you should have the determination to keep healthy. This may take constant effort and the use of a considerable time for the proper activities.

In addition to this determination there should be an adequate understanding of the reasons for good health, what constitutes it, and how it is retained. You should understand something about the structure of the body, or *anatomy;* the way in which organs of the body function, or *physiology;* and the rules for the preservation of good health, or *hygiene.*

And then you must form good health habits. You must act according to your knowledge and desire for health if you are to be benefited. In other words, you must practice the rules of health. Your concern now will be with the last of these three points—the formation of good health habits.

Health Habits. Health is governed by the practice of wise habits. The basic health habits are concerned with eating, sleeping, working, playing, and having a good posture. If you form regular habits concerning the use of the right kind and amount of food, sleep, work, and play, as well as correct posture, you should be in good health. It is estimated that a fair distribution of your time should be eight hours for work, at least eight or nine hours for sleep, and the remaining hours for recreation and duties not included in work or sleep.

Many men and women with physical handicaps have been made strong by the regular practice of good health habits. Theodore Roosevelt, formerly the president of the United States, was a good example of this change. As a boy, he was frail and sickly. Indeed, it seemed impossible that he could ever become a strong

© *Underwood & Underwood*

Theodore Roosevelt on a Ranch

man. His later health and strength, which you recognize in this illustration, were due to his faithful, strenuous practice of health habits. He had the will to persist in following the rules of health, which he knew he should follow.

The trend in the field of medicine is to prevent as well as to cure disease. The forming of health habits is a big step in this direction. Habits are usually formed through practice. This requires will power. First, decide what health habits you want to form and make a written or mental list of them. Second, be determined to practice these habits regularly and without exception. Third, ask your friends and folks at home to help you; they can do this in many ways. Fourth, keep a record of the progress you have made.

According to most authorities the following essential health habits should form the basis for your health program. Make a list of those you already practice, and watch your progress.

Food. Chew your food well. Do not overeat. Do not eat between meals. Eat ripe fruits and green vegetables often. Eat food suitable to your digestive system; that which is easily digested by one person may cause trouble for another person.

Drink. Drink plenty of fresh, pure water. Drink at least one pint of milk daily. Drink no stimulants, such as coffee or tea. Drink no alcoholic liquors.

Sleep. Sleep with the windows open to supply plenty of fresh air. Be sure to get at least eight or nine hours of sleep each night. Relax mentally.

Exercise. Spend at least one hour daily out-of-doors. Do not take too violent exercise at any time, especially right after eating. Never go in swimming sooner than two hours after eating.

Posture. Stand erect. Sit erect. Walk erect. Do not lean on anything. Wear comfortable shoes.

Cleanliness. Use soap and water freely and often. Do not eat a meal without first washing your hands. Use an individual towel and washcloth. Brush your teeth at least twice a day. Keep your finger nails clean, and do not bite them. Keep your hair and scalp clean. Keep your clothes clean.

Recreation. Allow yourself the proper amount of time for play. Take this recreation outdoors, if possible. Enter into at least one sport until you can thoroughly enjoy it.

Mental Health. Mental health is as important as bodily health. Mental health requires that you possess the state of mind in which you are capable of doing your best work. Living with the least possible friction will help you to think clearly. The following suggestions may be helpful to you in maintaining mental health. Practice these and you can develop a personality that will be pleasing to those with whom you come in contact:

Learn to understand yourself, your interests, and your abilities.

Avoid worry, as it makes matters seem worse.

Cultivate cheerfulness; this will aid your progress.

Work hard and play hard.

Develop self-control as it leads to mastery.

Health in the Home. Your parents will help you to maintain a routine which will establish in your life these simple and essential habits. Your home has the first responsibility for preparing you for school, and the school has an interest in aiding your home to maintain its own standard of healthfulness. Improved health in the home is one assurance of better health among children in and out of school.

Since much of your time is spent at home, it is essential that your home be healthful and comfortable. Your parents will give careful attention to such ways as these for making the home healthful:

The site for the house should be high enough to allow for good drainage.

Great care should be used when installing the plumbing and sewage system.

If there is a cellar, it should be kept sanitary by providing a cement floor, by whitewashing the walls of the cellar, and by securing proper ventilation.

There should be plenty of window space in the house to admit sunlight and air.

The kitchen, where the food is prepared, should be kept clean.

The bathroom should be airy and sanitary.

Heating and ventilating should be carefully regulated. The temperature should be about 70° F. The air should be kept fresh, moist, and circulating.

The lighting of the rooms in which you read should be sufficient so that you will not strain your eyes.

Test and Study Exercises

Aids to Learning.

1. Remember that health is secured by the practice of wise habits.

2. Habits are formed as a rule through practice, which requires the use of will power.

3. You have seen that mental health is as important as bodily health.

Test Exercises.

On a separate sheet of paper write the following sentences, supplying the missing words.

1. Physiology describes the way in which the ____ of the ____ work effectively.

2. Anatomy describes the ____ of the ____.

3. Hygiene consists of the rules for the ____ ____ ____ ____.

4. Food should be ____ well.

5. You should sleep at least ____ ____ ____ hours each night.

6. A temperature of ____ degrees is considered satisfactory if the air is kept ____ and ____.

7. Good health includes ____, ____, and ____ fitness.

8. A well-built house has plenty of ____ space.

9. To avoid worry is a part of a program of ____ hygiene.

Suggested Activities.

1. The teacher may assign a pupil to make a study of his own neighborhood, to learn what can be done to promote better health. This may include consideration of (*a*) drinking water, (*b*) street cleaning, (*c*) sanitation.

2. (*a*) Study the life of Theodore Roosevelt to see how he overcame poor health as a boy. You may refer to some such book as, *Boys' Life of Theodore Roosevelt,* by Hermann Hagedorn. (*b*) How did Theodore Roosevelt continue his pursuit of physical vigor even when president?

3. *Group Activity:* The class may draw up a list of health habits which they believe they should practice regularly.

4. *Group Activity:* The teacher may have several pupils keep a chart of the temperature in their homes every day for a week, to see whether it is satisfactory.

CHAPTER II

MENTAL FITNESS

PREPARATORY NOTE: Perhaps you have wondered why you should go to school. In what way will school contribute to your happiness? School people have puzzled over the answers to these questions for many years. Skills, attitudes, and ideals should be secured. Habits should be formed. In short, you will need the right kind of personality if you are to get the best results out of your education. This chapter will help you find ways to develop yourself.

Purposes of an Education. Education is growth. Schools exist to help young people until they are able to continue their own development alone. Teachers help the pupils to think for themselves. The purposes of your attending school should be to enable you:

1. To develop sound health by forming correct habits.

2. To increase your appreciation of home, realizing what it means to you and to those with whom you come in contact.

3. To have an interest in solving difficulties met in your daily life.

4. To know your responsibility as a good citizen.

5. To select and keep yourself employed happily in a useful vocation with an opportunity for growth and advancement.

6. To learn how to use your leisure to develop and broaden your interests, which will enrich your life and make you more interesting to others.

7. To develop a good character as a means of bringing about harmony between you and your associates.

A Liberal Education. In obtaining such a liberal education, you develop four different points of view. First, *Open-mindedness.* You will at all times be ready to learn the truth. You cannot always be right; therefore, you must be willing to admit that you may be wrong. You cannot know everything; therefore, you need not be afraid to admit that you do not know a particular fact. An open-minded person is ready, when he receives new knowledge, to compare it with what he previously had considered true.

Second, *Eagerness to learn.* To learn something you must first feel the desire to learn. You will want to know the truth and will be eager to learn. You will want to know the reasons for a statement.

Third, *Discrimination or critical-mindedness.* You will accept only that which you are satisfied is right and true. You will weigh both sides of a problem, intelligently search for the truth, and accept it.

Fourth, *Courage to do.* After you have accepted what is right and true, you will have the courage to put what you have learned into practice. If a new idea is sound, you will be convinced by it, and will accept it and follow it even if it is different from former ideas and former ways of doing things.

Personality Development. As a part of your education you should strive to develop a pleasing personality. According to your personality, which is the sum total of the traits you possess, you will be either liked or disliked, attractive or unattractive, interesting or uninteresting, popular or unpopular. Personality is made up of a large number of qualities. To the extent that you develop pleasing qualities, or worth-while traits, you have an attractive personality. Such traits as these increase your ability to get along well with others.

	S.	M.	T.	W.	T.	F.	S.
TEMPERANCE Eat not to Dullness; Drink not to Elevation.							
T.							
S.	*	*		*		*	
O.	* *	*	*		*	*	*
R.			*			*	
F.		*			*		
I.		*					
S.							
J.							
M.							
C.							
T.							
C.							
H.							

A Page from Benjamin Franklin's Notebook

Franklin's Method. Benjamin Franklin, the great statesman and diplomat of the Revolutionary War period, in an effort to improve his own personality, made a list of thirteen personal "virtues" which he practiced most faithfully. They were temperance, silence, order, resolution, frugality, industry, sincerity, justice, moderation, cleanliness, tranquility, chastity, and humility. Franklin tells us in his autobiography how he kept a notebook ruled off for these thirteen virtues and allowed seven days for the special practice of each one. Thus he would cover the list in three months and then start all over again. The sample page for the first virtue, temperance, will show you how Franklin indicated every day those qualities in which he had failed to keep up to his standard.

The mere effort to concentrate on certain virtues each week will not necessarily produce perfection. However, Franklin's method does have some advantages.

Desirable Qualities of Personality. The following list of desirable qualities is somewhat like his and will help you to use the plan of this great scientist and scholar of two centuries ago. You may want to check the weak and strong points of your own personality against such a list. The questions will help you decide whether you understand the differences in these various qualities. A discussion of these questions may prove very helpful to you.

1. *Ability to Change.* Is it easy for you to listen to what others are saying? Are you anxious to ask questions when new subjects or business plans are discussed? Do you fit in with other people's plans, methods, or ideas?

2. *Courage.* Are you afraid to express your opinion when asked? Are you too timid or too bold? Have you the courage to stand for what you think is right and best?

3. *Dependability.* Can you be relied upon to carry out plans entrusted to you? How often in the past month have you failed to finish your work on time? How often in the past month have you failed to keep your promise or an appointment?

4. *Enthusiasm.* Are you always enthusiastic? Do you inspire others to put their best efforts into their work? Are you interested in your studies in school?

5. *Friendliness.* Think of five people whom you like very much and determine your reasons for liking them. Do the same with five people whom you dislike. Do you make friends easily? Do you keep their friendship? Do you meet people halfway?

6. *Honesty.* Are you upright and truthful in dealing with your parents, your teachers, and friends? Are you able to overcome the temptation to cheat in examinations? If someone gives you too much change, do you give it back to him? Do you always play fair?

7. *Industry.* Can you keep at your work steadily until it is finished? Can you perform distasteful tasks with care? Do you put your work before pleasure?

8. *Initiative.* Are you a "self-starter" or a follower? Can you think and plan for yourself, or do you depend on others? Do you attempt original, creative work?

9. *Judgment.* Do you use good judgment in selecting your friends? Can you find several different ways

of solving any one problem in connection with your work? Do you have the ability to decide wisely an issue before you?

10. *Perseverance.* Do you give up hard tasks too easily? Can you hold yourself to the accomplishment of any duty regardless of other attractions?

11. *Self-Control.* Are you patient or do you lose your temper easily? Are you a good loser?

12. *Tact.* Do you work in harmony and co-operate with other people? Do you praise others for what they have done? Do you try to cheer others when they are unfortunate or unhappy?

13. *Tolerance.* Are you able to see the points of view of other persons even though these persons differ with you? Can you avoid racial or religious hatreds? Do you believe that all people have their good qualities?

14. *Unselfishness.* Are you considerate of others? Do you insist too often upon having your own way? Do you do what your friends ask of you? Do you talk too often about yourself and your own interests?

Study Habits. In obtaining an education, it is necessary to plan ways and methods that will remove difficulties in your way. It is essential that you make some very definite plans. An athlete in the track meet "gets set" before he runs the race. "Getting set" for him means making all the preliminary preparations necessary before the start. A student has considerable preparation to make before he "finishes the race" and obtains an education. You may have to work a few hours each week while you are attending school, but this need not be a hardship. Many others do it. If it does not take too much time or interfere with your studies, you will benefit by the experience. It will give you a sense of responsibility. It will make you appreciate your opportunity for securing an education.

The Best Place. If you want to obtain an education, it will be necessary for you to form study habits of place and of time. To obtain the best results, you should have a definite place in the home as well as in the school where you can study without being disturbed. The surroundings should have an atmosphere that will help you study. The room or corner of a room should be well lighted, well ventilated, and properly heated. The decorations should be pleasing, but not distracting. A dictionary and other reference books should be conveniently placed. During study hours you should be alone, if possible. If you try this, you will find that these conditions will make it much easier for you to study. You are merely "getting set."

The Best Time. Now that you are "set" with a definite place, you need to arrange for a definite time to study, in the home as well as in the school. Your budget of time is provided while in school by following a regular program. But while at home, you should make a schedule similar to that which you have in school. Your place for studying will be of no use unless you occupy it. Determine the number of hours you can spend nightly in your room or at your desk. Determine which hours are most suitable. Then make a timetable and stick to it. Offices, stores, factories, and mills are operated on time schedules. All methods of transportation are run on scheduled time. In all

"A PRACTICAL SCHEDULE — NOT AN IMPOSSIBLE IDEA"																	
A. M.					NOON											P. M.	
7	8	9	10	11	12	1	2	3	4	5	6	7	8	9
S.																	
M.																	
T.																	
W.																	
T.																	
F.																	
S.																	

A Week's Schedule

these fields of labor a time schedule brings order and increases the ability of people to do good work. It will do the same for you if you adopt and follow one.

Try the foregoing schedule for a week or two. Copy it on a large sheet of paper. Place what you did with your time in the lower space of each hour and adjust your new schedule for the next week accordingly. Schedule all school hours, meals, physical recreation, and hours for adequate study. Do not allow your schedule to run you, but do not overrun it.

Test and Study Exercises

Aids to Learning.

1. Notice the four different attitudes which you develop in your search for a liberal education.

2. Personality is the sum total of the traits which you possess and is made up of numerous qualities.

3. Observe the study habits of place and of time that you need when you acquire an education.

Test Exercises.

Match items in the first list with corresponding items in the second list by putting together on a sheet of paper the numbers of the two items which best go together.

1. Eagerness to learn.	1. Steady attention to business.
2. Ability to change.	2. Trustworthiness towards responsibilities.
3. Courage.	3. Upright dealings.
4. Dependability.	4. Ability to decide an issue wisely.
5. Honesty.	5. Harmonious working with others.
6. Judgment.	6. Originality and creative work.
7. Initiative.	7. Boldness to do the right.
8. Tact.	8. Desire to know the truth.
9. Industry.	9. Adjustment to the ideas of others.

Suggested Activities.

1. (a) Study the life of Benjamin Franklin to determine how he used his list of virtues effectively. Use some such book as *Boys' Life of Benjamin Franklin* by Helen Nicolay, or *Four Great Americans* by James Baldwin. (b) Which qualities on Franklin's list would not be considered so important today as they were in his time?

2. Which qualities on page 23 would have been regarded with suspicion in 1750?

3. Make a list of the different situations under which a person can be absolutely honest today. How does honesty differ from truthfulness?

4. Make a schedule of your free time from 7 a.m. to 10 p.m. How many hours will you have for classwork? for study outside of school? for recreation outdoors? for quiet reading at home?

5. As a test of your efficiency, keep a record for a week of the time you actually waste. Are you as efficient as a good piece of machinery?

6. *Group Activity:* The teacher may arrange for class discussions on personal traits which are desirable for all pupils.

7. *Group Activity:* The teacher may assign several pupils to interview business or professional people, to learn what their education has done for them.

CHAPTER III

MORAL FITNESS

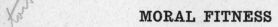

PREPARATORY NOTE: The following chapter shows that more important than health and more valuable than learning is good character. Character can be developed just as the body and mind can be trained. Ideas about right and wrong are constantly changing. These show the changing customs of different peoples in their efforts to improve themselves according to their own ideas of what is desirable.

Importance of Character. The world needs men and women of outstanding character in every walk of life. To develop a good character is, therefore, most essential. Without it, no one can be really worth while. A man can grow rich dishonestly, but that is not success. He knows his own wrong, even if others do not, and he suffers from it. We would not have confidence in our physicians if we felt they did not possess good character, or in our bankers if they lacked such a character. When your father needs a physician, he goes to the one who is known to have a good character, and in whom he has confidence. When he has money to invest, he is especially concerned about the character of the banker with whom he deals. When you have problems too hard for you to decide, you go to someone in whose character you have confidence.

If you were to rate the many traits of men according to their relative importance, surely you would rank traits of good character first. To be successful, to improve yourself, and to serve others, it is essential that you develop a good character.

Qualities of Good Character. Your character is what you really are, basically and deep-down. Others may not know all the qualities of your character because these qualities are not on the surface. Character differs from personality, in that character refers only to your most important traits, while personality includes all your traits. (See page 22.) Critical-mindedness, good judgment, sincerity, self-control, courage, honesty, and initiative are a few qualities which might be included in a list of character traits.

The "Golden Rule" is an old rule, but it is still as effective as ever. It bids you do to others as you would have them do to you, and to keep from doing anything to others which you would not want them to do to you. It works both ways. If you practiced this rule in your everyday living, you would develop ideal character and be happier and more valuable to your community. Try to live by this rule. *Do* only as you would have others do to you. *Say* only that which is helpful to others.

You are changed for the better or worse by the kind of thinking you do. The mind is affected by your thoughts just as the body is affected by your food. If you eat impure food, you build impurities into the body. Also if you think evil you build evil into your mind, and so affect your whole being. If you look for evil and for faults in another, you will be sure to find them; to look only for the good in others is far more profitable.

Development of Good Character. A good character is the greatest asset you can have. To develop it, it is necessary to practice using the best traits. To control yourself is a very valuable accomplishment. To achieve this, you must be determined and confident. Indeed every time you overcome a difficult task or a disappointment, you are made stronger to overcome the next and still more difficult task.

On the other hand, if you do not practice these traits which build good character, you will become weaker rather than stronger. Life cannot exist without change. If you do not improve your character, you will begin to live on a lower level. You will do discreditable things. You will lose self-respect as well as your reputation, which is the opinion that others have of you. Your personal worth will decline and you will suffer distinct loss of character.

To develop a good character, you must be conscious of your responsibility. You must possess high ideals. You must exercise those traits and qualities which will gain for you the confidence and trust of your fellow men.

Changing Times. The term *moral* refers to standards of right and wrong which are based upon long-established customs. As customs change from time to time and from place to place, so moral standards change. In Franklin's time, "silence" was evidently regarded as a virtue, since he included it among his thirteen most desirable traits. Today one would look upon "silence" as desirable only on certain occasions when talking would become a disturbance. A boy who tried to be silent too much might become sullen and gloomy. On the contrary, our ideals of religious tolerance and open-mindedness would have been

Opposition of Puritan Leader to Religious Tolerance

frowned upon by our Puritan forefathers because these traits would not have seemed desirable under their stern rule.

Morals in Different Places. Some nations and peoples have different customs or standards of morality from other nations. Marriage customs, and attitudes toward alcoholic drinks or kinds of food often change the moral standards of different peoples. Early child marriage is considered moral by the Hindus of India but not by Western nations. The use of alcohol is forbidden by Mohammedan rule but permitted under Christian rule. Also, three important world religions forbid the eating of pork while others do not.

Changing Conditions. Finally, a virtue may become a vice if carried to excess. Franklin praised thrift or saving, but excessive thrift is miserliness. Obedience is necessary on many occasions but if carried too far it becomes slavish submission. Critical-mindedness is excellent if it means an intelligent search for what is true; however, it might easily become an unreasonable criticism of everything, if not watched.

And so we see that moral codes change with different times, different places, and different conditions. This does not mean that there is no sure standard of right and wrong for us to follow. On the contrary, we should accept the highest standard we can find until we are satisfied that we have something better.

Value of a Moral Code. A satisfactory moral code is a set of rules, which assures justice and happiness to those who follow it. One who applies the teachings of his code will develop self-control. One who has self-control will have respect for the rights of others. Such a person is tolerant toward others, and morally grown up.

Boy Scout Code. An excellent example of a code of morals is that followed by millions of present and former boy scouts. Scouts undertake as part of their responsibilities the observance of twelve scout laws. These may be summarized by the statement that a

scout is trustworthy, loyal, helpful, friendly, cour-
teous, kind, obedient, cheerful, thrifty, brave, clean,
and reverent. This excellent moral standard influences
for good the characters of scores of thousands of our
boys today.

Boy Scout Jamboree to Nation's Capital

In addition to observing these twelve laws, boys
entering the membership of the Boy Scouts of America must take the Scout Oath:

"On my honor, I will do my best—
  1. To do my duty to God and my Country,
     and to obey the Scout Law;
  2. To help other people at all times;
  3. To keep myself physically strong, men-
     tally awake, and morally straight."

Test and Study Exercises

Aids to Learning.

1. Notice the difference between character and reputation.
2. Remember that morals change with different times, places, and conditions.
3. Character is developed by using the best traits you have.

Test Exercises.

On a separate sheet of paper write the following sentences including the missing words:

1. Character represents what a man really ____, but reputation is that which people ____ he ____.
2. Standards of right and wrong are called ____.
3. Moral standards change from ____ to ____ and from ____ to ____.
4. Thrift carried to excess becomes ____.

Suggested Activities.

1. Look up the customs of the South Sea Islanders, in an encyclopedia, to learn how their moral standards differ from ours.
2. Read an account of Charles A. Lindbergh in some such book as *We,* or his story "New York to Paris" found in *Junior Anthology— Book One,* by Wellons, McTurnan, and Smith. Which of the twelve Boy Scout laws did he demonstrate on that flight?
3. *Group Activity:* The class may discuss whether we ever attempt to justify the taking of human life today? by capital punishment? in self-defense? in warfare?
4. *Group Activity:* The class may consider how the boy scout is trained in the observance of each of his twelve laws. Is his method better than that Benjamin Franklin used with his thirteen virtues?
5. *Group Activity:* The class may choose sides for a debate on the question, Resolved: That trustworthiness is the most important of the twelve Boy Scout laws.

CHAPTER IV

VOCATIONAL AND ECONOMIC EFFICIENCY

PREPARATORY NOTE: Perhaps you are looking forward eagerly to the time when you will earn your own living and support yourself. It will soon be necessary for you to lay the plans for your own career. To do this intelligently you should understand certain ideas which will be important in any occupation you enter. Saving money is a valuable accompaniment of earning money, and buying wisely is necessary if you are to be able to have anything left over for saving and investing. The following chapter discusses some of these investments.

Importance of Planning for the Future. Everyone has a future. Everyone has a right to do what he can to make his future as long and as happy as possible. A planned future is more likely to be satisfactory than an unplanned one. With your present knowledge you can foretell certain things. If you eat green apples your immediate future is liable to be very unpleasant. You know that, so you do not eat green apples. If you are to have a swimming test in a week, but do not plan and practice you will fail in your test. You will never pass it until you plan your time and get your practice. That is true of your daily lessons also, as you know. If you stay up too late at night, you will be tired in the morning. That morning is the future of the night before.

Such a future is immediate. It is only one kind of future. The other is more distant. It is not an hour after the green apples, or the morning after the night —it is a period of years during your adult life. It is the time which will test most severely the planning you have done or have not done. It is the time of life when you will fail or succeed as a grown man or woman. That is the kind of future which plans may make happy and useful. But the habit of successful planning must be started when you are young. If you form the habit now of planning for the immediate future, plans for the distant future will be easier and more helpful. Have you ever carried out a successful venture without planning? Most people have not. Life is the greatest venture of all. Successful living demands thoughtful planning.

Responsibility of Earning a Living. Young children rely on their parents to take care of them. Some members of society, such as tramps and criminals, always depend on others for their livelihood. But the first responsibility of every adult citizen is to provide himself with the necessities of life. In other words, a self-respecting individual tries his utmost to earn his living. Many people who are unable to support themselves cannot find work because they are not trained to do work for which there is a demand, or because other conditions prevent their finding a position. To be able to earn a living in our modern world requires both planning and training.

Choice of Career. The important consideration in choosing a career and planning for it is the service you can render. Real service, of course, means more than merely acting with good intentions: it means providing the community with something it needs and wants. Suppose, for example, you have a garden in which good spinach can be grown even in the hottest months of summer. In many localities spinach cannot be grown successfully in July and August. If you grow good spinach and sell it in places where it cannot be grown, you will render a service and also make money. If, in the city, you can supply ice cream and cold drinks in communities distant from stores you can, in the summer months, render a service and also make money. These are types of work that you can do. Successful adults use the same general ideas in finding suitable careers in life. What you learn and do now will help you select your lifework later.

In addition to being able to render a service, try to choose a lifework you will enjoy. Many people find themselves trained for and doing work which does not really interest them. You may, for example, have no desire to sell things. You would rather be a producer. A salesman is dependent upon the producer; he must have something to sell. You may want to grow the spinach, and have some one else sell it. That is the way of the business world. The manufacturer seldom sells direct to the consumer. The farmer seldom sells his produce direct to the housewife. Distribution of goods is a business in itself.

You may discover the work for which you are fitted in a number of different ways. You can make a score card for yourself by listing the qualities or traits required or demanded by the vocation in which you are interested. You may possess many of these same traits, but you will be stronger in some than in others. If you mark those traits in which you score average with an *a*, those above average with a +, and those below average with a —, you can readily compare your traits with those required in the vocation you are considering. If you find that you have most of those traits required by the particular vocation, to the degree of average or above average, you seem to be fitted for that particular vocation and are likely to be successful in it. Perhaps, on the other hand, you will find that you lack entirely the traits required by this vocation, or you may have them to a degree below average. Then you should consider another vocation for study, because your score indicates that you are not fitted for that particular vocation. A more thorough study of this kind will doubtless be conducted when you are in senior high school or in college.

After carefully attempting to choose your vocation, begin to plan in every detail the way to master it. The standards and requirements are being raised for every vocation because of the increasing supply of workers. There is no room at the top for those who are not willing to work harder than the average person. By choosing wisely and planning carefully, you make a good beginning. Direct all your efforts toward planning your career, for it will mean more than merely earning a living. A successful career is more likely to enable you to get the most out of life. Economically, it should enable you to earn and save money above that needed for comfortable living. Socially, it should enable you to prepare yourself for enjoyable relations with your friends. Politically, it should enable you to take an active part in the affairs of your government. In general, it will give you a broader outlook on life and make you happier. This is better than anything that money can buy.

Wise Spending. It is not enough to plan to earn money. We must plan how to spend money wisely. There is a natural tendency for people to spend money in proportion to the amount they receive. The more money they have, the more they spend. A good way to determine the amount of money to be spent, as well as to be saved, is by the use of a budget. An expense budget is an estimated amount of money to be spent for the necessities and luxuries of life, for a certain period of time, usually a month or a year. It should be made up according to the individual's needs.

Sample Budgets. Here is a suggested budget form for a pupil traveling daily to school.

Expenditures	Per Week	Per School Year 38 Weeks
Necessities		
1. Lunches	$0.75	$28.50
2. Fare	.50	19.00
3. Schoolbooks	.25	9.50
4. Paper, pencils, etc.................	.10	3.80
Pleasures		
1. Recreation	.20	7.60
2. Charity	.10	3.80
3. Saving	.10	3.80
	$2.00	$76.00

Following is a general budget for a family of four, which you may compare with that used in your own home.

Expenditures	Per Month	Per Year	Percentage
Necessities			
1. Food ....$ 50.00		$ 600	30%
2. Shelter 33.33		400	20%
3. Household operation (Heat, Light, Service, Supplies, Fare)...... 25.00		300	15%
4. Clothing 20.00		240	12%
Advancement			
5. Health 8.33		100	5%
6. Education and Recreation....... 8.33		100	5%
7. Benevolences 5.00		60	3%
8. Savings and Insurance......... 16.67		200	10%
	$166.66	$2000	100%

A family budget will vary for many reasons, such as the number and age of children in the family, the health of each person, the type of employment of the wage earner, the education and even the social or religious interests of the family. Of course, expenses in the country are quite different from those in the city and expenses vary in different sections of the nation. You will see that the proportion of your income spent for certain items changes with increased earnings. A rich family does not eat ten times as much food as a poor family. However, it may spend many times as much money for clothing, for shelter, or for recreation as the poor family.

The following pictograph[1] shows where a typical family dollar goes. Compare these average figures

[1] **pictograph.** A chart presenting facts by the use of picture symbols.

with those given in the suggested family budget. You will see that on the whole they are very similar, although the average family apparently saves very little and spends more for transportation.

WHERE A TYPICAL FAMILY DOLLAR GOES

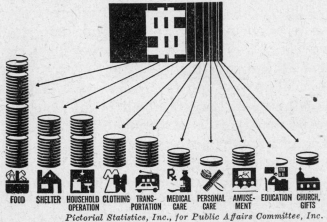

Pictorial Statistics, Inc., for Public Affairs Committee, Inc.

Each Coin Represents One Penny

Meaning and Importance of Thrift. Thrift means wise spending of money and wise saving. If you do not spend wisely and if you do not save money you may become a spendthrift. If you are thrifty you will use your income wisely. You will watch your expenses carefully and buy wisely, so that you will be able to save and invest a part of your income, to be used only for emergency and old age. To be thrifty does not mean to be stingy. The fact that you earn a little money in your spare time for some future need is an example of thrift. But to refuse to help promote a worthy cause, when able, is miserliness.

You can be thrifty in the use of your time and strength, by thoughtfully planning your time for study, work, and play, and then by using it as you planned. You can be thrifty with the things you use, as food, or clothing. If you are thrifty you will be careful how you use your own property, house, lawn, books, and furniture, as well as the property that belongs to other people. To break or deface public property is not only foolish, but wasteful, since the taxpayer always pays for it.

Conservation of Natural Resources. The importance of thrift, in the life of all people, has become so evident that there is a National Thrift Week, observed annually during the week beginning with Benjamin Franklin's birthday (January 17th) because Franklin wrote so much about the importance of thrift, in his "Poor Richard's Almanac." During Thrift Week we are urged to practice a wise economy in the use and care of our natural resources: coal, oil, timber, and minerals. The United States is rich in natural resources, but we cannot afford to waste them. The law encourages the planting of trees, and the national government has forest reservations as do some states and counties. Various methods are employed to prevent waste and to increase the practice of thrift among the people. One of the ways in which the national government saves its natural resources is through irrigation of waste lands. Desert lands in the state of Washington have been converted into fruitfulness by irrigation, as is shown in the photograph on the following page.

False and True Economy. Some people have the wrong idea as to how to save or to be thrifty. For example, they deny themselves wholesome food in order to dress well and to "keep up with the crowd."

Courtesy Northern Pacific Ry.

Irrigation in the Yakima Valley

Some people buy things because they are "bargains" rather than because they need them. They deny themselves some of those things really necessary for health. To sacrifice your health even for education may be false economy, not thrift. You may think it is economical to leave school a year or two before you complete your course, to start earlier to earn money. This would most likely prove to be false economy. Very likely it would be far wiser to complete your schooling.

To manage your money, property, and affairs with true thrift is wise economy. Before you buy something, do you consider whether you need it and whether you need it right now? Is it possible that you need something else more? Wise economy does not end when you have made a purchase, since it also includes the use and care of all your possessions. To be careful with your clothing, books, and everything you use, will make them last much longer. The time an article lasts should be considered in connection with its purchase price. For example, shoes which cost three dollars and wear but two months are really more expensive than shoes which cost six dollars if they wear six months.

Careful Buying. Great care should be taken to get value received for all money spent. Very frequently you find that the package actually costs more than the contents. This is true of many toilet articles and cheap perfumes. The advertising for which a company pays is frequently so expensive that the company has to charge more than the article is worth to you. Packaged breakfast foods, tooth pastes, and patent medicines are sometimes in this class. Many people are not good buyers because they do not know much about the materials they buy or their value. They accept shoddy[2] in place of wool goods, paper instead

[2] shoddy. A cloth of inferior quality.

of leather, and cotton in place of linen. When canned food contains less than is advertised, or the "fresh meat" is not actually fresh, or the scales have been tampered with to give short weight, you do not get your money's worth. You can save a large part of what you spend and still get better value if you make certain that you are getting exactly what you order and what you pay for.

Installment Buying. Many people buy on the installment plan because they can secure things immediately in this way, for which they could not possibly pay in cash. Much of this installment buying is for purchases which are not necessary and which burden the buyers with greater debts than they can possibly pay. When the buyer cannot make the payments on his purchase, the seller takes back the goods and the buyer loses both payments and the goods. In this class come luxuries such as jewelry or expensive automobiles or even unwise purchases of radios, books, or clothing.

Other installment buying may be very advisable for a person of modest means because of the advantages secured while paying the costs. Homes purchased by this means may be paid for as rent to the great advantage of the purchaser in many cases. Of course, there frequently is a considerable increase in the cost, not only because of the interest charge of six per cent or more but because of the various other hidden "service" charges. An automobile costing eight hundred dollars in cash might easily total nine or ten hundred dollars paid for over a year or two.

The caution that you should observe is to watch the total amount of these payments. Let us suppose that a man with a salary of two hundred dollars a month is buying a five thousand dollar home at a monthly cost of fifty dollars in addition to his heat, light, and other operating costs. Then he buys a six hundred dollar automobile at forty dollars a month and a hundred dollar radio at ten dollars a month. Half his salary is spent for these three articles alone before food, clothing, household operation, and various forms of advancement have been considered. He is spending fifty per cent where he should spend only twenty-five to thirty per cent.

Reasons for Saving. Many conditions arise that require unexpected expenses, for which one cannot pay with his regular income. The average man finds great difficulty in borrowing money from a bank unless he has adequate securities, such as good stocks or bonds to offer the bank. His only other source is the loan company, which charges very high interest rates and uses all kinds of pressure if he fails in his payments. It is much better to be prepared for such emergencies by having money on hand. A wage earner may become ill or he may lose his position temporarily. Parents want to save so that their children may go to college without too great a financial struggle. At times aged parents or other relatives have to depend on another member of their family. Emergencies make some form of saving necessary if one is to be able to meet them when they arise.

It has been shown by insurance companies that out of one hundred men twenty-five years of age, only one will be rich forty years later and four will be able to live comfortably. Five will be dependent upon their personal earnings, or upon charity, if they should lose their jobs; fifty-four will be dependent upon their relatives and friends for support, or perhaps upon charity; and thirty-six will have died. This shows the importance of saving and of investing wisely. Those persons who save sufficiently, as a rule, need not fear dependence in their old age.

Investment of Savings. To invest our savings is to put them to work for us. Our savings properly invested will earn an income for us and help other people as well. The money we invest is loaned to others for building purposes, or for operating a store, bank, factory, or some other business enterprise. Some of the money earned returns to us as interest on our investments, as payment to us for letting others use our money. Thus the whole community is benefited along with us. If we keep our savings idle, no one profits by them.

Investments may be of several kinds. You can put money in a savings bank or in the postal savings account where a small rate of interest is paid. Recently there were over forty million depositors in more than fifteen thousand banks throughout the United States. Usually these savings are perfectly safe, although several years ago hundreds of banks were closed and millions of dollars were lost to depositors because of the great depression following the

First World War. Since that time the federal government has worked out a plan to guarantee the deposits, so as to prevent any further loss.

Other types of investments are bonds, stocks, real estate, building and loan association shares, and various forms of insurance. All of these run into billions of dollars of savings each year, as millions of people are now holders of some of these forms of investment.

Bonds. A bond is a written statement showing that you have invested or loaned a certain amount of money, upon which you are to receive a fixed rate of interest for the use of your money. Bonds pay various rates of interest but seldom over five or six per cent. As a rule, many kinds are considered a safe method of investment. United States government bonds are the safest. Bonds issued by well-known and well-managed corporations are usually safe and pay four, five, or even six per cent interest. Among the corporations which borrow money by issuing bonds are railroads, electric light and power companies, other public utilities,[3] and some large industrial plants. Some real-estate bonds are safe and good investments, under normal conditions.

Stocks. Stocks are shares in a certain enterprise. If the enterprise makes money, the shareholder makes money. The profits of the enterprise are distributed to the shareholders in the form of dividends. In prosperous times, the shareholder often receives larger dividends than his money would earn if it were in-

[3] **public utilities.** Corporations controlling such public benefits as transportation, communication, light, and power.

vested in bonds. However, the return on stocks is not
so sure nor so safe. Stocks fluctuate in value and they
rise and fall in price, due to many conditions. When
buying bonds or stocks, one must investigate carefully
the company which issues them. Most of us need the
help and advice of others who are better informed
about investments than we are. Of course, our advisers
must be persons in whom we have confidence, such as
the banker, who is well informed and who is able to
give disinterested advice.

Building and Loan Associations. Investment in the
stock of building and loan associations sometimes pays
well, and is particularly helpful to those who want to
buy a home and cannot pay the entire cost at one time.
Many families have bought a dwelling by borrowing
from a building and loan association, and by repay-
ing the loan by monthly payments, when it would have
been impossible for them to pay the entire price at
one time.

There are many ways of investing your savings
safely. Be sure to put safety and sure returns ahead
of high and uncertain returns. The one who claims
to know how to "get rich quick" is not at all sure or
he would take advantage of it himself and not adver-
tise it to the public.

Insurance. One good form of investing your savings
is insurance. This provides for those dependent upon
you if something should happen to you. There are
many kinds of insurance. The person who buys insurance makes annual, quarterly, or even monthly payments called premiums, according to arrangement.

The younger one starts with insurance, the less it costs per year. An endowment policy is one that you keep up for a certain time stated on the policy, and at the end of that time you can draw out the cash value stated thereon. A specified payment policy is also for a certain time, stated on the policy, after which you cease paying the premiums. You cannot draw out the cash for it, but you do have a paid-up policy. An ordinary life policy continues until you die, after which your beneficiary, or the person named in your policy, will draw out the amount stated on the policy.

Insurance in a sound company is sure and safe, but pays little interest. The different kinds of policies are desirable for different reasons. For example, a ten-year endowment policy, taken out early in life, could be used as a method of saving money for a college education, but it is the most expensive kind of policy. The short-term life policy is the cheapest form of life insurance, as it is only for the purpose of protection rather than for investment also.

Some of the forms of insurance we have mentioned are partly forms of saving, since the sum contracted for is certain to be paid, either to the insured or to his beneficiary. The amount, however, is called protection as it protects the insured for a larger amount than that saved.

But there is another kind of insurance in which the amount of the policy is paid only if some special event occurs. Fire insurance is an example of this. Experience teaches us that of each thousand houses that exist, a certain number are likely to be destroyed by fire, partly or entirely, in a given time. However, no one can guess which particular house will be destroyed. The loss of a house is one which most families cannot afford. Let us suppose that each of the house owners pays a small sum annually into a general fund. Then the owners of the property which is destroyed can be paid out of that fund, and no one has to bear a large loss. He protects himself in this way against the risk of losing a large amount. This distributes the risk. The same principle underlies all types of property insurance. They guard against events involving losses which may prove too costly for a single individual to bear.

Life insurance companies receive three and a half billion dollars of premiums each year from about sixty-five million policy holders. This shows how important a form of saving and protection insurance has become. This is considerably more money than is spent each year for the entire cost of public schools. Fire-insurance premiums total another billion dollars each year.

Other forms of insurance emphasize protection rather than savings. Accident insurance resembles fire insurance and protects against sudden loss of earning power in case the insured meets with any severe accident. Automobile insurance includes risk of fire, theft, property damage, collision, and injury to any person. Furniture or other property can also be insured against fire or theft. All these are means of spreading a probable heavy cost among a large number of possible losers.

Test and Study Exercises

Aids to Learning.

1. Notice the three important considerations in choosing a career—service, enjoyment, and adaptability.

2. Observe the differences between wise and false economy.

3. Learn the ways in which you can be sure you will get value received for the money you spend.

4. Remember the advantages of the four kinds of investments discussed.

Test Exercises.

1. What are the important facts you should consider in choosing a permanent vocation?

2. Can you reasonably expect success in more than one kind of vocation?

3. What conditions determine the amount of money budgeted each month for shelter for a family of four?

4. Why is it true that "necessities" decrease in percentage with more salary, and "advancement" items increase?

5. What are the advantages of budget making?

6. Explain how thrift can become miserliness if carried too far.

7. What are the advantages and dangers of installment buying?

8. Should all people carry insurance? In your opinion how much should a married man carry if he has a three-thousand-dollar salary and two young children?

9. When is it advisable for a family man to carry term insurance and when endowment insurance?

Suggested Activities.

1. Play this insurance game. Use paper slips with sums written on for money. Pretend that five of your friends have pet frogs which they want to insure with your company. You figure out the probable life of each frog and insure each one for fifty cents to be paid in case of death. Suppose the premium is five cents a week. If Ed's frog dies in four weeks you pay him fifty cents and lose thirty cents. If Joe's frog lives thirteen weeks you pay fifty cents and have collected sixty-five cents—a profit of fifteen cents. Jack's frog lives eight weeks. You pay fifty cents and lose ten cents. Bill's frog lives twenty weeks. You pay fifty cents and have collected one dollar—a profit of fifty cents. Al's

frog lives twelve weeks. You pay fifty cents and have collected sixty cents, a gain of ten cents. What condition is your insurance company in at the end of the experiment? In the beginning you should have had at least two dollars and a quarter of your own, because all the frogs might have died in the first week. How would you have acquired this amount of capital? Could you have sold stock?

2. Choose several items which would be luxuries for a married clerk with an eighteen-hundred-dollar income but which might be considered necessities for a banker with a ten-thousand-dollar income.

3. *Group Activity:* The teacher may conduct a class discussion on the value of vocational education in preparation for the printing trade.

CHAPTER V

CIVIC EFFICIENCY

PREPARATORY NOTE: You will find in this chapter that many things go into the making of personality. We have already considered its physical, mental, moral, and economic parts. There is still left the social or civic point of view—your relation to your companions and to the community in which you live. You are a citizen of your school, and here you train to become a better citizen of your community. As such you will have certain civic duties, whether you live in the country or in the city. You will serve your community better if you become acquainted with some of these important duties.

The School Community. All through life you will be given opportunities to serve your community. You should accept these opportunities as they come and serve in the best way you can.

Has it ever occurred to you that your school system is operated and organized like a community? It has rules to guide and govern its citizens, and officials to enforce these rules. The pupils are the citizens. The older and better informed "citizens" or pupils are naturally expected to care to some extent for those that are younger and less informed.

An example of this care is schoolboy safety patrols who safeguard the lives of children in more than five hundred cities. Schoolboy patrolmen are awarded medals for lifesaving by the American Automobile Association. By this patrol service, many thousand children are safeguarded daily on their way to and

© *Underwood & Underwood*
Schoolboy patrolman helps children across the street

from school. The number of accidents and deaths during school hours has been greatly reduced by these patrols.

Use of Your Talents. Each individual has certain talents. Different individuals are adapted for different kinds of work and for different kinds of service.

It is only natural that you can succeed best by discovering and developing those talents which you already possess. In the same way you can render the best service by using those talents and gifts which you have.

Self-Reliance. Do not depend upon your parents, teachers, or other pupils to do your lessons or solve your problems for you. The reason for requiring you to do them yourself is that you may learn by your own experience. If you copy the work of a fellow student, or have someone else do your work, you are robbed of the experience that benefits you.

You are constantly before the eyes of your parents, teachers, pupils, and others. You should be careful of what you say and do and how you say it and do it because you are making a record of which you will want to be proud. Of course you cannot change your record once it is made. But if you see where you have made mistakes, try at once to correct them in the record you are making now. The fact that you see your mistakes shows that you are developing a fine sense of right and wrong.

Differences in Communities. A citizen's duty is to have a part in all good work for the improvement of his community. Opportunity for this will be different in a large city from that in a small village. In the city the individual citizen seems to count for little because he knows so few others. The villager knows everybody and all recognize his value to the community.

However, there are many ways in which the man in the large city can help his fellow citizens. Civic associations play an important part in keeping up the standards of the big city. City clubs or Chambers of Commerce, Kiwanis or Rotary Clubs all have their committees which try to keep down graft in politics, corruption in labor circles, and inefficiency in city control and in public schools. These groups resemble the town meeting in that the individual men can have a considerable influence, if they wish to give freely of their ability and time.

In the smaller town the capable individual naturally is able to take part in even more civic groups. He can be a member of the Board of Aldermen or the Board of Education. He can personally direct one of the divisions of the local government. He can be an important member of the civic organizations. But in both the large and small community it is entirely possible for the ambitious, intelligent citizen to do his share.

Obedience to the Law. In addition to taking an active part himself, the citizen should follow the wishes of the majority of his fellow citizens as expressed in the law. Obedience to the law is merely following the wishes of the people as decided by their representatives. It is necessary in a democracy for people to obey the opinions of the majority; otherwise there would be no lasting democratic government. Even though you do not understand or approve of all the laws, you should follow them as long as they remain laws. It is your privilege, however, to make every effort to have an unjust law changed by the people as soon as possible. You may not like to put a muzzle or a leash on your dog, but if the village ordinance demands it, you must obey for the good of the community.

Serving the Government. It is the duty of all citizens to serve their country and government at all times. A good citizen will think of these duties as privileges, since he is a part of his community, and he should be willing and anxious to have an active part in its affairs. There are numerous ways in which a citizen can serve the community, such as voting at all elections, serving on juries when called, paying taxes willingly, and holding those public offices for which one is best prepared.

Voting at all Elections. It is the duty and privilege of every citizen to vote at all elections. Before a citizen votes he should inform himself about the problems involved in the election. He should also study carefully the different candidates so that he can vote intelligently. All citizens should be interested in their government and its problems. The progress made by a community depends upon its people. Therefore, all citizens should take active part in the affairs which are their own. This can be done by voting and by getting others to see the importance of voting. As a rule nearly half of our citizens do not take advantage of their privilege of voting. This shows a lack of interest in their own welfare. If all progressive-minded people would vote, the elections would be influenced in the direction of good government. Satisfactory officials would more likely be elected. Practices injurious to the welfare of the community would be discontinued and persons who place self-interest above the progress of the community would be retired to private life. Economy of public funds would be practiced. Policies and measures that make for good government would be adopted.

Performing Jury Service. Service on juries gives a citizen the opportunity to protect the innocent and to punish the guilty. No citizen should lose this opportunity. In all cases the juror should have but one thing in mind. He should strive honestly and fearlessly to bring about justice to those concerned in the case. Juries have it in their power to enforce the law strictly and fearlessly. If this is done, crime will be reduced. Undue mercy on the part of juries usually tends to increase and encourage crime.

Paying Taxes Willingly. As any business enterprise needs funds to carry on the business, so the government must have funds to carry on its functions. These funds are raised by taxes for the most part. Taxes can be, and sometimes are, collected by force; but this should not be necessary if the people understand and appreciate their responsibility. Fortunately the majority of people understand this and feel the responsibility of paying their share toward the support of their government. If a taxpayer believes that the amount of his tax has been set too high, he has the opportunity to present his objection before a Board of Review appointed for such service.

Holding Public Office. A public office is a public trust which in turn is a compliment to the one holding the office. He should, therefore, do his duties in a manner that will gain for him further confidence and respect. He should not betray those who have honored him by electing him to office. A public official has the opportunity to render a real service to the public and to his government. He has the power to help reduce crime and to further all causes that will benefit the people. The ideal public officeholder will be honest, just, and fearless, and will put the interests of the public before his own. He will realize his responsibility and will endeavor to serve the people and his government according to the commands of his conscience and his best judgment.

Test and Study Exercises

Aids to Learning.

1. Remember that obedience to the law is but following the wishes of the people as decided by their representatives.

2. Review four of the ways in which citizens can best serve their government.

3. You can succeed best by discovering and developing those talents which you already possess.

Test Exercises.

On a separate sheet of paper write the numbers one through seven on the left margin. Then write *yes* or *no* after each number depending on your judgment as to the answer. If there is a difference of opinion regarding the answers, these should be discussed by the teacher.

1. Is a junior-high-school pupil a citizen of his community?

2. Is it honest to help another pupil copy written work?

3. Are there times when you should disobey a bad law?

4. Does a good citizen write his lawmakers urging them to pass particular laws which he thinks are desirable?

5. Is it worth while to vote at elections, regardless of graft in politics?

6. Does a good citizen accept jury service even though it is inconvenient at the time?

7. Are taxes essential for the efficient operation of government?

Suggested Activities.

1. Consult an almanac to find out the number of votes cast in the last presidential election. What percentage of the people voted? What is the importance of this fact?

2. Keep a scrapbook of newspaper clippings of local civic activities together with the names of the men and women who have a part in them.

3. *Group Activity:* With the help of the teacher, you may hold an election in your school following, as closely as possible, the local election plans. Have the various candidates present their views before the class, so that you may know which are the best candidates. Prepare ballots like regular ballots. Arrange booths for voting. Appoint judges and clerks of election. Have a preliminary registration of all qualified voters.

4. *Group Activity:* With the teacher's help, you may conduct a jury trial of a student accused of violating some school rule. Select the jury of twelve after permitting the attorneys on both sides to "challenge" any person suspected of favoritism. Present the evidence carefully. Allow each side to present witnesses. Instruct the jury to weigh the evidence fairly and decide on the basis of the facts only.

5. *Group Activity:* With the help of the teacher, you may select sides for a debate on the subject, Resolved: That professional people should not be exempt from jury service.

PART II

THE CITIZEN AS A MEMBER OF A GROUP

As we look back over the development of our country, we see that the Indian, in his day, was the only one in our history who was really independent, for he supplied all his own food, clothing, and shelter. The explorers and pioneers were partly dependent upon others for their necessities of life. Today we are almost entirely dependent upon others for our needs. The growing demand for different kinds of food, clothing, shelter, and luxuries has made it necessary to produce everything in larger quantities. Therefore, methods of production have been improved.

It is also true that every country is dependent in many ways upon other countries for raw materials[1] used in preparing food, clothing, and shelter. You will notice in the illustration some of those raw materials which we import almost entirely. Although we produce at home most of such raw materials as iron, coal, oil, and cereals, yet other necessary metals such as

---

[1] **raw materials.** Natural products not yet prepared for use.

tin, nickel, and platinum, as well as rubber, sugar, tea, and coffee are brought to us from foreign countries. Our whole social life is dependent upon different

SOME VITAL IMPORTS OF THE U. S.

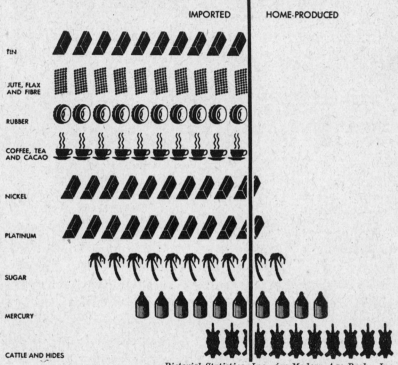

IMPORTED　　　　HOME-PRODUCED

TIN

JUTE, FLAX AND FIBRE

RUBBER

COFFEE, TEA AND CACAO

NICKEL

PLATINUM

SUGAR

MERCURY

CATTLE AND HIDES

Pictorial Statistics, Inc., for Modern Age Books, Inc.
Each symbol represents 10 per cent of apparent consumption

groups. Many and varied are the groups to which we belong as we grow older. The most important are the *Home,* the *School,* the *Church,* and the *Community,* each with its many interests and organizations.

CHAPTER VI

YOUR PART IN THE FAMILY

PREPARATORY NOTE: As a citizen of the community you belong to many groups. You have definite responsibilities to all of them and you secure many benefits from them. The home is the first and the most important of these groups. Here are your parents and other members of your family and here you first learn to meet and to fit in with strangers. As time goes on you begin to look forward to a home which you will build, where you will spend your grown-up years. You will find great interest in learning how to develop yourself properly for this task, as you read this chapter.

Meaning of Home. The first group a child enters as a member is the family, or the home. It is in the family circle that the individual normally gets his start in life. Here he learns to love and to respect his parents and to play and to work with his brothers and sisters. If all families of every community meet their responsibilities fully, the homes of these communities will be good places in which to live.

The ideal home is a place where people are bound together by ties of affection, where courtesy and consideration for others are extended, and where the young are guarded and guided. It is a place where one may find rest, comfort, and a sense of security; where fundamental culture is developed and passed on to the younger generation; where worthy character traits are taught, learned, and enjoyed. The ideal home is a sacred institution—a haven—a source of inspiration and encouragement.

"The home is the oldest unit of civilization. In it the mothers of ancient China taught their children politeness and obedience. In the home, during the Golden Age of Greece, Athenians practiced wisdom, courage, temperance, and justice. Christian parents have taught faith, hope, and love.

"At heart the home is a spiritual unit, a glowing fire of good will and mutual helpfulness. The worthy home guards its income and expenditures, strives for efficient material equipment and daily routine, maintains a stimulating life, seeks beauty, develops the best side of each of its members. Be proud of your home. Give it the best you have."

Ideal Condition for Children. At the White House Conference on Child Health, former President Herbert Hoover summarized his desires for our nation's children. The ideal for which we should strive is that all children should be born under proper conditions; they should live in hygienic surroundings; they should be properly nourished; they should have prompt and efficient medical attention and inspection; they should receive primary instruction in the elements of hygiene and good health; they should have the complete birthright of a sound mind in a sound body; and they should be encouraged to express in fullest measure the spirit within them.

Relationship to Parents. Without realizing it and without even appreciating it, you receive unending care and attention from your parents. In return for this, you learn to love, respect, and obey them. Your parents make many sacrifices for you. But as time goes on you begin to realize that you, too, have certain responsibilities. You want to do your share about the house, and as you grow older you become still more co-operative.

As a child and youth, you receive from the family more than you contribute to it. As a young man or woman, you naturally desire to contribute to the family welfare. As old age creeps upon your parents, there is frequently an opportunity for you to show your appreciation, by providing a home for your parents.

Relationship to Brothers and Sisters. To live in an ideal home, it is necessary to practice the "give and take" spirit. To accomplish this, you should be considerate of your brothers and sisters as well as of others. Be thoughtful of their interests, and be patient and sympathetic with them. Be willing to co-operate with them to help them accomplish their work. Try team-work in your family, and see what the results of this experiment will be.

In childhood the foundations for a satisfactory personality are laid and habits are formed. It is important to form right habits, whether physical or mental, for they tend to become fixed habits. If they are bad habits, they lead to unhappiness and inefficiency in adult life; if they are good habits, they produce happiness and efficiency.

Relationship to Outsiders. If the practice of being considerate, sincere, kind, and co-operative works successfully in your family, try it on outsiders. It will also work successfully in large groups. If home training fails to improve your life, the failure means either that you did not receive the right training or that you did not apply it in the formation of your habits. In either case you discredit those who gave you your home training. If you would reflect credit on your parents and increase your own happiness and well-being, you should cultivate those habits which will develop worthy character traits in your relations with other people.

There are many groups of people outside of the family with whom you come in contact. If you are unselfish with your friends, you will develop the habit of thoughtfulness when dealing with people. If you treat your neighbors as you would like to be treated, there will be a better understanding between you and other people. Since many of your waking hours are spent with your teachers, you should spend that time profitably. As a boy or girl, young man or young woman of today develops an unselfish regard for others, and a desire to help, so will the man or woman of tomorrow have the proper regard for those he meets. This is an excellent foundation for the solution of problems much later in life.

Importance of Homemaking. Through family life, civilization is improved. One of the most important steps in life is that of establishing a home. No problem requires greater care. To be successful, two homemakers should have a similar point of view and make their decisions with frankness and mutual understanding. They should use every effort to improve themselves by making the most of their opportunities and the best use of the talents they possess.

© *Underwood & Underwood*

Modern Electric Kitchen

Most young men and women want to have a part in building a home some day. They look forward to that time with a great deal of satisfaction. Therefore, they should be prepared for their new venture. The young man should have entered the vocation he has chosen to follow. The young woman should know how to manage the household on his income. In such a partnership each should contribute to its success and happiness. To secure lasting happiness, each should have a sound mind and body, strong character, useful work to do, and sufficient interests for leisure time.

Housekeeping and Homemaking. Good housekeep-

Primitive Utensils of Covered Wagon Days

ing requires the organizing of one's duties, the careful planning of time and effort, the choosing of materials or tools with which to keep house, the attractive placing of furniture, and the efficient arranging of household equipment.

During the past century, the tools of the household have changed along with other tools or machinery.

The kitchen of the covered-wagon days contained an open grate with an iron pot for boiling and a Dutch oven for baking. You can see in the photograph the churn for buttermaking, the tallow-candle dip, the bellows for blowing fires, and other utensils of the pioneer days. Compare this with the modern electric kitchen and you will appreciate the progress made in housekeeping today.

While good housekeeping is important, homemaking is far more important. The home, however simple, should be a source of comfort, peace, encouragement, and understanding. The ambition to improve, together with the spirit of sympathy and unselfishness, will help produce success in homemaking.

Real Homemaking. There are many things which have a part in real homemaking. *Household management* includes planning the family budget, selection and preparation of food, selection and care of clothing, and planning and furnishing the home. *Pleasant social relationships* result from the wise choice of friends and proper personal conduct and relationship with others. *Good health* includes the physical care of all members of the household, mental development by further schooling and reading, and moral health and character development.

Test and Study Exercises

Aids to Learning.

1. Remember that in childhood the foundations of your personality are laid and habits are formed.

2. Notice the distinctions between homemaking and housekeeping.

3. One of the most important steps in life is that of establishing a home.

Test Exercises.   ~put real number in ( )~

1. Why is the home the most important institution to which any individual ever belongs?

2. Why does a good home develop the best side of its members?

3. Which is the most essential trait for a child to observe—to love, to respect, or to obey his parents?

4. Name several important problems that occur in most homes, and explain how the co-operation of all members of the family helps to solve them.

5. How should children in the family assist in home-financing problems?

6. What modern household tools does the city housewife have which the country housewife frequently lacks?

7. In what ways do you differ from your brothers and sisters, physically, socially, and mentally?   ~stop~

Suggested Activities.

1. It is interesting to read about various prominent families of the past century, who have contributed so much to our history. The teacher may assign someone to read the story of the Adams family which contained two early presidents of the United States. (See *Compton's Pictured Encyclopedia*, I, pp. 12-16, or some other encyclopedia.) Two other presidential families are the Roosevelt and the Harrison families, each again with two presidents as well as other well-known citizens. What influence did their families have on these six presidents?

2. Contrast the different kinds of home life throughout the world. The *Junior Anthology—World Literature* by Wellons, McTurnan, and Smith describes country and city life—Norwegian, Japanese, German, English, Scotch, and American homes. You may make a list of some foreign customs such as these.

3. *Group Activity:* The teacher may have several pupils draw a plan of a kitchen in a city house, showing how the different pieces of equipment should be located to give the greatest efficiency and economy of time to the housewife.

4. *Group Activity:* The class will enjoy selecting scenes from Dickens' *Christmas Carol* for dramatization. They will find described here Bob Cratchit's happy household as well as that of Scrooge's nephew, Fred.

5. *Group Activity:* The teacher may wish to arrange a class discussion on the question as to whether strict obedience of children in the family is better than sympathetic co-operation of all members.

CHAPTER VII

YOUR PLACE IN THE SCHOOL

PREPARATORY NOTE: Another group to which you belong very early in your life is the school. Originally the home trained its children in almost every experience which they needed for later life. As civilization became more complicated this no longer was possible and so schools were started as training aids to the home. Our nation from its very start placed great emphasis on learning and so schools have grown and improved greatly during the last century. The development of complete personalities is one of the main purposes of schools today, as you will find in this chapter.

The Meaning of Education. Education is the growth of those talents which an individual possesses and the acquisition of new ones. One of the important aims of education is to combine knowledge with an ability to use it. Education requires learning, and education attempts to put the talents of people to use. Most important of all, education enables you to think for yourself. Education encourages self-reliance and initiative. Education adds to your character the ability to do and think what you know should be done and thought.

The rightly educated person knows how to make himself a useful citizen. He knows how to fit himself

74

to conditions which exist. He is able to judge what is best and has the courage to allow his better judgment to decide the issues that confront him. He is able to face and to try to solve the many difficulties of life. The main pillars of democracy are intelligence and strength of character. The school offers you an excellent opportunity to develop both of them.

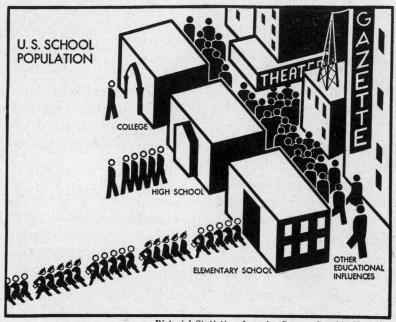

U. S. SCHOOL POPULATION

COLLEGE

HIGH SCHOOL

ELEMENTARY SCHOOL

OTHER EDUCATIONAL INFLUENCES

Pictorial Statistics, Inc., for Survey Graphic Magazine

Each figure represents one million full-time students

A prominent American journalist once said, "Learning is wealth to the poor, an honor to the rich, an aid to the young, and a support and comfort to the aged."

In a democracy such as ours, where the government rests upon and is controlled by the people, the government cannot be efficient or even endure very long unless the people are well educated.

The Interest in Education. America has more interest in education than in any of her vast industrial corporations. The value of all the school property in the United States, both elementary and secondary, is about seven billion dollars. Over two billion dollars are spent annually to maintain and operate these public schools. The entire teaching force is more than a million in number, while the pupils and students attending these institutions reach nearly thirty million, as you see in the pictograph. These facts support the common opinion that education is valuable, and even essential, from the viewpoint of the individual, the government, and society at large.

Although we regard the sums spent in the educational system as an investment, we cannot measure the profits. We are certain, however, that there is no better investment than an education. You will see proof later in your book that every boy and girl should try to complete at least a high-school course.

Methods of Learning. You learn directly and also indirectly. When you realize that there is an effort in acquiring knowledge, you are learning directly. For example, classwork sets up definite objectives to be attained. Certain information, skills, or points of view may be the objectives.

On the other hand, when you are not consciously giving your attention to increasing your skills or adding to your interests, you are learning indirectly. For example, when you secure subject-matter information in class, you also indirectly acquire training in habits, such as accuracy, neatness, or concentration. As a further example, athletic games have as their direct objectives the game itself and the recreation it affords, but they also teach character traits indirectly. Dramatics and public speaking teach indirectly a number of desirable traits. Among these are self-expression, self-control, overcoming of stage fright, ability to think on your feet, and the use of good English. The direct objective is acting the play itself, winning the debate, or winning the oratorical contest. So you learn both directly and indirectly in classwork and in extra-class activities.

School Activities—In Class. As you think over your school life, you will find it divided into two large groups: in-class activities and out-of-class activities. In-class activities are the subjects you study and the classes to which you belong. Out-of-class activities are your school interests outside the classroom. Included in the latter are any musical, dramatic, athletic, or literary clubs to which you may be attracted.

Of course the classes are more important than the clubs. When you read the benefits of an education given on page 80, you will see that these concern both the in-class activities and the out-of-class activities of the school. All of these benefits are found in one or more of such class subjects as English grammar and literature, spelling, arithmetic, geography, history, civil government, science, music, and physical education. They also play a part in the debating or dramatic club, the choral group or the basketball game.

In your classwork you are naturally interested in getting the best results from your efforts. Grades are only one indication of your degree of success but they are important in our present system. On them depends much of your later success or failure in high school and college. But more important than grades is the real understanding of your subjects. If you are interested in and understand your schoolwork you will make better grades more easily.

Do you understand *why* a given problem was solved in the way it was? Do you see the reasons back of the project in geography or history which you have just completed? For example, do you know why rivers and mountains are important in a nation's life and history? If you do not, you are failing to get the most out of your classwork. Naturally this requires effort on your part, and homework sufficient to read carefully all your assignments and to think over all the questions. Your teacher is available to help you when you encounter difficulties. Perhaps you will have to consult other books in the library, because it is difficult for any school text to present all that is important in a subject. Of course, you will have to be accurate and careful in your written work, and you will not allow anything to interrupt your attention either in class or in your own study room.

Finally, try to find a way in which the subject will ? of especial benefit to you. Does the history make ?r some point you have heard discussed or you may have read in the papers or magazines? Does the arithmetic problem concern something in which you are or will be interested? You will readily find such applications as these if you really look for them, and they will make your subjects far more interesting and valuable. You will find that all knowledge may be put to use. As a careful pupil you should understand that use, and make an effort to find and apply it. Such an effort will give purpose and value to your study.

School Activities—Out-of-Class. When your classwork is done, if you can spare the time, try to enter into one or more out-of-class activities. Membership in various clubs is very profitable. Time spent in the band, chorus, orchestra, debating team, dramatics, or athletics, usually is time very well spent. Perhaps you are qualified for service on the staff of the school paper or for duty on the school council. Be sure to take an active part in some out-of-class activity, but be sure to give your classwork your first attention. Avoid too many out-of-class activities, as they may lead to neglect of classwork, or overwork, or both. You will find that the world outside of school requires the talents of people who can do a variety of things well. In school you can get valuable training for later life if you broaden your experience and learn to get along with people.

School Spirit. When you put your school above any of its clubs, classes, teams, or individuals, you are loyal to your school. When you have respect for authority and co-operate with those in charge of the school, and when you boost and help promote any worthy cause of your school, you have the right school spirit. Anyone can cheer for his team when it is winning, but it takes a "good sport" to cheer for his team when it is losing, or to cheer for good plays made by the opposite team.

If you have the right school spirit, your conduct will readily show it. You will have pride in your school to the extent that you will not do anything to injure its reputation. You will not permit anyone to deface its property or mar its good name, if it is within your power to prevent it. An occasional visitor to your school will soon observe the presence or lack of good school spirit among the students. For where there is good school spirit, you and all pupils will be wholeheartedly interested and actively engaged in every department of the school. You will sacrifice your own wishes for the good of your school. This training in loyalty will also carry over into your later life. It will make it easy for you to see the value of loyalty to your country, your business, or your profession. Habits of loyalty help your character and add to your success in life.

The Benefits of an Education. A study was made some twenty years ago to determine the benefits which should result from an elementary and a high-school education. These benefits were grouped under seven heads:

(1) *Command of the fundamental processes,* or the tool subjects such as arithmetic, writing, spelling, and language, is emphasized throughout all grades. (2) *Good health* is based upon your study of sanitation and

physiology, and also upon your entire program of physical education which is intended to give you a sound body. (3) *Worthy home membership,* and (4) *civic participation* are traits which improve your personal development, influence your character and affect both your family and your neighbors. (5) *Vocational efficiency* comes from the proper training for a trade, business, or profession, which most boys and girls will need as a means of livelihood. (6) *Ethical character* is based on the proper understanding of right and wrong and is therefore good character. (7) *Worthy use of leisure* is the ability to use your spare time in such a way that it is thoroughly enjoyable to yourself and also helpful to your friends and associates.

If you are deriving the benefits described above, your in-class and out-of-class activities are helping you develop in the right way. If you want to know the value of your schooling, grade yourself on the progress you have made toward these objectives. By making an outline and adding subheads under each of these seven topics, you can obtain a more detailed account of your progress. If you grade yourself once or twice a year, you will learn whether you are actually growing, and you will find that your own development is more important than your accumulation of material goods. You will understand that going to school is building a foundation upon which to shape an intelligent and useful life.

Education for Earning a Living. In this workaday world where everyone must, or should want to, earn his own living, the better educated you are, the more valuable will you be to yourself and to an employer. When you stop to think about it, you will realize that the competition in industry, business, and in the professions is growing because standards are constantly being raised, and the number of trained individuals is constantly increasing. If you realize this, you will understand why an adequate education is becoming an absolute necessity. Sometimes parents allow boys and girls to leave school to help the family with their earnings, when this is not necessary. In such cases the parents fail to realize that an education is not a luxury, but rather an investment that will be of great financial aid in the future.

You can qualify for many kinds of businesses or professions by attending one of the many excellent colleges or universities available. But first you should discover the work for which you are best fitted. Even in well-equipped high schools a great many courses are offered which prepare boys and girls for definite kinds of work.

Education for Serving Others. But merely to earn a living is not enough. It is true that work is necessary to obtain money to buy the necessities of life, but money is only a symbol of value, a medium of exchange for material things and for work done. You must have some unselfish purpose in your work for the benefit of society, to be truly happy. When you cease to work for money only, you gain in proportion to the spirit you put into your work. Then your work becomes a joy and satisfaction instead of a hated duty and drudgery.

It has often been said that ignorance and selfishness are two great obstacles to human progress, in addition to being causes of human misery. Ignorance vanishes as you become educated, and selfishness disappears as you learn to love your fellow men and as you become interested in your fellow men's welfare. As you avoid being ignorant and selfish, you stand ready and willing to serve others.

A new social attitude is spreading through all classes, agencies, and organizations which shows that people are becoming more intelligent and unselfish in their desire to improve conditions. This new spirit is expressing itself in various ways. Underprivileged classes are being better cared for. Employers feel that they owe their employees something besides wages. Social settlements and philanthropic organizations are doing noble work. Schools and universities are announcing that the object of education is to fit men and women for service. Of course, churches are fitting individuals for service. Rotary Clubs have for their slogan, "He profits most who serves best."

A prominent judge once said, "Man in all stages, from poverty to riches, from ignorance to learning, reacts to the urge of service and the glow which it brings. Service to others, service to the community, service to the world, are ever apparent. To serve well, one must be honest, have the courage to stand for his convictions, and do the right thing."

Education for Enjoying Life. To enjoy life, one must have some measure of real success. What is success? Surely it is not a mere collection of dollars

and cents, nor an accumulation of any material products. Fame, social position, or political prominence,
do not always mean success. Service and love for
others must be one of your guides to living—service
that helps your fellow men. The Golden Rule must
show in the life that would be accounted a success.

To be sure, there is no short cut to success, no royal
road to learning. You cannot go through life without
paying your dues. You cannot get something for
nothing very long. It may take many a severe lesson
to learn this; it may cause great sacrifice, but it is
worth it in the end. As you learn, you become more
appreciative of the better things in life, and life becomes more enjoyable.

Education, more and more, develops your appreciation. Art appreciation, music appreciation, nature
appreciation are opening new avenues of thought and
instruction for you in school. To admire the beauty
of a sunset, or the flaming tints of autumn, is appreciation. But a deeper appreciation of the beauty in
life may be gained in the home. Here daily and hourly
contacts give you opportunity for the cultivation of
sympathy, understanding, and kindly attentions.

Appreciation of life, understanding of life's problems, and obedience to the laws of life make the only
road to happiness. The greater the appreciation, the
greater is the capacity for happiness. Real happiness
comes only when the mind is contented with its course.
Those whose real satisfaction consists in striving
toward an ideal, find life the most worth while.

Test and Study Exercises

Aids to Learning.

1. Remember that one of the most important aims of education is to teach you to think for yourself.

2. Observe that thirty million young people out of our total population are now enrolled in school. This shows how our country is far above other nations in the extent of free, public education.

3. Review the seven benefits to be secured from an elementary and high-school education.

Test Exercises.

1. Which of the seven fundamental benefits of education are illustrated by the subjects you are studying this year?

2. What are several ways by which you can tell a well-educated person from one who has had little formal education?

3. Should a course in citizenship primarily add to your information, increase your skills, or change your points of view?

4. Why should boys and girls remain in school, if possible, until they are at least twenty years old?

5. What out-of-class activities are most valuable as preparation for your chosen vocation?

6. Whom would you consider more successful in life, the man who had accumulated money only, or the prominent scientist who had discovered a cure for a common disease? The political boss of a wealthy state, or the poet, Longfellow? Why?

Suggested Activities.

1. Inquire from your principal how many of your grade-school graduates finish high school. Compare this with the average school by consulting your librarian. What does this signify to you?

2. Make a list of the out-of-school activities which pupils in your school enjoy. How do these activities show the results of the seven benefits of an education?

3. *Group Activity:* The class may discuss the reasons why a man without children should help support the public schools.

4. *Group Activity:* The teacher may assign pupils to consult the library and make a report to the class on the education of Abraham Lincoln as compared with that of George Washington. How did the school experiences of both differ from yours?

CHAPTER VIII

THE INFLUENCE OF RELIGIONS

PREPARATORY NOTE: The church plays an important part in the life of most communities, as this chapter indicates. It contributes to the moral betterment of life as well as to the improvement of cultural values. There are many religions which have influenced the world's thinking. Several of these religions, and especially Christianity, have raised the standards of living and bettered the conditions of mankind. The home, the school, and the church together have made our country what it is today.

Different Ideas about Religion. Religion has different meanings for different peoples. To the Chinese, Confucianism[1] is a code of morality emphasizing social service. To the Arab, Mohammedanism[2] means the careful observance of prayer and temperance. To the Jew, religion is a belief in one God and in virtuous living, tolerance, and peace. To the Christian, religion signifies that God is the Father of all and that all men are brothers. All of these religions have their lofty ideals of morality. Unfortunately, however, superstition and selfishness are also found there. Religion then

[1] **Confucianism.** The moral system of Confucius, a Chinese philosopher of the fifth century before Christ.
[2] **Mohammedanism.** The religion of Mohammed, the Arabian prophet of the seventh century.

86

is a matter of belief, a belief in the relation between ourselves and God.

The Christian religion is the prevailing one in this land of ours, and in fact, in the whole world as far as numbers go. Over one-third of the people of the world, about six hundred eighty millions are called Chris-

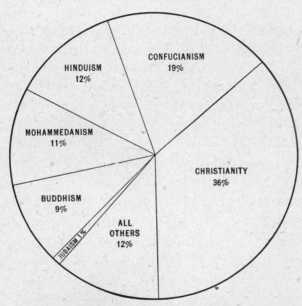

The Percentage Distribution of World Religions

tians, or followers of Jesus of Nazareth. Confucianism has nearly one-fifth of the world under its sway; Hinduism[3] and Buddhism,[4] the religions of India, have

[3] **Hinduism.** The ancient religion or beliefs of the people of India, based on the caste system.

[4] **Buddhism.** The religion of the Hindu prince Buddha, of the fifth century before Christ.

together more than one-fifth, Mohammedanism over one-tenth, and Judaism, the religion of the Jews, one-hundredth of the total population. Hundreds of minor faiths include a large part of the other inhabitants of the world.

Christianity like many other religions, is not united. The Roman Catholics include almost half the total Christian group, Greek Catholics about a fifth and Protestants the remainder. These again are subdivided—the Protestants into many different groups.

Among the important teachings of Jesus, the founder of Christianity, is the belief that God is the Father of all men and that all men are brothers. Jesus explained his social teachings in the Golden Rule. "To do unto others as you would have them do unto you" is the essence of this belief. This is the practical rule which applies to our everyday conduct.

Unfortunately people of different religions and even of the same religion have too often been eager to oppose one another in defense of their particular beliefs. History has been full of bloody wars brought about by man's intolerance. The practice of the Golden Rule, however, would do away with these senseless mass killings. Murder, crime, and war would cease if we did to others as we would want them to do to us.

The Benefits of Religion. Man's lack of concern for his ideals has caused most of the sufferings in the world. Selfishness and greed are usually back of this lack of concern. But despite this fact, most of the improvements in civilization today have their roots in the Golden Rule. Christianity teaches us to relieve all suffering, to help the oppressed, to make the world a better place in which to live, to be tolerant of other people, and to be merciful.

Relief of Suffering. The Hospitalers or Knights of St. John, during the Crusades eight hundred years ago, were among the first to take care of the sick and wounded. The monks used their monasteries for similar purposes for many hundred years. Florence Nightingale, a nurse, nearly a century ago carried out the same idea on the battlefields of the Crimean War. All of these indirectly received their inspiration for relieving suffering from the teachings of Jesus.

There are many other kinds of sufferers who need relief besides those wounded in battle. Medical missionaries today are trying to better the condition of the people in all the lands to which they go. They teach them the scientific use of medicine, how to take care of themselves physically, and how to avoid disease. These same practices are followed by the settlement workers in the slums of our big cities. Here the poor are massed together in such large numbers that they find it difficult even to live. Sanitation and health are cared for by the city government, but the visiting nurse or case worker has to teach people how to observe these health rules.

Improvement Through Education. One of the best ways to make people happier is to give them the knowledge by which they can care for themselves. Christians during the Middle Ages formed schools for training their children. These at first were religious schools under the control of the monasteries. The

early schools in our own country were started by the
Puritans and other settlers as places for religious
training. Thus schools had their beginning among
our ancestors as religious institutions. It was not till
the middle of the last century that free public education became popular.

By means of schools children were taught the newer
developments of their day. They became better citizens. They learned to enter business and the profes
sions. They learned how to enjoy life and to make
others happier. They began to look beyond their own
household and as they grew older, they gave more
attention to their neighbors.

Settlement houses like Hull House in Chicago,
started by Jane Addams a half century ago, were the
first means of helping the poor in our large cities.
Institutions for the care of the blind or the aged also
grew up out of this same interest. The Young Men's
Christian Association came into being at about the
same time. Most of these were associated with religious
interests in one way or another. And so in ways such
as these religion, together with education, helps to
make a better world.

Teaching Tolerance and Mercy. It took many centuries, however, before religion became tolerant and
merciful to its enemies. Early men believed in killing
their foes, even including the helpless women and
children. The early Christians frequently followed
the same practice. The first settlers in America were
merciful neither to the Indians nor to their religious
opponents in other settlements. It was not till this

last century that the quality of mercy and the spirit of tolerance became commoner.

Florence Nightingale practiced this in the Crimean War by caring for both friend and foe. You see in this photograph from a recent moving-picture film,

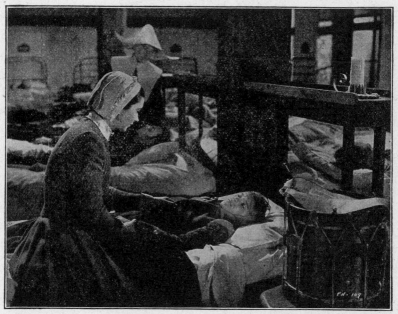

Photo Courtesy of Warner Bros. Studio

Florence Nightingale Administering to the Wounded

how she aided the wounded in her hospital. The Red Cross has always aided the wounded and dying of both sides on the battlefield. Religious wars have about ceased and man is becoming more tolerant of those who differ from him in religious beliefs.

However it is still hard to be tolerant of differences of opinion. People differ harshly on some of the minor points of religion or politics. Education still has a long way to go to teach men to look at both sides of a disputed question and to recognize the good points of their opponents. Open-mindedness is necessary if you are to be tolerant.

Your Responsibility to Religion. Even though you accept all this as true, what is your part in bringing it about? What can you do to spread these ideals in your community? In the first place, you should have sympathy and an understanding of the conditions of those who are less fortunate than you as well as of those who hold other beliefs. Understanding the problems of others leads to tolerance. You may think you dislike certain groups of foreigners but you find it hard not to like the foreign boy or girl whom you know well in the playground or clubroom. You think *he* or *she* is different when really *you* are the one who takes the different point of view.

Co-operation and Participation. Churches would not flourish if all people were merely tolerant. You must co-operate and play your part if you are to give as well as to receive the benefits of religion. Your relation may take the form of membership in the activities of some religious group. This should include participation in its undertakings.

More important than all these contributions of religion is the influence religion has on the right living of its members. Religion is more than a code of morals. Morals, as you have learned, vary from time to time and from place to place. Religion supplies reasons for right and wrong. The faith you have in the ideals of your religion is one of the most important guides that cause you to do what you believe is right and to avoid what you consider wrong. By holding to this faith you make yourself a better person and a more valuable citizen of your community.

Choose 5 complete copy

Test and Study Exercises

Aids to Learning.

1. Observe three of the ways in which religion has improved our civilization.

2. Remember that various people give different meanings to religion.

3. Education teaches you to look at both sides of a disputed question and to be tolerant of differences of opinion.

Test Exercises.

1. What are the advantages of a community with an active church in it?

2. Are there more followers of Asiatic religions than of Christianity?

3. What organizations for helping those less fortunate were started by religious groups?

4. What international boys' organizations are closely related to the church?

5. Is Christianity merely a personal religion or is it also based on social teachings—the relation of man to his fellows?

6. What are several important ways in which Christianity has aided modern civilization?

7. What are examples of cruel treatment because of religious differences?

8. In what ways were the early colonial schools connected with religious interests?

Suggested Activities.

1. The teacher may assign pupils to color outline maps of the different continents of the world showing where the world religions are located.

2. **Refer** to your encyclopedia for information about the Knights of St. John, and see what part they had in the Crusades.

3. The teacher may assign pupils to report more fully on the life of Florence Nightingale and her influence in preparing the way for the Red Cross.

4. Look up the life of some famous missionary such as John G. Patton, Father Xavier, or David Livingstone. How did they relieve suffering and in what ways did they really educate their people?

5. You may read part of Jane Addams' *Twenty Years at Hull House* or some other biography of her to learn of the changes that were made in this neighborhood under Miss Addams' guidance.

6. *Group Activity:* If you live in a town, your teacher may arrange to have the class visit some social settlement, boys' club, or old peoples' home. Discover how religious influences are making life happier for these people.

CHAPTER IX

YOUR INTEREST IN THE COMMUNITY

PREPARATORY NOTE: The next chapter explains that you are not only a member of a family, a school, or a church; you are also a member of a community, whether it be a farm community, a small town, or a large city. The way in which your own community has developed is of great interest to you. You will find it interesting to learn more about the early communities from which your own grew, and also the different kinds of communities found all over the nation. You have a definite part to play in the betterment of your own community.

Changing Communities. You are a member of the community in which you live even though you are not old enough to vote. Sometimes a state or a whole nation is spoken of as a community. However, for our study here, we mean a village, a small town, or a local neighborhood in a large city.

Whenever a group of people live together in the same locality, have interests in common, and are subject to the same rules or laws, we refer to that group as a community. As a member of your community, you should be interested in its progress and welfare, just as you are interested in the progress and success of your school, church, or club.

The members of these organizations are responsible for the good or bad reputation of their organization. The same is true of a community. The community may be known as the best one for miles around, or it may be known as a place to avoid, depending on the attitudes and actions of its members.

Community spirit depends to a great extent upon the home training of its members. If you are considerate of those about you, you will be interested in helping your neighbors make your community a more pleasant and a more attractive place in which to live.

Communities in the history of our country may be classified according to the time in which they were developed. A number of things, such as the time in which they existed, the circumstances under which they were formed, their particular problems, and their kinds of people made these communities what they were. Thus we have the original community where the Indian lived, the frontier community where the early white settlers lived, and the modern community of today.

The Original American Community. The Indian produced his own food, made his own clothes and dwellings, and occasionally even dug his own grave before he died. He depended upon very few for assistance of any kind. He was independent in making a living, but on the other hand, he was superstitious. Thus independence and superstition were the two outstanding conditions found in the original community. As time went on, these two conditions changed, as you will notice.

The Frontier Community. The early white settlers traveled and lived together within communities. One of their chief problems was to protect themselves from the Indians. They were obliged to work together in order to help one another against the common foe. This way of doing things naturally developed a spirit of co-operation. They hunted and fished together, worked together, and took turns in guarding the community night and day. On the other hand, they were better educated and, consequently, less superstitious than the Indians. The life of Daniel Boone will serve as an excellent example of life in the frontier community.

Two features of frontier community life were co-operation and training. This training, however, was not sufficient when compared with the amount of training needed later. As time went on, the co-operation found in the frontier increased. As a result, the modern community requires a total dependence upon others, and also more and more attention is given to the training of its citizens.

The Modern Community. Today there is no such thing as independent living. Everyone is dependent upon someone else in many ways. Even the hermit can hide in the mountains for only a short time. The millionaire, with his great wealth, needs the help of others. The city people need the farmer's grain, and the farmer needs the machinery made in the city. Industry requires the help of labor as well as the use of capital. This is also true of sports. You know that a football team needs players in the line and players in the backfield. You know that a baseball team needs players able through special practice to play certain positions.

In this day of specialization many dozen people are needed to make one pair of shoes, whereas years ago one man made the pair by himself, even though it required much more time to do so. Formerly two men would kill and butcher a hog or a steer, but today, in the meat-packing house many men are engaged in preparing them for food. The result is that several thousand hogs, sheep, and cattle are slaughtered and prepared in a single day in a single meat-packing house. Dependence on one another has been brought about by the necessity for greater production due to greater demand.

The two outstanding conditions of our community of today, as compared with those of the original and frontier communities, are almost total dependence upon each other and improved training. As time has advanced, the independence of the early communities has changed to the dependence of our modern community. Ignorance and superstition have been replaced by knowledge.

The Beautiful Community. A community still surrounded with its native scenery is frequently a beautiful community. On one side, off in the distance, there may be snow-capped mountains that seem to meet the blue sky; on the other side a lake into which the sun's rays pour their light. The background of the lake may be a forest with its green and shapely trees, and on the edge of the community a long winding stream where one can enjoy fishing for hours. Such a community is attractive, especially if it has a wholesome community spirit. An example of this is seen in the photograph of Yakima, Washington. Off in the distance towers snow-capped Mt. Adams surrounded

Courtesy Northern Pacific Ry.
Yakima, Washington, and Mt. Adams

by forests, while on the other side flows the river, bordered by beautiful orchards.

On the other hand, a community may have created its own beauty. An artificial lake may border its edge. Trees may be planted, houses painted, and lawns and terraces created. Such a community also is an attractive community, if it has a wholesome community spirit.

An ideal community in which to live should have real beauty, natural or artificial. But above and beyond that beauty, it must have people in it with ideals, principles, and good habits which will produce peace and justice.

Study of the Community. It is a good thing for a community to take an inventory of itself occasionally. A community needs to survey its strength and weakness, its progress, and the places where progress still should be made. A community should learn its needs in their order of importance. Then it should plan ways and means of satisfying these needs.

Your Duty to Your Community. If you are interested in your community and its affairs, you will want to do your share to improve it in whatever way you can. You will obey its rules and have respect for the rights of others. You will be fair in all your dealings and support your community in every possible way.

You will be loyal to your community by working for it. You may hear school children speak disrespectfully of the policemen and firemen. They forget that these men are constantly risking their lives for the protection of the public. These men safeguard the community. One way to be loyal to your community is to respect and support its officers.

The Community's Duty to You. The officials of your community who have the proper spirit and a sincere desire to benefit all its members, will accept their responsibilities and solve its problems to the best of their ability. They will endeavor to safeguard public health. They will endeavor to protect life and property within the community. They will provide education and recreation for everyone. They will aid the handicapped and unfortunate. They will plan the city so that there will be beauty, convenience, and efficiency. They will endeavor to have all members of the community do their part in the community. These are some of the principal problems found in all communities, but there are many other minor problems constantly coming up for solution.

If the officials of a community fail to meet and solve these problems, whether because of inability or lack of desire, they can be replaced by more capable and more willing officials if the people so decide. The people select their own officials and thus control the future of their community. A community is just what the people make it.

Just as an individual has duties to perform and problems to solve, so communities have their duties and problems. If neighboring communities will co-operate, rather than criticize one another, all will benefit and a desirable community spirit will be the result.

A Growing Responsibility. Every individual should want to do his part in his community. Some will see how they can be helpful sooner than others, depending on how well they have learned to be helpful and to co-operate at home and at school.

At home a child learns that he should not destroy his toys, the furniture, or other things about his home.

He also learns that he should not injure his neighbor's property.

At school he learns to be neat in placing waste paper in the basket instead of throwing it carelessly on the floor or street. He learns not to destroy or deface his school building or other public buildings. He learns not to break windows in buildings whether they are occupied or not. When he is willing to respect these rules, he shows that he is a good citizen and has taken his first step in the affairs of the community.

As a youth we expect more of him. He begins to realize that there are standards by which he may guide himself. He knows that the record he is now making will count for or against him in the future. He is more eager than ever before to take his place in the development of his community.

As an adult he takes his place in industry and the community. He has the opportunity, if he is qualified, of being elected or appointed to hold public office. He may be asked for counsel and advice on matters of importance. He is in a position to render great service to his community. He will be expected to use his influence for good among the youth of his community. As he grows older he becomes still more experienced and therefore a wiser counselor and a firmer supporter of his community.

Contrasting Communities. We have discussed your place in the home, the school, and the church. These three institutions are very important in all good communities. You will now see that there are many kinds of communities; some are large, others are small; some are industrial, others purely residential. Of the industrial communities some are mining towns, some are manufacturing towns, some are railroad centers, some are oil towns, and some are seaports.

There are also rural and urban communities. The rural communities consist of farms and small villages. Here houses are far apart and naturally association between people is more difficult. In the urban communities, people can mingle with each other more than in a rural community because they live closer to each other.

The Rural Community. The rural community supplies the urban community with its food. Also it provides the city with raw materials to make its clothing. No longer is life in the country considered lonely and inconvenient as was formerly the case. Rural folks have been brought into closer touch with the city by means of transportation and the radio. Cars, trucks, and good highways make it possible for the farmer to deliver his produce more quickly than ever before and at less expense. The farmer can now go to the city to buy in less time and at a cheaper rate. He can also go to town oftener for recreation. Even airplanes and refrigeration are having their part in very rapid transportation of perishable produce.

Many a farmer today has nearly the same conveniences as his city neighbor. He talks to him over the same telephone system. He listens to the same concert or market report over his radio. He uses gas, oil, and electricity from the same source as does his city neighbor. He has free delivery of mail. Frequently he

reads the same daily newspaper and magazines, and he
borrows books from a public library. He may attend
a similar theater, lodge, or church. His children can
attend the same kind of high school or college. Unfortunately this is not yet true of all farmers, as the
illustration shows, but the number who have these conveniences is continually increasing.

FARM EQUIPMENT

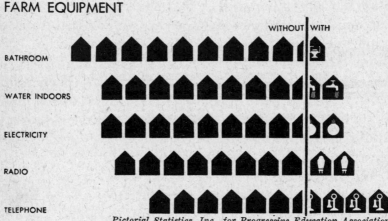

Pictorial Statistics, Inc., for Progressive Education Association

Each symbol represents 10 per cent of all farms.

The farmer in addition to this lives a more independent life. He enjoys the sunshine and fresh air,
which is free from the smoke and dirt usually found
in the city. He can go to the city whenever he chooses
since he works under his own direction. During certain periods of the year he has more leisure. As a rule,
he is not under the same pressure as is the city man.

The Large City Community. The urban community
supplies the rural community with ready-made clothes,

machinery, and all kinds of equipment. While the resident of a large city has many advantages over his country friend, he also has disadvantages. City people live very busy lives. Most of those who work there have a considerable distance to travel to and from their work daily. The city man often lives in a large apartment house high above the street. He may have fewer neighbors and real friends in that same building than the man who lives in a small community. Every city has its problems. The larger the city, the more numerous and the greater are these problems.

On the other hand, the city is a center of culture and learning. Here are most of our newspapers, high schools, colleges, churches, theaters, large stores, and many other cultural opportunities. The city offers comfort, amusement, and education, but it also has poverty, vice, and the slums.

We need both types of communities, urban and rural. They depend upon each other and work together, each respecting the other.

The Small City Community. This type of community depends upon both the rural community and the large city communities. It has many of the advantages of both. It is, as a rule, a residential village, without many large industries. Here a general spirit of friendliness and common interest are found because everyone knows almost everyone else. People attend the community centers, they are interested in civic affairs, and they are concerned with the welfare of everyone else in their community. They can go to the big city or to the country whenever they choose. If the small city has the right community spirit, it is perhaps the

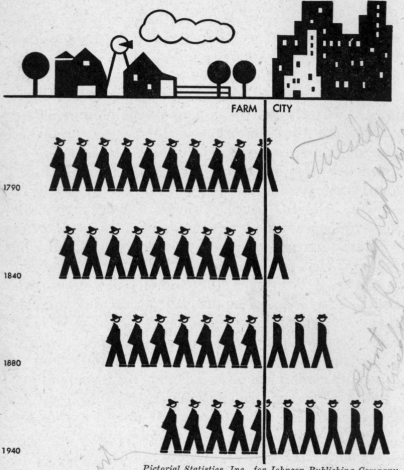

Pictorial Statistics, Inc., for Johnson Publishing Company
**Each symbol represents 10 per cent
of total population in farm and city.**

most attractive of all communities in which to live.

From Farm to City. The number and proportion of people living in towns and cities has been constantly increasing. About one hundred fifty years ago, only one-twentieth of the inhabitants of the United States lived in towns or cities, with a population of twenty-five hundred or more. One hundred years ago only one tenth lived in towns and cities. Sixty years ago this number had increased to nearly one third and since 1920 to over one half. As a matter of fact, in 1940 there were twenty million more people in towns of twenty-five hundred and over than in 1920. You can see in the pictograph the trend to the city during the life of our nation.

If rural people continue to move to large towns and cities, we shall have ever-increasing problems. The crowding of too many people into small areas causes housing difficulties. The difficulty people have in finding adequate houses or apartments naturally causes dissatisfaction. Poor housing is one of the reasons crime increases. Unless people begin to return to the small communities, life will become even more complex in our cities than it is today.

Test and Study Exercises

Aids to Learning.

1. Note that a group of people living together in the same locality, with common interests and common laws, make up a community.

2. Observe the changes in regard to co-operation and training in the original community, the frontier community, and the modern community.

3. Notice how the proportion of people leaving the rural districts has created vital problems in our cities.

Test Exercises.

On a separate sheet of paper give the letter for the correct answer for each statement.

1. A community may best be defined as a group of people associated together in (*a*) a school (*b*) a church (*c*) a club (*d*) a state (*e*) a town or village.

2. In the original American community the Indian was (*a*) independent (*b*) co-operative (*c*) well-educated (*d*) highly specialized (*e*) industrialized.

3. The farmer is usually dependent on the city for (*a*) food (*b*) roads (*c*) raw materials (*d*) machinery (*e*) water supply.

4. The city man is dependent on the farm for (*a*) machinery (*b*) food (*c*) transportation (*d*) houses (*e*) recreation.

5. An outstanding advantage of the city is its (*a*) quietness (*b*) neighborliness (*c*) culture and recreation (*d*) slums (*e*) congestion.

Suggested Activities.

1. Consult *Compton's Pictured Encyclopedia* or some other reference book for the village life of the American Indians. In what ways were they very superstitious?

2. Find out what new kinds of food the Indian taught the white man to use.

3. Read the *Life of Robinson Crusoe* by Daniel Defoe, or *Swiss Family Robinson* by J. D. Wyss, to learn how people cast on a desert island are able to live by themselves.

4. Write to one of the large air-transport companies, and ask them what kinds of perishable produce they carry from the farms to the cities.

5. Consult an encyclopedia or almanac on the growth of the city of Chicago. What were the important reasons for its very rapid growth?

6. *Group Activity:* The teacher may take the class to visit some industry where mass production is shown. The stockyards, an automobile-assembly plant, a shoe factory, or a newspaper-printing plant will illustrate the specialization of each man's job.

7. *Group Activity:* The teacher may assign several pupils to visit a nearby fire station and report to the class. They will learn the ways in which firemen protect the property of the community, even at the risk of their own lives.

8. *Group Activity:* The teacher may have different pupils report to the class the source of the common foods we eat everyday.

PART III

THE COMMUNITY WORKING THROUGH ITS CITIZENS

A community is what its members make it. It is within the power of its members to make it an ideal community by working together for the common good. If its members are indifferent and are not concerned about their community, it will not become progressive. It may even become slow and backward.

Any organization, such as a baseball club, football team, school, church, or lodge, must have rules by which it can be governed. It cannot exist long without some rules. If it is to be successful, it is necessary that the members give their support by obeying the rules.

A community, too, has its laws which are the wishes of the majority of the people as decided by its representatives. These laws must be obeyed by its members if the community is to be successful and prosperous. For example, the laws of a community provide for the protection of the health, life, and property of the members of the community. Surely all its members should want to obey these laws as they are all

benefited by them. The laws of a community also provide education, recreation, and aid for its dependents.

It is the duty of officials to see that laws are enforced.
The intelligent members of a community will not only
obey its laws, but they will insist that careless and
indifferent members also obey them. If a baseball or
football team is to be successful, its members must
co-operate. If a community is to be successful, its
members likewise must co-operate. When laws are
to be made or officials are to be chosen, it is the duty
of the members, as citizens, to work together in the
enforcement of the laws and in the support of its
officials. This working together is essential for success
in any organization, large or small.

Co-operation comes as a result of a thorough understanding of the community's needs and a desire to assist in its success and prosperity. People should understand what the community does to maintain *public
health* and to provide *protection of life and property*.
Citizens and taxpayers should understand the community's efforts to provide public *education and recreation,* even though they have no children of their own
attending school. They should understand the needs
of those of the community who are handicapped and
dependent and will therefore be helpful to the *community's dependents*. They should do their part in
adding to the beauty of their town through *city and
regional planning*. They should understand the structure of *modern industrial life*. Finally, citizens of the
community should encourage and help those *immigrants* who want to become citizens.

CHAPTER X.

PUBLIC HEALTH

PREPARATORY NOTE: We have considered the value of good health to the individual. Equally important to the community is the good health of all its citizens, as this chapter shows. A disease which threatens the existence of a town can come from the humble home of the poorest citizen. Community health depends on many features. Air and light, water and food, housing and sanitation—all must receive careful attention if a community is to maintain public health. To accomplish this result many laws are drawn up and boards of prominent citizens see that they are carried out.

The Importance of Good Health. The importance of good health cannot be stressed too much. To keep "a sound mind in a sound body," you should learn the laws of good health, how to acquire good health and how to keep it. Good health is essential for all the groups of which you are a member.

First of all, the family should be healthy. Healthy parents are necessary if their children are to be well-born. Intelligent parenthood is essential if children are to be guarded against unnecessary disease. No longer is it considered desirable to expose babies to the common ailments so that they will be free from them later on. Too often simple diseases such as

111

measles and whooping cough leave weaknesses or even worse afflictions that could have been avoided. Therefore the wise parent sees that his children are vaccinated or inoculated[1] to prevent their contracting such germ diseases. He also makes certain that his children's hearing and sight are entirely sound, that they have no throat disorders such as diseased tonsils, and that all organs of the body are in good condition.

The same care is required in school or industry. All well-ordered communities require vaccination and periodic health examinations for schools and business organizations where many people are brought constantly together. The common cold reduces the efficiency of both pupil and worker tremendously. If more care is taken to prevent colds and adequate treatment is given when they occur, unnecessary loss of time and suffering of the patient as well as others can be prevented. If a cold is allowed to continue, sometimes it causes partial deafness which becomes a life handicap. Don't attempt to wear out a cold. Take care of it immediately. If you are ill, do not expose others to your colds or contagious diseases. The prevention of accidents is as important as concern for good health. This includes the regulation of automobile traffic and special instruction in the use of dangerous, exposed machinery.

In any community, in the country or city, the constant health of its members requires that certain precautions be taken. Pure air and water, wholesome food, cleanliness and sanitation, the prevention of dis-

---

[1] **inoculated.** Given a mild form of disease to prevent its later occurrence.

case and epidemics, and the care of the physically and mentally incompetent are all very important problems for the well-being of the community. Although these primarily require community action, yet they are also the concern of every member of the community.

Pure Air and Sufficient Light. We think of pure air as found only in the country because city air is so frequently filled with dust, smoke, and gas. Soot-laden smokestacks, engines belching black smoke, and automobiles pouring forth poisonous gas from their exhausts encourage diseases of the lungs. Dusty country roads may produce similar results, but the number of people exposed to them is much smaller than in cities and towns. Much of this air pollution in the city, however, can be remedied by the careful firing of furnaces and boilers, and by attention to the proper construction of cars so that most of the gas is carried away through the exhausts.

Adequate light is also necessary if you are to avoid eyestrain. Excessive glare is as bad as insufficient light. Light coming over the shoulder is always desirable when you are writing so that you will avoid shadows. Your eyesight is one of your most valued possessions and no effort is too great to protect it. If your eyes become strained, they should receive immediate attention and an examination, to see whether you need to be fitted with glasses.

The Water Supply. We need an abundant supply of pure water in the home for drinking, bathing, and cleaning purposes. The community needs water for protection from fires and for cleaning the streets.

Industry needs water also for supplying power. Agriculture is in need of water for irrigation, as water is required by all forms of plant life. Various business houses, such as bakeries, laundries, and dye establishments use a large amount of water.

It is the community's problem to seek unpolluted sources of water. Some smaller communities have wells. Other communities bring in the water from great distances. This is planned by engineers, who search for water wherever it can be found. Reservoirs or containers may have to be built and the water piped from its source to the reservoirs and thence to the houses where it can be obtained under pressure simply by opening the water faucets. Los Angeles brings her water in aqueducts from the snow-capped Sierra Nevada mountains and from the Parker Dam over two hundred miles away. New York has tapped the great watersheds of the Croton and Schoharie rivers and constructed two systems of reservoirs and aqueducts from the Catskill Mountains which together make the greatest water supply system in the world. Chicago, Detroit, Cleveland, and Buffalo, on the contrary, get their water through tunnels running several miles out into the Great Lakes. Cities like Cincinnati and Omaha located on rivers usually get water from those rivers. Of course such water must be thoroughly purified and tested before it can be used.

Deep well water is usually pure enough to drink, but all other water should be purified by being sterilized or treated with a germicide,[2] usually chlorine,

[2] **germicide.** A substance that kills germs.

to destroy germs; it should be treated with alum to clarify it when very muddy; or it should be filtered or passed through sand beds to remove other particles.

Most cities and towns own their water plants, and the people are charged with a water tax to help pay for the securing and purifying of the water. The

Courtesy Northern Pacific Ry.

Grand Coulee Dam

supply of water must be sufficient, pure, and steady for use all the time. The state sometimes takes over the control of the rivers and other bodies of water to prevent pollution or to utilize the water power. Different states may agree, with the consent of Congress, regarding their use and control of water supplies.

The United States, through its Department of the Interior, has constructed vast irrigation works for farming purposes for the dry lands of the west. It also uses water power for industry. The Wilson Dam at Muscle Shoals in Alabama and the Grand Coulee Dam on the Columbia River are examples. The dam at the Grand Coulee, which is shown in the photograph, will serve to irrigate all the surrounding lands, to generate an immense amount of electric power, and to harness the flow of the water by a reservoir in order to check floods.

Wholesome Food. Laws are made and certain standards are set up by the government to assure us of wholesome food. Tests and inspections of all houses handling food sold to the public are made by government agents. The reasons for these measures are to avoid disease caused by eating poorly prepared food, and impure or spoiled food; to guard against the sale of perishable foods, such as milk, butter, meat, eggs, fish, fresh fruits, and vegetables that have been kept too long; to prevent the spread of disease by those who handle food; to assure cleanliness, sanitation, and purity of food by means of official inspection; and to guarantee correct weights and measures.

All the units of government co-operate to protect us from impure food. The local government has food inspectors who visit bakeries, dairies, markets, and other stores to insure the proper sanitary care of food. Also care is taken regarding all persons handling food to make sure that they have no contagious diseases. States have laws to protect the food supply within their borders. A federal pure-food law prevents impure food from being carried in interstate commerce. The Department of Commerce regulates weights and measures by testing and inspection. The Department of Agriculture inspects cattle before they are slaughtered, and inspects their meat afterward. It inspects foods and drugs to prevent false labeling. It fights pests and blights on crops.

It is just as necessary that the right kind of foods be eaten as that the food be pure. Food is essential as fuel for the body just as is coal for a furnace. Some food is also valuable for rebuilding the cells of the body. Still other food regulates the functions of the body. The best *fuel foods to produce heat and energy* are fats such as butter, milk, cheese, oils, and fat meats. Other heat producers are sugar and starches found in bread, cereals, and potatoes. The best *cell-building foods* are lean meat, eggs, milk, nuts, cheese, and beans. Other builders are minerals found in milk, eggs, cheese, liver, spinach, and prunes. The *regulating foods* protect us against certain diseases. Green vegetables, fruit, whole grain cereals, as well as water are among this group.

You will notice that milk is valuable for several purposes. That is why milk is so important an item of food for both children and adults. Plenty of milk, fruits, and vegetables, together with bread, cereals, some meat, and a considerable amount of water are desirable for most people.

Cleanliness and Sanitation. If the people of a community are to be healthy, the community must be kept

clean. Almost every community has a sewage system
through which the sewage is carried in underground
pipes from the houses to a body of water or to septic
tanks.[3] Garbage must be disposed of. It may be
dumped into bodies of water or in some outlying section, both of which are unsanitary and costly methods.
It may be burned in the city incinerator,[4] a sanitary
method if there is not too much odor. Or it may be
reduced; that is, the greases and fertilizer may be
extracted for use and the remainder burned. This is
both a sanitary and an economical method.

Some rubbish and waste of a community may be
used by careful thought and planning. For example,
ashes may be used to fill in swamps or waste land.
Rags, newspapers, magazines, old rubber, and bottles
may be sold and reclaimed by those who can utilize
them again. A small amount of money is paid for
such rubbish, and in this way rubbish becomes a source
of revenue instead of a nuisance.

A progressive community will clean its streets by
sweeping and flushing them regularly. The state and
nation help the local community maintain cleanliness
and sanitation by preventing the pollution of streams
of water. Sometimes the action of Congress is necessary to do this. They may prohibit manufacturing
plants from polluting air or water by smoke and waste.

Prevention or Cure. We are coming to realize more
and more that preventing disease is better than taking
the chance of getting a disease and then trying to cure

[3] **septic tanks.** Tanks in which sewage is kept to decompose.
[4] **incinerator.** A furnace for burning waste and garbage.

it. The community is constantly busy with this task.
Epidemics are checked or avoided by quarantining
those who have a contagious disease and by vaccinat-
ing or inoculating those not yet afflicted with the disease. Food, water, and milk, as well as those who
handle the food, are inspected by government officials
to prevent disease and to promote health conditions.
Swamps and stagnant water are sprayed to kill the
larvae of mosquitoes, called "wigglers." Germs are
analyzed and new serums[5] or antitoxins for prevention
of disease are discovered from time to time. In addition to these measures the community can reduce illness by doing its duties regularly and efficiently, by
cleaning the streets and alleys, by disposing of its
waste, by supplying pure food and water, by teaching
laws of health through its schools, by maintaining a
good hospital, and by inspecting its factories for health
conditions.

Care of the Sick. You have seen how essential are
pure air and sufficient light, pure water and a wholesome, well-balanced diet, the disposal of waste material, and the prevention of disease. All of these are
required to keep people healthy. And yet despite all
our modern scientific knowledge and all our efforts,
disease still exists and people become ill.

During the past generation the death rate from
tuberculosis[6] has been cut from two hundred to about
sixty out of every hundred thousand persons. Heart

---

[5] **serums.** Blood fluids used for inoculation for the prevention of certain
diseases.
[6] **tuberculosis.** A disease of the lungs, intestines, bones, or other parts of
the body, characterized by small swellings in the tissues.

disease, cancer, cerebral hemorrhage,[7] kidney trouble, and pneumonia[8] exceed tuberculosis now as causes of

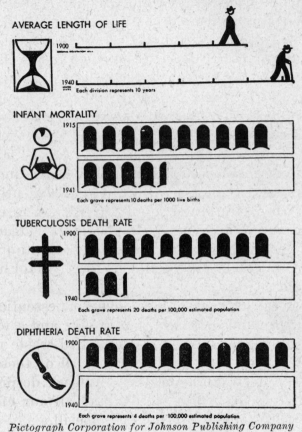

AVERAGE LENGTH OF LIFE

1900

1940   Each division represents 10 years

INFANT MORTALITY

1915

1941   Each grave represents 10 deaths per 1000 live births

TUBERCULOSIS DEATH RATE

1900

1940   Each grave represents 20 deaths per 100,000 estimated population

DIPHTHERIA DEATH RATE

1900

1940   Each grave represents 4 deaths per 100,000 estimated population

Pictograph Corporation for Johnson Publishing Company

America's Improving Health Record

death. As the pictograph shows, the diphtheria death rate has also been greatly decreased and infant deaths

[7] **cerebral hemorrhage.** The bursting of a blood vessel in the brain.
[8] **pneumonia.** Inflammation of the lungs.

have been lessened considerably. As a result, the average length of life is gradually increasing. However, over ten per cent of our population is ill at any one time and the average city person is sick two or three days a month. Deaths from certain diseases have been gradually becoming fewer each year, and yet over eight million persons are admitted to hospitals every year.

Since Florence Nightingale made the cause of nursing so important an aid to health and since Pasteur discovered the relation of germs to disease, medical science and hospital care have been improving. More than half a century ago Pasteur vaccinated twenty-five sheep for anthrax, a bacterial disease usually fatal with animals. A similar number were not vaccinated but all were injected with the disease bacteria. The crowd of skeptical physicians who watched him found the first lot alive and well, while the others were dead or dying. This famous demonstration of the power of vaccination is portrayed in the film on the life of Pasteur, as shown in the photograph. Careful determination of the nature of the disease, the use of the X-ray and radium, inoculation and vaccination for contagious diseases, and the use of anesthetics[9] for operations have made hospital treatment more and more successful.

Besides the physically sick are the physically handicapped—the lame, the blind, the deaf, and the dumb—and also the mentally sick or deficient. The last group includes those who are insane, or entirely lacking in

[9] anesthetics. Drugs which remove the feeling of pain.

mental powers, and the feeble-minded. The feeble-

Sheep Vaccinated by Pasteur

minded may be slightly under the normal person or

they may be not much above the baby in ability to care for themselves. The way in which a community cares for these unfortunates shows the kind of a community it is. The way in which you look upon the physically handicapped shows what kind of person you are. They are not objects of either pity or scorn. Except for those wholly unable to care for themselves, they are regular, ordinary people with special personal problems.

Boards of Health. Every community recognizes that good health is necessary for effective effort in every line of endeavor—in school, in play, and in work. To this end many communities have a Board of Health which is responsible for the health conditions within the community. The aim of the Board of Health is to learn the cause of disease, to prevent disease, and to care for and cure the sick. This Board of Health draws up a code or a set of rules for the prevention of disease and for the maintenance of sanitary conditions within the community.

The duties of a local Board of Health vary with the size of the towns. In the larger towns the general duties include the following items:

1. To maintain sanitary conditions within the community by cleaning up swamps, destroying vermin and other pests.

2. To inspect foods and drugs and all places where food is handled.

3. To maintain hospitals, clinics, and places for the free distribution of medicine for the sick.

4. To maintain laboratories for the analysis of

water, drugs, and food, and in the large towns for the manufacture of vaccine and antitoxin.

5. To protect against such diseases as diphtheria, smallpox, and typhoid by using serums and by quarantining houses containing these diseases.

6. To maintain infant welfare stations where mothers may bring their babies and receive instruction on their feeding and care. From these stations visiting nurses are sent out to homes where their service is needed.

7. To record vital statistics of the community, such as births and deaths. By its death rate (number of deaths per one hundred thousand people) the community will know whether its battle against disease is gaining or losing.

8. To educate the public on health questions. This is done by means of the radio, motion pictures, lectures, and posters.

State and Federal Assistance. States co-operate with their local Boards of Health to improve health conditions. The State Boards of Health draw up state sanitary codes. The states may impose quarantine against an epidemic upon an entire community or upon a neighboring state. They also conduct educational campaigns to inform the rural population about soil pollution and dangerous disease.

The United States co-operates with state and local Boards of Health to improve health conditions throughout the entire country. Congress has passed many laws to regulate foreign and interstate commerce.

The *Pure Food and Drugs Law* was passed over thirty years ago to prevent the shipment between states of foods and drugs which were improperly labeled. Many preservatives are forbidden entirely and all substitutes must be clearly indicated on the label.

The United States Public Health Service is under the new Federal Security Agency. One of its important tasks is to prevent any contagious disease, such as yellow fever, smallpox, or the bubonic plague,[10] from being brought into the country by immigrants. Accordingly every ship entering any of our harbors is met by a revenue cutter and is forced to remain in quarantine if there is any danger. The uprooting of yellow fever and malaria at Havana, Cuba, and in the Panama Canal Zone is an excellent illustration of the efficient handling of disease by this service. The Public Health Service also carries on scientific research in the causes of disease and publishes reports containing the results of its studies.

Enforcement of Health Laws. The success of public-health work lies in the co-operation of all Boards of Health, health officers, and of all the people. A single individual having a contagious disease endangers the entire community. From a single case an epidemic may spread and many may die of the disease before it is checked. To avoid this, public health measures are essential. But unless the laws are enforced strictly, public-health work cannot be satisfactory. Public health promotes good health for all. If health for all

[10] **bubonic plague.** A dangerous disease which is accompanied by fever and chills, and which is spread by rats.

is to be maintained and protected, the laws pertaining to health conditions must be enforced without fear or favor. It is far wiser and cheaper to enforce health laws than to permit an epidemic to overrun the community, state, or nation.

Test and Study Exercises

Aids to Learning.

1. It is important to remember that if you would keep good health you must have pure air, sufficient light, unpolluted water, wholesome food, and thorough cleanliness.

2. Note that it is just as necessary that the right kinds of food be eaten as that the food be pure.

3. Remember that the prevention of disease is far better than the attempt to cure the disease after it is contracted.

Test Exercises.

Match the items in the first column with those in the second column that best complete the sense, by placing their numbers together on a separate sheet of paper.

1. Antitoxins	1. secures its water from a dam two hundred miles away.
2. The common cold	2. are called wigglers.
3. Butter and milk	3. inspects bakeries and dairies.
4. Yellow fever	4. are cell-building foods.
5. The local board of health	5. causes a great deal of lost time in school and at work.
6. Los Angeles	6. is a means of removing the sense of pain.
7. Larvae of mosquitoes	7. are excellent energy producing foods.
8. Inoculation	8. are used to prevent disease.
9. Lean meat and vegetables	9. is causing a mild form of disease to prevent its reoccurrence.
10. An anesthetic	10. was practically uprooted in the Panama Canal Zone.

Suggested Activities.

1. Ask your school office to tell you the number of absences during a school year caused by such diseases as diphtheria, scarlet fever, measles, mumps, and whooping cough. Which sickness caused the most absences and which the least?

2. Make a list of the foods you have eaten during the past week. Classify these foods as energy-producing, body-building, and regulating foods.

3. Look up the meaning of calories and vitamins in your physiology book or in *Compton's Pictured Encyclopedia* (Volume 5, pp. 144-146). Which of the foods mentioned in the list you have made contains the largest amount of calories? What different vitamins do they contain?

4. Ask your librarian's help in investigating the contributions made to our nation's health by such men as Wm. C. Gorgas, Walter Reed, and Alexis Carrel.

5. *Group Activity:* The teacher may arrange a visit to the town waterworks to see how your drinking water is purified and how a constant flow is made available.

6. *Group Activity:* The teacher may select several pupils to visit a nearby dairy to learn how milk is pasteurized and how the bottles and equipment are sterilized, and then report to the class.

CHAPTER XI

PROTECTION OF LIFE AND PROPERTY

PREPARATORY NOTE: A second concern of every community, after public health is taken care of, is the protection of the life and property of its citizens. The more careful a community is to correct the conditions which lead to crime, the less crime it suffers. The more attention given to overcoming carelessness and neglect, the lower are the fire losses and the accidents. The costs of these failures to the community are tremendous, as this chapter will prove.

City Police. It is the duty of the government to enforce the laws, to maintain order, to protect lives and property, and to prevent crime. In the early history of our country, when there were fewer people and less crime, the policemen usually were men with little experience and no training in police duties. Today it is necessary that policemen be trained for their various duties so that they possess skill in marksmanship, physical ability, and an understanding of crime prevention and detection.

Some specialize in certain fields, such as identification work or detective work. The identification department consists of experts on fingerprints, photography, guns and ammunition, and bloodstains. There are public and private detectives who become expert in tracing criminals by these means. Policewomen are being used in most of the larger police departments. They handle cases involving women offenders and the protection of working women. Mounted policemen, in the employ of the city or the state, are trained in horseback riding. Their horses also are well-trained, so that they will push a crowd back when they are spurred and are ridden along the curb. They will remain standing at a place untied until their masters return, and will often follow their masters even when they are not led.

Each city police department is usually organized and supervised by a commissioner, or chief appointed by the mayor, to whom the commissioner or chief is responsible for the success of the police department. The number of captains, sergeants, and patrolmen is determined by the size of the city and the character of its people. A captain has charge of an entire district, a sergeant has charge of a squad within a district, and a patrolman has charge of a beat, consisting of a block or several blocks. Detectives are assigned to cases requiring special attention. They are all paid out of public funds.

The duties of the city police are quite varied. First of all they try to safeguard the public in all ways possible. The patrolmen are constantly on the lookout for lawbreakers of every kind and endeavor to protect the innocent. This may involve battles with desperate criminals against whom they must use all the

possible devices of modern science. Or it may mean
merely the warning of first offenders to stop their
unlawful efforts.

A second duty is that of the traffic squad which keeps
pedestrians and vehicles moving along the city streets.
Automatic lights aid them in this regard, but the city
crowds are so great at certain hours of the day that
many policemen are required at busy corners. They
slow down automobile speeders, guard against accidents, and handle those accidents which occur. City
ordinances of various kinds must be enforced, such
as those concerning begging, and the parking of automobiles in busy streets or on the wrong side of the
street.

The detective squads are used to locate criminals
and to catch them when they have escaped. As *plain-
clothes men* they have better opportunities for detect-
ing such wrongdoers than have the uniformed police.
A careful system of fingerprinting is kept of all
known offenders, and many other means of identification are used.

There are many ways in which the police can be
helped by private citizens. The adult or child who
looks upon the police as his friends, can help them
by his sympathy and understanding. Too frequently
there is graft in city politics which involves the police
department. But the average patrolman is just as
anxious as the ordinary citizen to put down crime and
to make his city a better place in which to live.

One particular help is the juvenile-police plan.
Traffic problems are greatly lightened by schoolboy

patrols who guard children as they cross the streets on their way to school. Accidents are reduced as most drivers gladly respect the authority of these volunteers in their effort to promote safety.

In doing their duties, policemen are constantly risking their own lives to protect others. It is very difficult, and in many cases impossible, for policemen to obtain life insurance because their work is too dangerous. Every day policemen somewhere in the country are losing their lives. Because of this fact we should respect them, and help them whenever we can.

State Police. Some states have laws that govern the organization of state police within their borders, provided they do not conflict with the federal laws, which are the laws of the nation. The state police are able-bodied men from eighteen to forty-five years of age, organized, supervised, and maintained by the state government. The governor may also call upon the militia, or national guard, to aid the public in any disaster like storm, flood, fire, strike, and riot, or to assure order at large public gatherings, as state or county fairs.

The Pennsylvania state police is an outstanding example of efficiency. The Texas Rangers are also among the most famous of the state police forces. The immense territory and varying population they patrol is only exceeded by that of the Royal Canadian Mounted Police who cover more than a million square miles of territory, much of which is extremely cold and desolate. Both "rangers" and "mounties" are said never to give up till they "get their man," no matter where his trail leads.

New York and Massachusetts have somewhat similar organizations. These men usually number from three hundred to five hundred and are organized into troops with barracks in different sections of the state. The men are carefully selected. They must pass rigid examinations and must take thorough training for their numerous duties. They enforce the law in general by helping the local police catch criminals, settle strikes, and put down riots. Some act as fish, game, or fire wardens. They recover stolen property and protect against thefts. State police forces are also maintained by public money.

National Police—Army and Navy. As stated in the Preamble of the Constitution of the United States, among the functions of government are the establishment of justice, the insuring of domestic tranquility, and the providing of common defense. Accordingly, the national government has the power to protect the life and property of its people and to assure them protection against foreign invasion and domestic violence. Congress, therefore, makes laws providing for the maintenance of an army and navy with their air forces, and for organizing the state militia. The President of the United States is the Commander-in-Chief of the Army and Navy, but delegates the supervision of these to the Secretaries of War and of the Navy. Thus the nation is constantly protecting its people on land and sea. The army and navy are maintained at great expense by public money raised by taxation or by borrowing. In addition to the army and navy, the federal government in its various departments has a staff of officials who perform police duty.

G-Men. The agents of the Federal Bureau of Investigation of yesterday have become the G-Men of today. Formerly they were, by profession, largely lawyers and accountants, trained and experienced only as investigators. But today they are also trained as expert marksmen. However, not more than five per cent of the bureau's activities have to do with the criminal who shoots back. The agent may spend most of his time trying to find out why false entries were made in a bankrupt's books.

An applicant for appointment as agent must be between twenty-five and thirty-five years of age, and must be a graduate of a recognized law school, a competent accountant, or else have displayed ability in investigation. He must also have had not less than two years' actual experience in business. After the applicant has met these preliminary requirements and has passed a written examination, his entire past is investigated. As far as possible, all his teachers and associates even from babyhood are interviewed. If passed upon favorably he is called in for a talk with one of the inspectors for the purpose of appraising his ability. After graduation from the training school, and after three months' test training, he will either have proved himself fit for a permanent appointment or he will be dropped. Each agent is reported on at regular intervals and occasionally special reports are sent in. The discipline is rigid but the method is successful.

The value of the training is so well recognized in the business world that requests are often received from ambitious young men who want to go through the course and do the work without pay. Agents are often offered positions in commercial organizations and it is the policy of the bureau to raise no objections in such cases.

The Bureau is not under civil service.[1] Positions are not filled for the good of the man but for the good of the service. Promotions are made on merit and are made quickly when they are deserved. An agent begins on a salary of thirty-two hundred dollars a year, which is increased as service warrants it.

Causes of Crime. The causes of crime are constantly being studied in an effort to reduce them. The fact that approximately fifteen billion dollars goes to pay the costs of almost a million and a half major crimes committed in one year in addition to over fourteen million less serious offenses, not including traffic violations, shows how vast the problem has become. What makes people steal or murder, burn buildings or kidnap children?

Scientific study indicates that many criminals are not sufficiently capable mentally to stand the strain of competition. They break down and turn to crime instead. Some are even mentally sick and should be classed with other mental defectives.

[1] **civil service.** Appointment to public office by competitive examination.

You will notice in the pictograph the fact that over half the people arrested are under thirty years of age. Boys may become criminals because of poor home surroundings or a lack of home training. Indifferent,

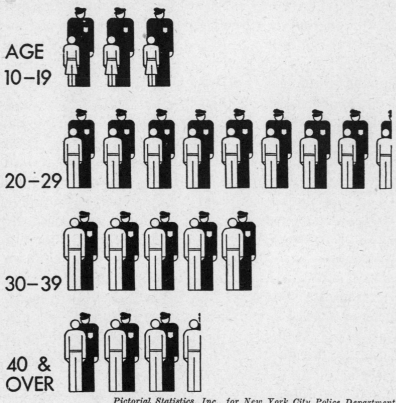

AGE 10-19

20-29

30-39

40 & OVER

Pictorial Statistics, Inc., for New York City Police Department

Arrests in New York City by Age Groups

Each symbol represents 5 per cent of arrests reported to Federal Government

drunken, or vicious parents drive them into the streets where bad companions soon lead them astray.

But other criminals do not have these excuses. They are superior physically and mentally and fail chiefly because of their inability to distinguish right from wrong. Moral defects can frequently be overcome by proper education, which teaches everyone the whole truth concerning crime. This will show what a complete failure those who follow a criminal life are bound to make. By this means, an attitude toward crime can be developed that will help to reduce crime or even abolish it altogether in some communities.

Development of Fire Apparatus. The purpose of the Fire Department is to prevent fires, to fight fires, and to teach people to be careful in the use of fire. In the early days, fire was fought by volunteer firemen who used buckets to carry water, hence the name *bucket brigade*. Some small communities today still have volunteer firemen, and buckets are still used to prevent the spread of a fire just started. The early hose cart was drawn by volunteer firemen. Some small communities still have one. Then came the horse-drawn steamer and the hook and ladder.

Because of the growth of cities, firemen soon were employed to devote their full time to fighting fires. Because of the growing fire hazards, fire extinguishers are found today on trains, steamships, elevators, and other public conveyances. The horse-drawn steamer has been replaced by the motor-driven fire engine in the larger cities so that greater speed can be attained. Keeping in mind the importance of preventing fires, the aviator now flies above the great forests to watch for small fires, so that they may be put out before they get much of a start.

Organization of Fire Department. Each community has its own fire department organization. Usually there is a commissioner or chief appointed by the mayor to whom the commissioner or chief is responsible for the work of his department. There are captains in charge of certain districts or sections of the city. The firemen of each section of the city have their own organization so that each fireman has a certain task to perform, thus avoiding overlapping of duties and saving time. Firemen become valuable to their company and are, therefore, promoted in position and rank as they gain experience. Firemen, like policemen, risk their lives continually to protect the lives and property of others. State and national forest preserves maintain forest rangers whose duty it is to prevent, and when necessary, to fight fire in the forests.

Fire Loss. The loss of property by fire in the United States every year is enormous. A few years ago property valued at more than one-half billion dollars was annually destroyed by fire. This means that there was a loss of nearly one and a half million dollars in fires every day throughout the entire year. Fortunately the amount has been cut nearly in half since 1930, as you see in the graph. It is estimated that there is usually a fire somewhere in the United States every minute of the day. Can you imagine the enormous waste?

These same fires are costing the lives of thousands of men, women, and children every year. In a recent year, nearly ten thousand lives were lost because of fires. This number is equivalent to that of an entire city. Thousands are thrown out of work every year because of fire, and hundreds of thousands are affected directly in various ways by these fires.

Causes of Fires. The causes of fires are many, and nearly all of them can be traced to carelessness and thoughtlessness. Let us name some specific causes and see which ones are due to carelessness or thoughtlessness.

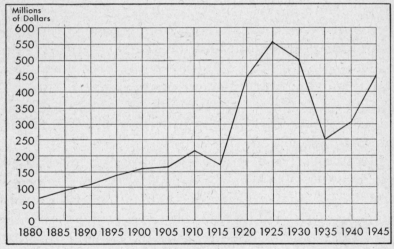

Annual Fire Losses

Children are permitted to play with matches, to burn dry leaves, to start bonfires, and to light firecrackers. It is thoughtless to permit small children to have matches at any time without supervision.

Women use kerosene or gasoline to start fires; they use naphtha for cleaning; and they neglect electric appliances until they become overheated. All this is carelessness.

People throw lighted matches, cigars, or cigarettes into heaps of rubbish, dry grass, or leaves. This, too, is carelessness.

Tourists leave camps without putting out their fires. The wind fans them into flames that spread until whole forests are destroyed.

Defective wiring, poor chimneys, and faulty flues cause fires because of carelessness in workmanship.

It is estimated that about ninety-five out of every hundred fires that occur could be prevented, because they are traceable to carelessness. It is also true that in no other civilized country are there so many fires as in this country. This implies that we are more careless with both life and property than any other civilized country.

Prevention of Fires. It is essential that we reduce the number of fires. We cannot afford to sacrifice many billions of dollars' worth of property every year. We cannot afford to sacrifice thousands of lives every year and we do not want the world to think of us as the most careless of all the civilized nations.

If we are to prevent such a wholesale waste of lives and money, we must educate ourselves and others. We should be careful in our use of matches. We should not throw any lighted material away without putting out the flame. Open fires should never be left unguarded. Electric wiring and chimney flues should meet careful inspection tests. Waste paper or clothes, oils, paints, or other inflammable materials should be

carefully protected. Electric appliances and dangerous cleaning solutions should be used only with the
greatest care. Finally, we must realize that all of us
help pay the costs of fire through our insurance. Only
by careful effort can we prevent the tremendous waste
of lives and money from mounting higher and higher.

Public Safety. In many large cities there is a separate department, the Public Safety Department,
whose duty it is to pass upon new buildings, inspect
old buildings, and counsel as to safety measures to
protect the public. In most smaller communities this
work is done by the Police Department or by a special
officer.

Public buildings are inspected for fire hazards; sufficient and convenient exits of public buildings are
required by law; the seating capacity of public buildings and theaters, and the capacity of elevators are
usually regulated by law with a view to reducing accidents and fire hazards. Bridges, railroad crossings,
and viaducts are safeguarded by the Department of
Public Safety.

Increasing Accidents. Although many such efforts
have been made to keep down the number of accidents,
the total is mounting every year. There has been an
increase from eighty thousand deaths to one hundred
ten thousand each year during the last twenty-five
years. Among these fatal accidents those due to automobile traffic and home accidents have increased while
most others have decreased. Automobile accidents
caused thirty-six thousand deaths in one year recently
and those in the home due to falls, burns, and other

forms of carelessness reached nearly as many. In addition to these fatal accidents, there were three or four times as many people permanently disabled, and lit-

WHY AMERICA'S SHAMEFUL
AUTOMOBILE ACCIDENT RECORD?

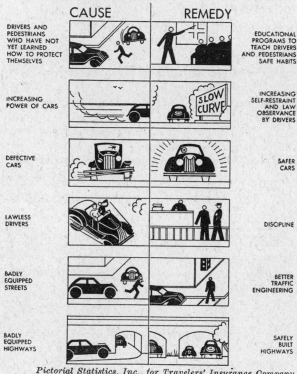

CAUSE	REMEDY
DRIVERS AND PEDESTRIANS WHO HAVE NOT YET LEARNED HOW TO PROTECT THEMSELVES	EDUCATIONAL PROGRAMS TO TEACH DRIVERS AND PEDESTRIANS SAFE HABITS
INCREASING POWER OF CARS	INCREASING SELF-RESTRAINT AND LAW OBSERVANCE BY DRIVERS
DEFECTIVE CARS	SAFER CARS
LAWLESS DRIVERS	DISCIPLINE
BADLY EQUIPPED STREETS	BETTER TRAFFIC ENGINEERING
BADLY EQUIPPED HIGHWAYS	SAFELY BUILT HIGHWAYS

Pictorial Statistics, Inc., for Travelers' Insurance Company
Education Engineering Enforcement

erally millions who received other smaller injuries. The cost of these accidents in one year reached three and a half billion dollars—nearly twice as much as the total cost of all public education throughout the nation. The reasons for automobile accidents are given in the foregoing pictograph, together with the remedies which are possible. Are you doing your part to reduce this disgraceful loss of life?

Test and Study Exercises

Aids to Learning.

1. Remember that the inability to distinguish right from wrong is one of the chief reasons for crime.

2. Notice the vast amount of money spent each year in the attempt to suppress crime.

3. It is important to learn and remember that most fires and most accidents are caused by carelessness.

4. Observe that more than a hundred thousand lives are lost each year through accidents of various kinds.

Test Exercises.

On a separate sheet of paper write the following sentences including the missing words.

1. Police who regulate automobile speeders are on the ____ ____.

2. Those police who use fingerprints and other forms of identifications to trace criminals are called ____.

3. In addition to the city police there are the ____ police and the ____ police.

4. The G-Men are taken largely from ____ or ____.

5. Many criminals are ____ sick.

6. The cost of crime each year amounts to nearly $____.

7. The chief reason for fire losses is ____.

8. The largest number of accidents in our country occur from ____ and at ____.

9. The total cost of accidents each year is nearly ____ the entire cost of public education.

10. Among the reasons for lawlessness are poor ____ ____ and lack of ____.

Suggested Activities.

1. Make a list of all the causes of crime you can think of in addition to those mentioned in this text.

2. Check the causes which you think are most important and explain the kinds of crime to which these lead.

3. In reading the daily papers determine whether policemen and firemen are not even more heroic at times than soldiers during war. Why do they get less recognition for their bravery?

4. *Group Activity:* The teacher may arrange a class visit to the neighboring police or fire station so that all may learn how our civilian fighters live.

5. *Group Activity:* The teacher may arrange a discussion of the work now conducted by the present director of the Federal Bureau of Investigation. How are the G-Men successful in securing convictions of most of their cases? Will the certainty of some immediate sentence prevent crime?

6. *Group Activity:* A group of pupils may constitute a committee to draw up safety slogans to prevent accidents.

7. *Group Activity:* The teacher may appoint a committee to arrange a program for Fire-Prevention Week in October. Perhaps your fire marshal will talk on "How to Prevent Fires." Reports can be made on the fire drills used in school. Different pupils can inquire from their parents about the fire insurance they carry at home.

CHAPTER XII

EDUCATION AND RECREATION

PREPARATORY NOTE: The best way in which a community can maintain public health and free itself from crime and property losses is to raise the standards of its educational opportunities and provide proper recreation for all its citizens. A community can advance no faster than the intelligence of its members permits. Our public schools have improved wonderfully during recent years, and yet the average citizen in our nation has not had the benefits of even an elementary school education. This chapter shows that an investment in intelligent citizenship is worth every cent it costs.

Free Education. If the people of a country are to be self-governing, they must be educated. Providing public, or free, education in a democracy becomes a duty of the state. The privilege of attending elementary and secondary schools is offered to almost anyone who is interested in securing an education. In many communities a junior college or even a municipal university is maintained and operated where its residents can secure two or four years of a college education with little or no cost.

Intelligent citizenship is essential in a democracy, where the people rule. Americans advocate free education for all who are interested because they know that it gives an individual greater opportunity for securing vocational advancement, as well as for rendering real service, and for increasing his enjoyment of life. They also know that it gives the community better-educated citizens. This means that there will be more capable workers, fewer dependents, and a trained leadership. The state and nation must help the local community provide for intelligent citizenship if the people are to continue to enjoy democratic government. In a democracy the responsibility for the education of all citizens rests upon the government. In our country this responsibility is placed upon the state governments.

Compulsory Education Law. The states have passed child-labor laws which prevent children from being employed, when they should be in school taking advantage of the free education provided for them. Most states have also made laws compelling children under fourteen, sixteen, or eighteen years of age to attend school for their own good. With the coming of large numbers of immigrants, this problem of enforcing child-labor laws and compulsory education laws became more complex. Fortunately, during the past generation, illiteracy, or the inability to read any language, has been gradually decreasing as the pictograph on the next page shows.

The real problem is to make all the people realize the value and importance of an education, and to have them appreciate their opportunity of receiving it without direct cost. In the larger communities where immigrants settle in large numbers, it is often necessary

to have the courts use their power to require many of
these parents to send their children to school to secure

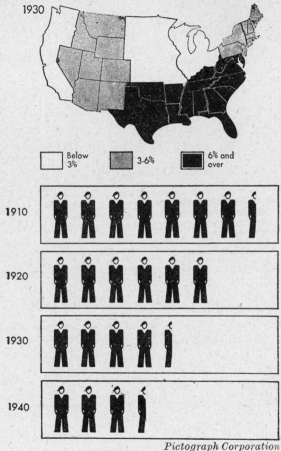

Pictograph Corporation

Illiteracy Vanishing
Each symbol represents 1 per cent of all persons
10 years or over

an education even though it costs them very little.
Sometimes the children do not want to attend school,

and sometimes the parents do not want their children to do so. They prefer that they work to help support the family, but in such cases parents are shortsighted and have little regard for the children's future. They should realize that a child can help his parents and himself much better after obtaining an education, than he can without an education.

Part-Time School. In cases where children are really needed to help support the family they are excused by the authorities from attending regular school in order that they may work. In such cases, though, they are required to attend a continuation school a certain number of hours a week. They may attend a continuation school conducted at the expense of their employer, or a public continuation school.

The community makes arrangements also whereby adults can attend evening school after their regular work. Frequently this, too, is entirely free. Here some can continue their education where they left off as children. Others can improve their employment by preparing for promotion within their present position or by preparing for another vocation.

Schools of Yesterday and Schools of Today. Educational opportunities were by no means the same for the early colonists as they are today. Three hundred years ago only the well-to-do classes sent their children to school or employed private tutors to care for them. The children of the poor had little formal education. At about this time the Boston Latin Grammar School opened as the forerunner of our modern high school. This differed very much from our high school, however, as it was not entirely free and it was primarily a preparation for college.

In 1821 the first public high school was established in Boston. Until after the War between the States there were only a few of these high schools and only a small number of the children attended them. About fifty years ago there arose a greater interest in education and so the number of pupils in both elementary and high schools began to increase rapidly. Since 1890 the number of pupils in elementary schools has nearly doubled—from twelve to twenty-three millions. In the same years, high-school pupils have increased thirty times in number—from two hundred thousand to over six million, and college students have reached a total of over a million today in about seventeen hundred colleges throughout the country. (See pictograph on page 75.)

However, we must remember that this increase in the number of pupils in our schools and colleges has all been very recent. There are still large masses of our population who have had little education. It is estimated that only two or three per cent of the adults in the United States have college degrees and only eleven per cent more have had a high-school education. You will see, in the following graph, that less than half of the grammar-school graduates finish high school, and that less than one-sixth of the high-school graduates secure a college degree.

Before the Revolutionary War there were only nine colleges, all founded primarily to train ministers. Many of these are now universities.

Name of College	*Date of Establishment*
Harvard	1636
William and Mary................................	1693
Yale	1701
Princeton	1746
University of Pennsylvania.........................	1751
Kings (now Columbia)............................	1754
Brown	1764
Rutgers	1766
Dartmouth	1769

In the simple days of early American life, children grew to manhood and womanhood without seeing more

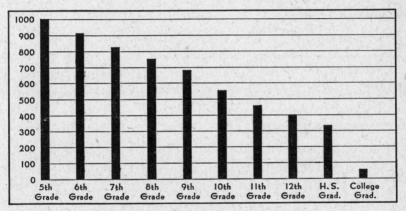

Survival of 1000 Fifth Grade Pupils

than the few score people in their immediate neighborhood. Today the child at an early age is expected to adapt himself to many different kinds of people. Sometimes hundreds or even thousands of children are brought together in one school building. Modern methods of travel make it possible for a child to see and know many other people and the problems which confront them. The youth of today sees industry conducted on a vast scale, and society and politics undergoing many changes. For youth of the early days life was far simpler.

Therefore it is much more important and necessary to obtain an education today than it was in the early days. Competition is always becoming stronger. Instead of offering only one course of study, as was the case in the early days, the schools offer many courses today, so that a boy or girl may plan for whatever work he or she desires to do. Boys and girls today have the benefit of counsel and advice from well-trained experts. This, too, was lacking in the early days of American life. In the words of a philosopher, "Education is life." American education is engaged in the process of putting this ideal into practice, making life real and worth while.

School Support. Public schools in most states are supported and maintained principally by local taxation. A large portion of the property tax is collected by the county or the local community for this purpose. Property is taxed according to its value whether the owners have children in school or not. States give money from the state treasury to help local districts extend equal opportunities to all pupils in their schools. The national government also grants money for certain uses, such as vocational education.

When a new building is to be built, a large additional sum of money is usually required. Therefore, the people of the district are called upon to decide by vote whether or not they want to incur this debt. Because it is an unusual expenditure and apart from the ordinary school expenses, the sum of money is usually obtained by the sale of school bonds, or borrowings, which need not be paid for a long period of years. People who buy these bonds receive interest on their investment. The bond buyers are thus repaid for the use of the borrowed money while the building is in use.

It costs on the average more than one hundred dollars a year to educate a boy or girl in a high-school course. The people as a whole are paying this money through taxes so that you and others may get an education. If you "make good" the money will have been well spent. But if you fail in your subjects you will have wasted that money.

Reasons for Public Support. There are many reasons why the public schools should be publicly supported rather than dependent on private funds. First, if our government is to continue to be a democracy in the best sense of the term, the voters must be educated to think for themselves. This certainly will mean that they must have at least a high-school education. As you remember, only a small fraction of the people of this nation have a high-school education now. Schools for all the people will be necessary if more voters are to be better educated.

Second, when conditions of unemployment prevail, young people should remain in school until they are at least eighteen or twenty years old. Most of them are unable to find employment in the city or on the farm, and therefore they should continue to prepare themselves for better citizenship until they can enter some permanent form of work. This, of course, will require free public schools.

Third, the changing conditions of life today are producing large numbers of drifters in our population. Boys and girls are in danger of falling into criminal companionship if they are idle. It is not only much cheaper to send boys and girls through high school and even through public college than it is to allow them to develop bad habits which may lead them to the penitentiary, but it is also much better for all concerned. There are several million young men and women of high-school age who are not yet fully employed. They should be kept in school if it is at all possible. The only way this can be done satisfactorily is at public expense.

Fourth, the advances of science during the past generation have been so great that at least a high-school education is necessary if boys and girls are to be kept adequately informed. This information will help them find the new and more profitable vocations upon which science will depend in its further march of progress. The same is true of the changes in history and other fields of study. The boy of today requires a longer and more thorough schooling than his grandfather did. More advances have been made in science, industry, and education during the past century than during all the centuries preceding. Free public elementary, secondary, and collegiate education is necessary. This is the only way in which we can secure an open-minded intelligent, and democratic citizenship.

Costs of Education. This public education for all who will take it costs over two billion dollars each year. This is an immense sum, and is much more than the cost of education a generation or more ago, as you can see in the following graphs. Sixty years ago the

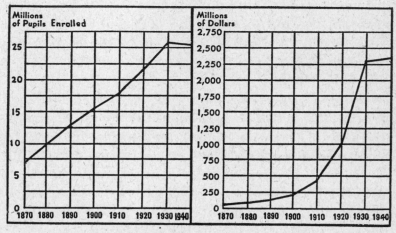

The Growing Costs of Education

total cost was less than one hundred million dollars annually. However, the decrease in the amount of purchases that can be made with a dollar today as compared with twenty years ago, the longer school term, the great increase in attendance, and the wonderful improvement in the quality of the whole school system have accounted for this thirty-fold increase between 1880 and 1940.

But when we compare the total cost of public schools
with other national expenditures we realize that it is
not relatively large. The cost of either gasoline or
tobacco products each year is about half that of
schools. The annual cost of national defense including all its related items usually considerably exceeds
that of public education. Life-insurance premiums
are considerably larger, and the purchase and operating expenses of automobiles are over twice as great.
The total crime bill each year is seven or eight times
as large. Studied in this light, education is relatively
inexpensive.

School Management. The schools of a village or
city are supervised by a *board of education.* The members of this board usually are elected by the people
and serve without pay because they are public-spirited
men and women interested in the childhood and youth
of their city. The board of education is given the
authority by the state to organize and operate the
schools under its care. It is entrusted with the public
money raised by taxation to support the schools. It
employs a well-trained and well-qualified person to
serve as *superintendent* of schools. Together they plan
the policies for the school system and employ teachers
and such other assistants as are needed to carry on
the work within a school system. They also employ
janitors to keep the buildings in a clean and sanitary
condition; they plan the curriculum, in accordance
with state requirements; they purchase supplies; and
they select and adopt textbooks, keeping in mind the
welfare of the boys and girls. The superintendent,

who is their administrator, is interested in carrying out the plans and policies in such a manner that the best results may be obtained.

The schools of a county are under the direction of a *county board of education,* and a *county superintendent* of schools. The county superintendent frequently recommends teachers for certificates. His chief task is to spend most of his time supervising the urban and rural schools in the county.

The state has final control of education. The schools of a state are under the direction of a *state board of education* and an administrator, usually called *superintendent of public instruction* or *commissioner of education.* The superintendent of public instruction is responsible for issuing and registering teachers' certificates to public-school teachers in the state. In addition to this, he inspects and accredits all schools within the state. He collects information about school attendance and school finance. He is responsible for dividing the state money for education among local school districts. The well-prepared superintendent is the educational leader of the state.

There is a federal Office of Education now under the Federal Security Agency. Here, facts concerning the nation's schools are collected, tabulated, and published for the benefit of the public. The Office of Education also carries on many studies regarding teaching problems, costs of education, and other subjects which individual states would not be able to undertake. The control of public-school policies is entirely in the hands of the states. The managing of schools and the pro-

viding of funds for the costs of education rests as a
rule on local communities. The federal Office of Education is intended to offer advice to states and towns
and to assist them with its studies and publications.

Thus the local community, the state, and the nation
co-operate in making possible a free education for all
who are interested.

Informal Education. Thus far we have been concerned with public schools for boys and girls. We have
referred to evening schools for adults but we have
not yet mentioned the vast number of other educational
agencies besides the public schools. Among the most
important of these *informal* or *out-of-school* kinds of
education are the following: correspondence courses
carried on by mail; libraries, museums, and art galleries; lectures, and concert courses of all kinds; radio
broadcasts and motion-picture programs; and finally
the vast number of magazines and newspapers which
cover the land with their influence.

The dividing line between informal education and
recreation is hard to determine. A movie may be
highly educational or it may be purely recreational.
In fact, the same performance may be different in its
influence on different people. You may, for example,
find only excitement in airplane pictures, but your
friend may learn something about group flying or
solo stunts. One person may see in a picture, based
on historical facts, only the thrill of the story, while
others will find whole scenes in history made clear for
them. But this is as it should be. The closer education

comes to recreation in its appeal, the more efficient it is likely to be.

Values of Informal Education. Try to imagine what modern life would be without any of these informal agencies. Millions of people are benefited by them. Libraries are especially important in this list. Most of us cannot afford to buy all the books we want to read, so we call on our public libraries to lend us books without direct cost to us. Some of these libraries are small but others are very large. The Library of Congress in Washington, D. C., is one of the largest libraries in the world, because it contains two copies of every book published in this country as well as many foreign books—about five million volumes in all.

We have had the radio and the movie for only a few years but their influence is probably greater than that of almost any other agency in the country, as nearly every one listens to the radio or attends the movies. The average movie weekly attendance in the United States is said to be nearly one hundred million.

And so education is obtained from these informal agencies as well as from our public schools. Education is the result of all the forces that guide our action or our thinking. School and home are the most important of all influences but, in many ways, these other agencies overshadow both school and home influence. And next to them in importance for the youth comes recreation in the form of physical or mental relaxation.

Need for Recreation. In order to do good work, one should find time for recreation. In the old days there was little time for recreation because people were too busy working at tasks necessary for their livelihood. Under modern living conditions, where the machine does so much of our work, the individual is given more time for leisure. Suitable recreation for mind and body has become necessary as an aid to health. It also is extremely important for character development, and for relieving the monotonous routine of office, store, or factory work. The many demands made upon workers, under the crowded and strenuous living conditions in the large cities, and the worries and cares common to all people require them to have some form of recreation and relaxation.

Work breaks down the cells and the nerve tissues; recreation, including sleep and rest, builds them up again. Thus we have a constant breaking down and building up of cells and tissues. Recreation is the process by which we re-create, renew, regain, or build up. It may be accomplished by rest, sleep, entertainment, taking active part in playing some game, reading, or even doing different work for a change.

Some people have a hobby at which they work for pleasure, or for the change it gives them. It seems that the less you actually enjoy your work, the more recreation you need; and the more regulated recreation you have, within proper limits, the better work you will do and the more contented you will be.

A community is wise if it maintains as many forms of recreation as are required to meet the needs of all its inhabitants. The laboring people as well as the wealthy need recreation, whether it be golf, baseball, tennis, or swimming. An ideal community should provide all its inhabitants with some form of recreational facilities suitable to their needs and desires.

Maintenance of Recreation. The community creates and maintains playgrounds, parks, and golf courses for you and for all other citizens, and it pays for them with public taxes. Municipal golf courses are usually self-supporting because a small fee is charged to use them. Money spent by a community for purposes of recreation is a good investment because it improves the health of its inhabitants, thereby making them physically fit for more and better work. Furthermore, recreation causes contentment and happiness. Playgrounds keep children off the streets, thus reducing automobile accidents, and at the same time they develop character and physical fitness. The community supervises its parks and playgrounds by hiring competent, well-trained leaders for that purpose. Municipal golf courses and parks are supervised by specialists.

Local Provision for Recreation. In addition to providing playgrounds where organized games may be enjoyed by all children without direct cost, cities or villages provide parks with their beautiful flowers, drives, and walks. Some parks have a zoo or a swimming pool. They furnish concerts and various games for the benefit of the public. Cities also establish libraries, art galleries, and museums where days can be spent profitably reading, or viewing works of art, and other exhibits.

Private recreation agencies may be commercial in that they exist primarily for the profit which their owners make. A large part of our recreation is under the control of private individuals who may or may not be concerned about the benefits which the public receives. This accounts for bad movies and dance halls and for high charges for various forms of recreation. When money-making is the first consideration, service may not be considered so important.

But many forms of recreation are under the control of semipublic agencies whose first concern is to benefit the public. The Young Men's and Young Women's Christian Associations, the Young Men's Hebrew Association, and the Knights of Columbus, all were started and managed by religious organizations. The Boy Scouts, Girl Scouts, Camp Fire Girls, and Four-H Clubs are also very valuable means of furnishing both out-of-school education and recreation of the highest order to boys and girls.

City authorities issue licenses to private or commercial agencies and supervise recreation supplied by them, such as dance halls, skating rinks, theaters, movie houses, and lecture and concert halls. Thus the local community is responsible for the kind of recreation carried on within its borders. This recreation should exert a wholesome influence upon the community.

State Provision for Recreation. In order to provide space for recreation and to make the beauty of nature accessible, states acquire and maintain their own parks. The various states differ in the features of

special interest in their parks. Nearly all have forest
preserves for hunting, fishing, and camping, which

Courtesy Northern Pacific Ry.
The Thrills of Yachting on Puget Sound

are regulated by fish and game laws. One state may
be noted for its lakes, another for its mountains, an-

other for its waterfalls, another for its caves, and another for its canyons, but each one furnishes some opportunity for physical recreation. The photograph of yachting on Puget Sound, in the northwest corner of the nation, is an excellent illustration of the pleasures that may be secured in our state waters.

The state capitol frequently has museums with exhibits of the history, origin, and development of that particular state. A trip through one of these museums provides both recreational and educational advantages.

National Provision for Recreation. The United States maintains national parks as playgrounds for the nation. There has been a considerable increase in the number of visitors to these parks during recent years. Congress may set aside land which contains great natural beauty and scenic wonders for national parks. After the president proclaims it open to the public, the Department of the Interior takes charge of it. A few of the most famous national parks in the United States are: Yellowstone, Glacier, Yosemite, Grand Canyon, Great Smoky Mountains, and Carlsbad Caverns. In the photograph, vacationists are seen near the top of Mt. Rainier in that national park in Washington noted for its beautiful glacier system.

The Library of Congress and the Smithsonian Institution are among the outstanding institutions of their kind in the world. Weeks can be spent here, in the nation's capitol, viewing the great works of art and literature, and the original histories dealing with the origin and development of our country and government. A trip through its buildings is highly educational as well as recreational. High schools arrange for their senior classes to go to Washington, in some cases from great distances, because of the educational and recreational values of these trips.

Courtesy Northern Pacific Ry.
Mountain Climbing at 12,000 Foot Level—Mt. Ranier

One of the recent types of combined education and recreation entirely managed by the federal government is the Civilian Conservation Corps which has employed more than five hundred thousand young men at one time. Although its chief purposes are to perform conservation work in forests and fields, as well as to rebuild young manhood physically, yet it has many educational and recreational features. Informal education of many kinds as well as some regular school classes are supplied to those who are enrolled. A recreation program is given these young men who otherwise would be deprived of such opportunities. By this means the federal government is trying to build into strong and worth-while manhood, hundreds of thousands of young men each year.

Test and Study Exercises

Aids to Learning.

1. Review the reasons for the great increase in the annual cost of public education.
2. Remember that education is the result of all the forces that guide our action or thinking.
3. Note how informal, or out-of-school education, is quite closely related to recreation.

Test Exercises.

On a separate sheet of paper give the letters for the correct answer for each statement.

1. Final control of education is in the hands of the (*a*) individual state, (*b*) federal government, (*c*) local community, (*d*) local school board.
2. Public schools now cost annually about (*a*) one billion dollars, (*b*) two billion dollars, (*c*) five hundred million dollars, (*d*) five billion dollars.
3. The largest part of the cost of public schools is usually paid by (*a*) the federal government, (*b*) the individual states, (*c*) the parents of school children, (*d*) the local community.
4. The local community creates and maintains (*a*) natural caves, (*b*) national parks, (*c*) playgrounds, (*d*) the Library of Congress.
5. The local community supports through annual taxes (*a*) the radio, (*b*) the Y.M.C.A., (*c*) community centers, (*d*) the Boy Scouts.

Suggested Activities.

1. Find out where national parks are located in your state or in neighboring states. Be prepared to describe a visit or an imaginary visit you have made to such a park.

2. Your teacher may help you find what your own state does regarding: (*a*) the requirements of the compulsory education law; (*b*) the way in which financial support is given local schools by the state.

3. Make a list of the movies you have attended during the past three months and the radio programs you usually hear. Arrange them in two lists placing first in each list those programs which, you believe, have the greatest educational value and last those which are merely recreational.

4. *Group Activity:* The teacher may appoint several members of the class to compare the local public recreation facilities, such as playgrounds, parks, skating rinks, and community centers with those in neighboring towns.

5. *Group Activity:* The class may be asked to report the daily or weekly papers they take at their homes and also the different magazines and other periodicals. Which gives the best treatment of local news or foreign news? Which gives the best articles on science, literature, travel, or political happenings?

6. *Group Activity:* The class may report similarly on the books each one has read, in addition to school assignments, during the past year. Which books in the total list were on (*a*) travel, (*b*) literature, (*c*) biography, (*d*) popular fiction?

CHAPTER XIII

COMMUNITY DEPENDENTS

PREPARATORY NOTE: In every community some citizens
are more gifted than others—in ability, possessions, or
opportunities. Those that have less may not be responsible for their own condition. They may be handicapped
physically or mentally or they may be the victims of circumstances over which they have no control as you learn
in this chapter. A community is frequently judged by the
way it treats such persons. Most of them can be helped
by a sympathetic understanding of their needs. The rest
should be handled in a way to prevent them from becoming harmful to their community.

Kinds of Dependents. There are many persons
who do not take a regular part in community life and
its affairs, either because they cannot or will not.
Those who cannot, may be divided into the following
classes—(1) *the physically handicapped:* the blind,
the deaf, and the crippled; (2) *the mentally handicapped:* the feeble-minded and the insane; (3) *the
unemployed:* those incapable of work, the misfits, and
the victims of depression; and (4) *the orphaned:*
those children left in the care of the state or in private
institutions. The community should care for these
people or help them to care for themselves as much
as possible.

Those who will not play their part are the (5) *criminals* or lawbreakers : those who have low or wrong ideals, with little or no will power to restrain them- selves, who must therefore be controlled and super- vised by governmental forces. The community guards against these undesirable citizens by maintaining jails and reform institutions where they can occupy them- selves by doing constructive work and where they can be helped to cure themselves of their criminal desires.

Blind. There are over sixty thousand persons in the United States totally blind, and many more who are nearly blind. The chief causes of blindness are heredity, sickness, and accident. It is said that nearly two-thirds of the cases of blindness might have been prevented. The remedies suggested for the prevention of blindness are better care of the eyes of babies at birth, prevention of unnecessary strain on the eyes of both children and adults by providing adequate lighting, protection of the eyes from dangers of infec- tion, and purchase of carefully adjusted glasses for those that need them.

The first institution for the blind in this country was established in Boston, Massachusetts, by Dr. Howe in 1830. It became known as the Perkins School for the Blind. Since that time many other schools have been established where the blind are taught to read by the use of raised letters called the Braille system. They are also taught to do things such as weave, make brushes, tune pianos, mend and repair furniture, and play musical instruments. Today nearly every state maintains a school for the blind where they can receive free instruction. These schools are well-equipped and have well-trained teachers. It is far better for the blind to attend these institutions than to remain at home because here they can learn to contribute to their own happiness and usefulness.

One of the Men Guided by the Seeing Eye Dogs

One of the most remarkable cases on record where a handicapped person has adjusted herself to life activities is that of Helen Keller who in early infancy lost her sight, hearing, and speech. A special teacher was provided for her in childhood and with her constant help and sympathy, Miss Keller gradually acquired a high-school and college education, and even learned to speak, though with some difficulty. As a result of her own success, Miss Keller has devoted her life to travel and even to lecturing with the help of her constant companion, in an effort to raise funds for the American Foundation for the Blind.

The "Seeing Eye" has recently been established to make blind people independent. They teach dogs to guide blind workers anywhere they want to go. These dogs make it possible for blind professional or businessmen and women and students to be entirely independent in getting about alone. The time and cost of such training have limited the number of such dogs that are available, but the Seeing Eye provides a real opportunity for the intelligent and ambitious blind.

Deaf. There are nearly sixty thousand deaf persons in the United States, and many thousands more nearly deaf. Many of these are also unable to speak. The cause of deafness is either an injury or disease affecting the inner ear, or heredity. Much of this is preventable. As most deafness is acquired and not inherited, it is necessary to guard against the causes to keep down the rapidly increasing number of cases. Severe attacks of scarlet fever, measles, or influenza cause infections leading to deafness, as does also meningitis.[1] You should try very hard to be patient when recovering from any illness. You may seem well, but you need rest after being sick. You will have less danger of serious results of sickness if you take enough

[1] **meningitis.** A very severe disease of the membranes of the brain and the spinal cord.

time to recover fully before being active. Modern preventive medicine will do much to lessen the inroads of these severe diseases.

The first permanent institution in the United States for the deaf was established in Hartford, Connecticut, by Gallaudet in 1817. Since then more schools have been established where the deaf are taught to read, write, and to converse by signs. The United States has the only institution in the world for the higher education of the deaf—Gallaudet College at Washington, established in 1864. The deaf are also taught to understand others by a method called lip reading.

Inasmuch as the percentage of those totally deaf is relatively small, wherever possible greater emphasis is being placed on the use of that part of the hearing which is left. This is done through the oral method of speaking and reading from the lips. However, the pupil who can neither speak nor hear touches the teacher's throat with his finger-tips when she speaks, and by this method learns to imitate better the throat movements producing speech.

In schools for the deaf vocational training is given in shoemaking, cabinetmaking, dressmaking, laundry work, and many other trades. Pupils play musical instruments and even are members of football teams. All this helps to avoid distinctions between deaf boys and girls and others, and helps to prepare them for self-support and useful citizenship.

Crippled. Clinics are organized all over the country to help the crippled. Instruction is provided for those who cannot go to school because of their handicaps.

There are also schools for crippled children confined to wheel chairs, and fresh-air schools for those affected by tuberculosis.

The federal government has a vast program of retraining former soldiers for new vocations. This is in charge of the Veterans' Administration, a special board for the purpose of caring for the veterans of the World Wars. More than fifty hospitals have been operated for this purpose and nearly three hundred thousand veterans and one hundred thousand of their dependents have been cared for at one time. Crippled veterans are trained for whatever work they are best able to do.

The vocational rehabilitation[2] division of the Office of Education co-operates with the various states in carrying on a similar service for other physically disabled citizens. The government assists by contributing to the cost of this training. The Dowling School for Crippled Children in Minneapolis is an example of state care for this kind of handicapped individual.

Feeble-minded. Feeble-mindedness is a mental defect present, as a rule, from birth. Feeble-minded persons are those whose brains never develop beyond that of a child. They may be divided into three classes. The *idiot* has the mind of a child one or two years old. Such persons are entirely helpless just as a child of that age would be helpless. Therefore, they should be placed in institutions where they can receive the best care from trained workers. The *imbecile* has the mind of a child from three to six years old. Because imbe-

[2] **rehabilitation.** Training the handicapped for new vocations.

ciles have abilities merely of children, they too, should be cared for in institutions equipped for aiding such persons. Some of them, however, can do routine work if carefully supervised. The *moron* has the mind of a child from seven to twelve. Morons need not all be kept in institutions because some can help themselves. They can do certain kinds of manual work but they need to be helped and guided all the time.

The first school in this country for the feeble-minded was established in 1850. Since that time other schools have been established where the feeble-minded are taught to care for themselves properly and to fit themselves for simple vocations. Today many states maintain institutions for both feeble-minded and insane persons.

Insane. Insanity is a form of mental sickness. An insane person at one time had a normal mind which became sick because of some extreme mental strain and worry, some injury, disease, or hereditary taint or blemish. Some forms of insanity are temporary and can be overcome by proper treatment. Other forms of insanity are violent and dangerous and therefore must be cared for in institutions which are properly equipped to treat such cases under the supervision of trained workers and specialists.

Mild cases of insanity can sometimes be treated by requiring a quiet and simple life. Extreme exertion and excitement must be avoided and much rest is needed. To prevent an increase in feeble-mindedness and insanity, it is necessary that people with these mental defects or sickness be denied the right to have children.

Recently there were nearly four hundred thousand patients in state hospitals for all kinds of mental disorders. Unfortunately this number has been increasing very rapidly during the past ten years, owing partly to a real increase, and partly to the increased efficiency in recognizing and caring for these people. Scientific care is making it possible to cure or permanently benefit a large part of this group.

Those Incapable of Work. In recent years unemployment has caused more dependents than all other reasons together. We may divide the unemployed into three classes.

The first class includes the aged and the ill. Some people of these groups really want to work but are frequently discharged and replaced by younger, stronger, or more efficient people. Such unemployed groups in the past have usually been cared for by relatives and friends, who are naturally interested in them and feel some responsibility for them as individuals. In the case of the failure of interested relatives and friends, these persons have been cared for by our local units of government, chiefly counties and cities. Most counties in the United States have county homes where old people may go to live. In many cases, the county aids some relative or friend of the aged or infirm person by furnishing a small monthly allowance, probably five or ten dollars a month.

Local governments, churches, and generous wealthy individuals have furnished hospitals in which those seriously ill may be treated free or at a very small cost. Governments have provided regular pensions for the aged and needy among soldiers, sailors, firemen, and policemen who have a claim on the government for services. Until recently this covered all that governments have done in directly aiding dependents. Social Security Acts are now granting aid also to the aged, the unemployed, and other types of needy individuals.

The Misfits. The second class of unemployed consists of those who for some reason seem to be misfits in society. They do not have family or friends to help them and these misfits are too lazy to do their part in providing a living. For this reason they become tramps and beg for food and clothing and use such shelter as they can find. Frequently such people pretend they are hunting for work, but work is the last thing they want to find. They seem to have no self-respect nor pride and are perfectly willing or even anxious to accept charity from anyone. Of course they have no claims on the general public. They are worthless as citizens, and are lacking in the American ideals of independence, self-respect, and personal pride. If it were not for the sympathetic spirit of our people they would have to work or starve.

The Victims of Depression. The third class of unemployed consists of those who want to work and support themselves and their families. These people worked and maintained happy homes for years, when perhaps some machine was invented which did the work they had been doing so much more cheaply that it was installed and the laborer lost his job. Or maybe an economic crisis or depression, like that of 1929, came and factories shut down. Apparently through no fault of anyone, and certainly through no fault of

ESTIMATED UNEMPLOYMENT

Pictograph Corporation
Each figure represents 600,000 unemployed

the laborers themselves, hundreds of thousands of people were thrown out of work.

It is this class that presents our greatest problems. They have the same American ideals of independence,

self-respect, and personal pride as all other good
American citizens and yet they are suddenly made
helpless by circumstances over which they have no
control. Their greatest danger is the temptation to de-
generate into the class of tramps and beggars described
above.

The depression of 1929 caused millions of people
to be added to this class of unemployed. Various estimates have been made of the exact total. It reached
its highest point in 1933 and has declined exceedingly
since that time, as is shown in the pictograph. Something had to be done by the federal government. The
problem was too big for local government and community help, and it was not a case for charity. These
people were not subjects of charity but victims of
circumstances over which they had no control. The
federal government proposed, with the aid of the
states, three kinds of remedy for the situation. First,
direct relief until something better could be done.
Second, the creation of employment by providing
public works. The Works Progress Administration
(W.P.A.) was created and employment instead of
direct relief was furnished most of the unemployed.
Third, an attempt to provide a permanent remedy for
the unemployed.

The proposed remedy consists of two Social Security Acts passed by the federal government. One was
an act providing for unemployment insurance. The
old-age pension act authorizes a tax upon each employer's pay roll and upon each employee's pay. This
tax began, in each case, with one per cent in 1937 and

is planned to increase gradually. Unemployment compensation is secured also by a pay-roll tax beginning at one per cent and later reaching three per cent. The purpose of these laws is to accumulate in the treasury at Washington huge sums which are to meet all payments required later.

The federal government requires that each state, whose citizens participate in the benefits of these social-security laws, also set up social-security reserve funds from which the state can meet its share of the payments. This means that state laws must be passed arranging for some kind of taxes to raise the money for a large reserve fund in the treasury of each state. These laws are still in the experimental state. It will be years before they get into full operation and the various reserve funds provided, reach the huge totals expected. In the meantime, unforeseen changes are apt to arise which will have to be dealt with as they arise.

The Orphaned. The Children's Bureau of the Department of Labor was organized in 1912 to investigate and report upon all matters pertaining to the welfare of children. One of its important divisions cares for dependent children. The White House Conference on the care of Dependent Children was called first by President Theodore Roosevelt and later by President Herbert Hoover. The federal government, therefore, has taken definite steps to look after those children who are not cared for by their own parents. Laws have been passed granting money to the states, in addition to the sums spent by the states, for the care of dependent children.

Each state is the guardian of all children who are not cared for by their parents. Child welfare bureaus have been established in many states to handle this task. Also county boards of child welfare have been developed in a number of states. Altogether there are nearly three hundred thousand children in different kinds of institutions for the dependent and neglected. These institutions include county farms or orphanages, state institutions, and private homes established by religious or fraternal agencies. Homes and vocational schools are supported by many of these groups for the dependent and orphaned children of their members. In some cases "house mothers" care for small groups who are housed together as families. Through such adequate care, boys and girls who lack the advantages of their own homes are kept away from bad companions and trained in self-support and good citizenship.

The Criminals. The criminal is the dependent who must be controlled by governmental force because he lacks ideals or will power to control himself. The least worthy and most expensive dependent of the community is this lawbreaker. It sometimes costs thousands of dollars to catch, try, and convict a murderer and if he is sentenced to life imprisonment, it costs thousands of dollars more to feed and keep him. And that does not begin to pay for the life or lives he has taken. It is said that every day of the year there are nearly one hundred and fifty thousand persons confined in the jails and prisons of the country. Can you imagine the cost of maintaining these prisons and prisoners?

There are two general kinds of criminals: First, the criminal who commits crime as a habit, just as you tie and untie your shoes by habit. He does it so often he forgets how to keep from doing it. Having started while young and apparently having succeeded with small crimes, he tried something worse each time. Such criminals seldom rid themselves of the habit.

Second, the occasional criminal, who commits crime on the spur of the moment and who may never have committed a crime before. He may even have been forced into crime. He is likely to repent and is usually sorry for his acts. It is to give these criminals a chance to reform and make good citizens, that the parole system has been established. Wisely used, it may be of great value to society.

Classes of Crime. Crimes are usually divided into two general classes by our state laws. Those that are considered less serious, such as small thefts, are called *misdemeanors* and are punished by small fines or imprisonment in our county or city jails. The more serious crimes of murder, burglary, or robbery are called *felonies* and are punished by imprisonment in a penitentiary. In the case of intentional murder, kidnapping, and a few other serious crimes, the criminal may be put to death. Those who break certain federal laws, as mail robbers and counterfeiters, are sent to a federal prison.

Prison Reform. Much is being done to try to change
the criminal. The effort is made to reform and, if
possible, make him an industrious, law-abiding citizen.
This cannot always be done, but it is worth attempting. The safety of the public, however, must not be
sacrificed or endangered in so doing. With the hope
of reforming criminals, prisons are made modern and
sanitary, prisoners are taught trades, the term of imprisonment may be shortened by good conduct, the
prisoner is given as much liberty as his conduct permits, and after a part of his term is served he may be
paroled.[3]

We must not forget that every prisoner who has
served his sentence and is released, must fit back into
the world from which he has been separated for so
many years. Unless he is prepared with a trade or
occupation and assured of another chance at a job, he
will as a rule drift back into crime. The parole officer
tries to give him that help and at the same time watches
him to be sure that he does not fail.

A noted prison authority has said that, in one of
the largest states only "about twenty-five per cent of
those paroled were declared violators" of their parole.
Many of these had merely failed to report promptly
to their sponsors, and only part of this group had
committed new crimes. The majority of those paroled
"are well on their way to becoming law-abiding citizens." With the constant improvement of the parole
law and the increase in the number of parole officers,
former prisoners can be more carefully watched and

[3] **paroled.** Released on good behavior.

helped to become worthy citizens again. Only those prisoners who have shown themselves entirely trustworthy should be paroled before their term expires. The rest should be assigned to special institutions where they can be guarded until such time as they are cured of their desire to live by criminal means.

Test and Study Exercises

Aids to Learning.

1. Remember the five classes of dependents whom society must provide for in various ways.

2. Distinguish between misdemeanors and felonies.

3. Recall the ways in which the blind, the deaf, the crippled, and the aged are being helped to care for themselves.

4. Observe the effort of the social-security laws in providing a permanent remedy for the unemployed.

Test Exercises.

On a separate sheet of paper, write the numbers one through fourteen on the left margin. Then write *yes* or *no* after each number depending on your judgment as to the answer to the questions below.

1. Can a large part of blindness be prevented?

2. Did Helen Keller learn to speak although she was deaf and dumb?

3. Is deafness usually caused by diseases or injury of the inner ear?

4. Can all deaf persons learn to hear again?

5. Can feeble-minded people be made normal through education?

6. Is insanity a form of mental sickness?

7. Has the moron the mind of a child two years old?

8. Are mental disorders apparently increasing very rapidly?

9. Are old-age pensions being provided under the Social Security Act?

10. Are all unemployed people given jobs by the federal government?

11. Is the number of prisoners greater than the number of blind persons?

12. Are pickpockets sent to the federal prisons?

13. Are modern prisons made sanitary?

14. Are more parole officers required if paroled prisoners are to be helped adequately?

Suggested Activities.

1. Read Helen Keller's *Story of My Life* and learn how her struggle for an education was finally rewarded.

2. With your teacher's help, write to "The Seeing Eye" in Morristown, New Jersey, for information about the ways in which dogs are trained as guides for blind people.

3. Search in your history or your readers for the names of famous people who were blind, deaf, or crippled but who still succeeded in accomplishing their ambitions.

4. Keep a scrapbook of the newspaper articles relating to governmental efforts to help unemployment, such as the C.C.C., N.Y.A., W.P.A., and other new agencies.

5. *Group Activity:* The teacher may ask several pupils to look up the use of the Braille system of reading for the blind and report this to the class.

6. *Group Activity:* The teacher may take the class to an institute for the care of the blind, the deaf, or the aged, if there is one nearby, so that the pupils may observe how society helps the handicapped.

CHAPTER XIV

PLANNED COMMUNITIES

PREPARATORY NOTE: As a community guards against those things which may destroy its usefulness, it also plans for the future in a way which permits its best development. It may already have beautiful surroundings or it may have to make its own beauty. It must watch its buildings and its traffic problems. It must guard against slums and crowded living conditions. These are necessary steps if it is to become a "city beautiful" which this chapter suggests.

Future Needs. City planning is building for the future. Planners should keep in mind the health and convenience of the city inhabitants, and also the beauty of the city itself. Regional planning is the same for territory outside the city and between cities, making possible the growth and spread of the city. An up-to-date community, even though small, will think of its future in mapping out its possible growth. A commission is usually appointed whose duty it is to study the city's needs, its defects, and its possible growth, and then to plan accordingly. For our purpose here, let us summarize the many aspects, or divisions, of city planning under the following heads: (1) *housing and zoning,* (2) *civic beauty,* (3) *communication and transportation.*

Housing and Zoning. Housing and zoning plans

include regulation of the construction of buildings, both public and private, and carefully planned zoning laws for the division of the city into districts.

A community is responsible for the buildings erected within its boundaries. Therefore it regulates the construction of buildings by means of laws, or ordinances. Large cities, with their congestion and their many building problems, require a building code. This is a set of rules governing the construction of all buildings, as well as the kinds of material used. It provides that the walls, floors, and ceilings of large buildings be made secure; that elevators and stairs be built safely; that plumbing, heating, lighting, and ventilation be adequate and sanitary; and that the buildings be protected against fire. Large cities have a tenement-house[1] law which regulates conditions of dwellings in the poorer parts of the city to assure sanitation and protection against fire.

Zoning Laws. City planning today requires careful zoning laws. For this purpose the city is divided into districts which are restricted for certain uses. The city sets aside residential districts in which home owners are protected. Bungalows are permitted in certain areas and large apartment buildings in others. Residential districts are naturally in the most favored portions of the city where quiet and beauty are found and yet where there is a convenient approach to places of business. Frequently, zones of quiet are set apart near the hospitals.

---

[1] **tenement house.** A dwelling house found in large cities, divided for the use of many poor families.

Large manufacturing plants or factories are usually in outlying sections or along railroad lines. Here the land is cheaper, operating costs and taxes are less and sources of power and methods of transportation are more convenient. The wholesale business district lies nearer the center of the city but it is connected with the factories by trucking and by rail lines. In the heart of the city and at various important outlying centers are the retail business sections. The retail sections must have streets wide enough to permit heavy automobile traffic and must be near to local transportation lines.

Unfortunately all cities are not adequately zoned, else there would be no slums, the areas where large numbers of poor people are crowded together in worn-out buildings. These tenement buildings are usually old dwellings, several stories high, which are divided into small apartments and rented to people who must live near their work. The buildings have very unsatisfactory heat, light, ventilation, plumbing, and sanitation. They are frequently rickety firetraps. Because of these facts a constant effort is being made to condemn them as unsafe and to replace them with more satisfactory houses.

The federal government has recently taken a leading part in replacing slum areas with low-cost groups of houses in various parts of the country. This is a part of the Public Works Administration (P.W.A.) to furnish employment and may not become a permanent program. Similar help is being given by the Department of Agriculture in those rural areas where there is great need. Farm families have also obtained tools, animals, seed, and other equipment necessary to carry on farming. Although all these efforts are still recent and have not yet been·perfected, they point the way to a gradual improvement of housing conditions.

Civic Beauty. It is very important that communities recognize the value of civic beauty. It is natural that people prefer to have pleasant surroundings. Human nature responds to beautiful things, whether they consist of natural scenery or man-made gardens. The presence of unsightly surroundings, such as unkept lawns, vacant lots used as dumping grounds, huge billboards, and dirty alleys, which are found in some communities, causes lack of respect for the community and discontent among its people.

Well-kept lawns and trees, freshly painted houses, clean alleys, flower gardens, and the absence of smoke and dirt and unnecessary noise play an important part in creating contentment as well as interest in the community. A community that advocates and provides for civic beauty creates for itself a feeling of co-operation among the inhabitants. Most individuals take pride in such a community and will do their best to live up to its standards. An excellent example of this city planning is found in the photograph of the civic center of one of the new industrial cities of the northwest. You can see the beauty of its carefully arranged streets with their lawns, shrubs, and trees lining the drives.

Development of Civic Beauty. Realizing the need for civic beauty, citizens are doing more and more to make their own community beautiful and attractive. You can play a very real part in this program by helping to keep your house and yard attractive. You may keep your lawn neat and trim, free of long grass and litter. You may plant flowers and take care of

Courtesy Northern Pacific Ry.
Civic Center of Longview, Washington

them, set out shrubs, and in other ways contribute to the beauty of your neighborhood.

Many communities have ordinances encouraging those who would make their city more beautiful. They will not permit the existence of unsightly billboards, dirty alleys, or unattractive streets, yards, or houses. Some communities have laws which call for the prompt removal of snow from the sidewalks, or the clearance of weeds from vacant lots. If the owners fail to do either of these, the city may have it done and charge them for the labor. This shows that these communities not only advocate civic beauty, but also make every effort to enforce ordinances that will improve their city. Today civic beauty occupies a prominent place in the minds of those who plan cities. They believe it is wiser and cheaper to plan a city properly while it is growing than to be confronted with the problem afterwards of locating parks and playgrounds in providing for civic beauty.

Results of Civic Beauty. There are many results obtained from planning and keeping a community beautiful. The people located in such a community will be happy and contented. Therefore, they will take pride in their city and will promote its interests. Civic planning will increase the value of property. Business and industrial plants will be attracted to the city. Many more desirable people will come to the community to live.

Communication and Transportation. People will always require the exchange of ideas and goods. Therefore, a community should plan carefully for the arrangement and management of communication and transportation. These will include postal service, telephone, telegraph, and radio; streets, highways, railways, waterways, air routes, subways, elevated-railways, and ferries. In establishing these means of communication and transportation, it is important to keep in mind the idea of rendering the best service to the public at a reasonable cost. These methods must be rapid, convenient, safe, and yet as inexpensive as possible. The city, state, and nation all co-operate in the development and regulation of communication and transportation because they are so essential for our progress and prosperity.

Streets and Highways. One of the most important features of a city plan is that of its streets. Some of the streets will be through streets or boulevards on which the traffic will have the right of way. Because of the increasing difficulty of traffic problems, these streets must be arranged so as to permit convenience of travel, and they must also be wide enough to admit sufficient air and light into the high buildings alongside of them. Heavy traffic has made necessary much wider streets and roads than were previously needed. Eighteen-foot roads formerly were considered sufficient but now forty-foot roads are none too wide, and some arterial highways or main thoroughfares are as wide as eighty or one hundred feet. The surfacing of roads has also become very important. Mud roads are long since out of date and gravel roads are fast giving way to macadam and concrete roads. The change from the horse-and-carriage on dirt roads to the automobile on hard-surfaced roads is shown in the following pictograph.

In village and city planning special attention is given to the way in which new streets are arranged. The *checker board* or *gridiron design* brings all roads together at right angles. This is satisfactory in small villages where the ground is level and rivers and lakes do not interfere.

Sometimes it is much better to have diagonal streets running straight to the center of town so that time may be saved in reaching important buildings. Accordingly, the *spider web design* has been found more satisfactory for many cities. The main avenues go out diagonally as spokes from the center of town and cir-

HIGHWAYS AND VEHICLES

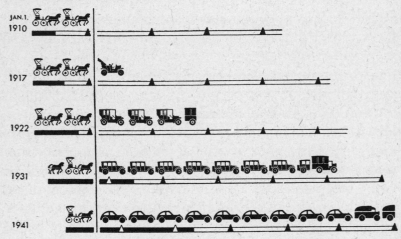

Pictograph Corporation

Each horse-and-carriage represents 10 million horses. Each motor vehicle represents 3 million motor vehicles. Distance between milestones represents 500,000 miles of road—surfaced portion dark

cular streets connect these avenues. Detroit is a good example of the use of the spider web design for streets, while Washington, D. C., modifies the plan by using both diagonal and right-angle streets. Chicago's new planning also combines both of these designs. It uses right angle streets for the most part with various diagonal streets jutting out from the main business district or the "loop." The beautiful boulevards in Chicago running along the lake shore and bordering the inland rivers serve as connecting links for automobile traffic. On the other hand Boston's crooked, narrow streets in the older part remind us of the tradition that they were originally cow paths.

Traffic Problems. These different arrangements of streets are designed to produce the most efficient flow of traffic. Fifty years ago traffic was made up of horse-drawn vehicles. Today various kinds of electric and steam railroads and multitudes of public and private busses and automobiles make traffic problems increasingly important in every village and city. No longer is it desirable for main avenues of traffic to cross each other on the same level. Even with automatic stop-and-go lights and traffic policemen, too many automobile accidents occur at road intersections. To prevent such accidents, one road is elevated over the other, and connecting passages are made so that all cars will go in the same direction.

Street lighting is very important as a means of increasing safety in driving and walking. The use of a sufficient number of street lights does much to prevent crime, to promote safe driving, and to increase the beauty of the location. Finally, the removal of all obstructions to the view is necessary. Chief among these are the numerous signboards that are blotting out the beauties of the landscape as well as making both country and city driving unsafe. Safety on the road requires that the driver give all his attention to the road and to his driving.

Local Transportation. In connection with the arrangement of streets and alleys should come the proper location of transportation lines and terminals. In locating these lines and terminals the safety, convenience, and comfort of the people must be kept in mind. Parks and playgrounds can well be mapped off at this time, too. Natural scenery will help to determine their location. If there is no natural scenery, parks can be made by planting trees and flower gardens, by constructing artificial lakes, and by making drives and walks.

Government Regulation. The city or village plans, builds, and keeps in repair many forms of communication and transportation within its own borders. As the village grows, these facilities of communication and transportation must be expanded. Many new problems in this connection arise continually and must be solved by those in charge. A city makes rules to govern traffic, and authorizes its policemen to enforce them. It grants rights to public service companies, and it may own and operate its own transit lines. You can do your part by learning the rules of the road, the proper use of the telephone, and other means of communication. An increased pride in the value of modern improvements will help you to understand life better, and appreciate it more.

The state builds highways, canals, and bridges, and keeps them in good repair. It also patrols or guards them to assure safe traveling. The state regulates transportation within its borders and also regulates those public-service companies which deal with communication.

Congress has the power to make laws for the development of our postal service and the radio, and for the regulation of commerce with foreign countries and among the states. It appropriates money to build

© *B. and O. Railroad*

Horse-Drawn Car of a Century Ago

national highways and to promote other forms of travel. The Great Lakes to Gulf Waterway now connected through the Illinois Waterway System, is an example of co-operation between city, state, and nation in advancing methods of transportation.

Modern Improvements. The development of means of communication under federal regulation is very marked. It now takes the air mail only one half day to go the distance which formerly required ten days by the pony express. In almost no other way have we seen

© *Underwood & Underwood*
Modern Streamlined Train

greater speed and improvement than in our mail system during the past two generations.

In recent years very great changes have likewise been made in transportation. The streamlined trains found in many parts of the country today travel at greatly increased speed because of improvements in their design and construction. The Diesel-electric engines of some of these streamlined trains use cheap grades of oil in place of coal as fuel and develop great power with remarkable economy. The principle of streamlined design was first used in airplane construction and now has been successfully applied to railroad trains, automobiles, steamships, and other forms of transportation. The previous photographs show the passenger car on one of our leading railroads a century ago and a modern streamlined train.

Test and Study Exercises

Aids to Learning.

1. Observe the ways by which city planning regulates the growth of the city and at the same time increases its beauty and effectiveness.
2. Notice how transportation has developed with emphasis upon the best service at a reasonable cost.
3. Observe the growth of slum areas in the large cities due to the crowding of many people in unsatisfactory dwellings.

Test Exercises.

1. What are the most important aspects of city or regional planning?
2. Indicate the way in which a large city is zoned for factories, stores, residences, and civic centers.
3. What are some of the most effective ways used for making the average village beautiful?
4. What has made it necessary to increase the width of roads and to use a more nearly permanent surfacing?
5. What are the advantages of the "checker-board" and the "spider-web" designs for city streets?
6. How is through traffic safeguarded at road intersections?
7. Trace the development of transportation and communication during the past fifty years, showing which new methods arose in each decade.
8. What is the objection to permitting stores and factories to be built in residential districts? Would tenement districts spring up there as a result of such action?

Suggested Activities.

1. Read some such book as Jacob Riis' *How the Other Half Lives,* Mary Antin's *Promised Land,* or Israel Zangwill's *Children of the Ghetto,* and be prepared to report on a story of slum life.

2. With the help of your librarian, read articles in recent magazines describing the federal government's plan for substituting new houses for old slum tenements.

3. Study auto maps showing plans of large cities such as New York, Chicago, Philadelphia, Cleveland, Boston, San Francisco, or Washington. Which street designs seem to be commonest, those meeting at right angles or those coming out diagonally from the center?

4. Investigate the various means of transportation between your home town and the large cities in your state.

5. *Group Activity:* The teacher may assign members of the class to write to airline companies, such as the American Airlines, to secure their maps and schedules. How nearly are all the large cities in the country served by the different air transport lines?

CHAPTER XV

MODERN INDUSTRIAL LIFE

PREPARATORY NOTE: The growth of industry makes problems for the modern city or nation. Nations are influenced
accordingly as they handle their trades and industries. A
knowledge of some of the important principles on which
modern business is built is a necessary part of the education of every citizen. Our present system of money and
credit and the methods of business management explain
many of the problems of labor and also explain government's relation to business and labor, treated in this chapter.

The Industrial Revolution. Until a century and a
half ago families produced their own food, clothing,
and other necessities, just as had been done for hundreds of years past. All members of the family even
including the young children, did their part. But trade
developed in Europe, and by the eighteenth century
families in England began to specialize in particular
forms of work. One family made cloth, another finished leather, and other trades were developed by
other families. Thus there came to be household manufacturing in the cottages of the English villagers.
When a family specialized in one kind of manufacturing they learned to do the work faster and better.

197

Gradually the invention of certain forms of machinery in England and America—Hargreaves' spinning jenny, Whitney's cotton gin, and Watt's steam engine —paved the way for the Industrial Revolution. This was the rapid speeding up of the mechanical changes

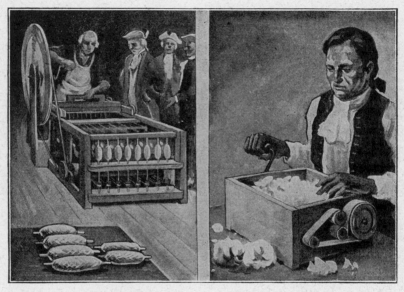

The Early Spinning Jenny and Cotton Gin

which had been taking place for centuries. These changes brought about the development of factories. It became cheaper for the owner of machinery to group together in one building many workers who could turn out much more work with the power machines under their control. Unskilled labor could be used in place of the skilled craftsmen who had given their lives to learning a single trade. Goods became cheaper and the people, especially the poorer classes, could have a great many things they were not able to have before.

Money. But the development of factories required constantly improved machinery and more money. Money had long ago become a *medium of exchange.* It proved much more convenient for the farmer to sell his cow or sheep for certain coins rather than to have to find another farmer who was willing to trade his hens or eggs for a sheep or a cow. At first, money was very crude and had no certain value. Later governments placed their stamp or seal on this money and it became accepted as a standard or *measure of value.* Then the farmer could say that his cow was worth a certain number of coins or dollars rather than so many chickens.

Money is also used as a *standard of deferred payment.* A man may want to buy a suit of clothes but will not have the money to pay for it until several weeks have passed. So he gets credit from the merchant and agrees to pay him for the suit after a certain number of weeks. If a farmer sells his hogs and cattle to a buyer who does not have the ready money, he takes a promissory note for them in place of the money. He can then turn this note over to the bank as credit to apply on some debt he may have, such as a mortgage on his farm.

Money is only one of the forms of wealth with which man has to deal. All his material possessions, such as land, stock, or houses, which can be measured by money, constitute *wealth.* Wealth may, therefore, be *real property* which is fixed, such as houses and land, or real estate, or it may be *personal property* which is movable, such as furniture, clothing, or money itself.

Money is now coined or made in this country only by the federal government, so that it will have the same value everywhere and will not be counterfeit, or false. Money may now be coined in silver, nickel, or copper. Money may also be engraved on paper notes. These are called greenbacks, certificates, or bank notes and are engraved by the Bureau of Engraving and Printing of the Treasury Department at Washington. A special paper containing silk fibers is made for this purpose. Great care is taken so that neither the steel engravings nor the paper can be duplicated and money made by others than the government employees in the Treasury Department.

Banks and Credit. Such transactions require the help of banks, which are institutions organized under the law to deal in money or credit. Banks are organized under the authority of the different states or of the United States. They receive the people's deposits of money and pay them interest on their deposits. This money is then loaned to others at a higher rate of interest than is paid to the depositors. In this way banks earn money just as stores do on their goods, buying at a low price and selling at a higher price. National banks also issue bank notes which circulate as money. Federal Reserve banks do a banking business with other banks. Credit transactions permit banks to lend at least three-fourths of all their deposits and still be able to meet all normal demands for cash.

Because of the repeated use of credit, bank deposits in the United States in 1937 totaled over fifty-two billion dollars while the actual money of all kinds in circulation for the same year was only about six and a half billion dollars.

That is to say, credit money is far more than actual money. A man deposits a check for fifty dollars in his bank and then pays his debts by drawing checks against this amount. Those who receive his checks do the same although perhaps none of them has received any actual money. So one check for fifty dollars may cover several hundred dollars' worth of transactions.

Business is based on credit. A businessman does not need to have cash enough for all his transactions if his credit is good. This means that if his past record has been satisfactory and he is known to be able to pay his bills when they are due, he can then borrow money when he needs it to pay emergency bills.

Business Management. Business may be under the control of a single individual who owns the entire plant and equipment. This is a *proprietorship* and is found most frequently in the small retail business employing only a few workers. A man may associate himself on equal terms with one or more additional helpers and so form a *partnership*. In that case they share responsibility for profit or loss equally. If the business is large and the owners prefer not to have individual responsibility, they form a *corporation*. This is a joint stock company authorized by the state, and it issues shares of stock showing shares of owner- ship.

Economic Activities. The various activities of a business fall into a circle of four parts. First, the growth, manufacture, or preparation of goods is called *production*. These products may be grown on the farm, manufactured in a factory, or made serviceable in a store. Second, the sale of these products is called *exchange*. In the sale, money is used as a medium of exchange. Third, the use of the products necessary to satisfy our needs is called *consumption*. Fourth, there is a division of income to determine how much profit has been made and what wages should be paid; this is called *distribution*. This term is also used to refer to the transportation of goods. These four activities are necessary in all business transactions and must remain well-balanced or confusion occurs. In a depression, money is scarce and so the consumption of goods declines. This means there are high prices for goods sold and few sales are made. As a consequence fewer goods are produced. Or, if the production of goods is faster than consumption requires, prices are lowered and unused stocks of goods pile up.

When goods are produced, there are four classes of income. The *land,* or property on which the goods are produced, will yield *rent* to its owner. If a farmer owns his own land, he does not pay real rent, but he pays in other ways, such as taxes, repairs, and improvements, which would equal rent. *Labor,* or the workers who produce the goods, will receive *wages*. If the worker is the farmer's son he may not receive real wages, but he will get his food, clothing, shelter, and education — things equal to wages or greater than wages. The *capital,* or money borrowed by anyone to buy the equipment for producing the goods, will draw *interest* for the person that lends the money. Finally the *management,* or those who own or plan the business, should receive *profits* for their ability and knowledge. No one of these features can be ignored in a healthy business.

Employee Welfare. When the employer carried on his trade in his own house and his helpers lived with him all the time, it was a simple thing for him to know their needs. Whether he took satisfactory care of them depended solely on his own desires as there were no rules or regulations for him to follow.

With the growth of factories, management got farther away from labor and the close association between management and labor was broken. The health and safety of the workers became more of a problem because of the increased use of complicated machinery. Various problems arose in which the interests of capital, management, and labor were shared, and it was necessary that all of these be protected.

First in the list of these considerations is the health and safety of the workers. Moving machinery requires safety devices to prevent accidents from occurring. Great care must be taken to keep down the possibility of fire. Sufficient lighting and ventilation are necessary in all places where workers have to spend hours at a time. It is just as important for workers to have good light at their work as it is for you to have good light for your studying.

The working day was originally from "sun up to

sun down," both on the farm and for the trades. This twelve or fourteen-hour day gradually gave way to ten hours, and then to eight hours as a standard. Today the forty-hour week is the goal reached in many industries.

CHILD LABOR

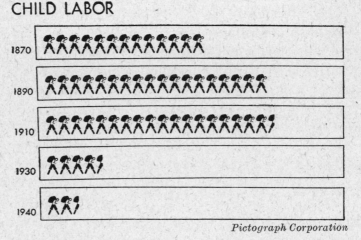

Pictograph Corporation

Each child represents 1 per cent of all children 10 to 15 years old

Regulations for the employment of children are very recent. Children once worked in mines and factories for as many hours as their fathers did. Many of these boys never saw daylight for days at a time. They went down into mines before dawn, and came out of them after sunset. Gradually this was frowned upon until most of the states now have laws which do not permit children under fourteen to sixteen years of age to work, and which limit their working hours from forty to sixty hours per week. Fortunately, during the past generation, the percentage of employed children has been decreasing, as is seen in the pictograph. This is but a step in the right direction. An amendment to the Constitution prohibiting the labor of persons under eighteen years of age was proposed in 1924, but it has been ratified, or approved, thus far by less than half the states.

Labor Problems. Progressive states have labor laws which safeguard the worker in various ways. A maximum of eight hours a day, with one day of rest in seven, is provided in most vocations. In many industries five days is the regular working week.

Buildings must be fireproof, and have sufficient fire exits with doors opening outward. A fire-alarm system and fire extinguishers must be installed. Every part of the factory must be kept clean. Good drinking water must be supplied, and also individual drinking cups and towels. There must be sufficient light, heat, and ventilation.

Dangerous machinery must be guarded and safety devices installed. Inspections of shops and factories are made by inspectors of the state labor departments. If injured at work, a workman receives a money allowance from an insurance fund, the amount to be in proportion to the seriousness of the injury. If a workman is killed at work, his family receives compensation.

Women in Industry. The number of women employed has been increasing during the past two generations, as the pictograph shows. Many new occupations are now open to women as well as to men.

Increased educational opportunities for women have also added to their interest in regular employment. Some states give women workers special protection

WOMEN IN OCCUPATIONS

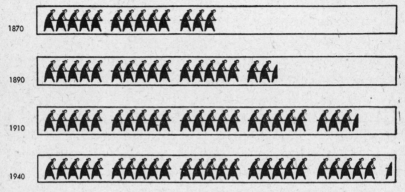

1870

1890

1910

1940

Pictograph Corporation for Keohane and McGoldrick's
"Government in Action," Harcourt Brace & Co.

Each woman represents 1 per cent of all women 10 years or over
(1940—14 years or over)

through their labor laws. These include the following provisions:

The working day is limited to eight hours and the week to forty-eight hours.

The employment of women is prohibited in certain vocations unsuitable for them, such as mining.

A minimum-wage law provides that an employer may not pay less than enough for a decent living.

High Cost of Child Labor. The employment of children for pay in shops or factories is called child labor. Children working in homes or on farms are usually not thought of in connection with child labor, even though they may be paid for their work. Children should be safeguarded by the community more than any other class of workers, because of the greater dangers they meet.

This is the community's most expensive labor problem. A child works at a great cost to himself, to industry, and to society at large. The cost to the child is that it deprives him of an education; it exposes him to accident and to disease; it deprives him of play and recreation so necessary to his growth; and his future chances and life itself are sacrificed or forfeited. The cost to industry is that he wastes material; he breaks machinery; he must be taught frequently; he is more careless and not so productive as an adult would be; his efficiency is lowered when he becomes an adult, because of his weakened condition. The cost to society is that it increases the number of ignorant workers; it wrecks young lives; it deprives the child of the benefits of home training; and it increases the possibility of more crime, because of insufficient education.

Labor Organizations. As factory conditions changed, there was the tendency for labor conditions to grow worse rather than better. The regulations for the welfare of employees which we have been considering have grown up over a period of many years. One of the reasons for this improvement was the growing practice of workers to organize into unions. Although labor organizations have existed almost since our national government was established, they did not become important until much later. The American Federation of Labor, composed of more than a hundred national or international trade unions, was formed over fifty years ago. More recently, another form of union based on industries was called the Committee for Industrial Organization. This includes an entire industry such as the coal industry, rather than just one craft in it.

Shorter hours, higher wages, the rights of *collective bargaining*,[1] better working conditions, and higher standards of workmanship are considered the objects sought by these different unions. On the other hand, strikes of increasing violence, *picketing*,[2] and *boycotts*[3] against companies said to be unfriendly to labor are considered disadvantages of such a system. It will be seen in the pictograph that strikes occur in times of prosperity rather than during depression.

Certain industries or companies maintain an *open shop* or hire any kind of labor, union or non-union. Others use *closed shops* and employ only union help. At times, during strikes called by union labor, *injunctions,* or court orders, may be issued by the court forbidding such action as picketing. Employers sometimes work against labor by *lockouts* or closed factories during labor disputes.

Government and Business. As business develops it comes in contact more and more with government. Of course, business must be taxed to bear its fair share of the cost of government. However, business requires

[1] **collective bargaining.** The system under which the officers of a labor organization carry on negotiations with the employer for improved working conditions.

[2] **picketing.** The act of persuading labor not to work during a strike.

[3] **boycotts.** Agreements to prevent dealings with a group opposed to your interests.

charters, or franchises, permitting it to operate under certain conditions. It desires that contracts be carefully preserved. It requests protective tariffs[4] so that it may avoid foreign competition during its growing period. Certain types of businesses such as banks and

WORKERS INVOLVED IN STRIKES AND LOCKOUTS

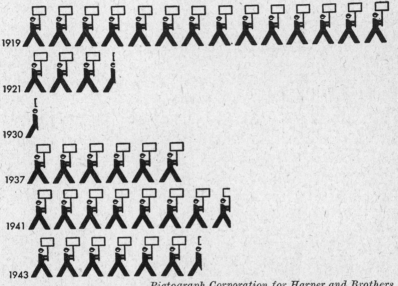

Pictograph Corporation for Harper and Brothers

Each symbol represents 300,000 workers

railroads, in which failure would cause loss to a great mass of citizens, are occasionally assisted by government loans during periods of depression.

Government Regulation. But business objects to certain forms of government regulation, feeling that

[4] **protective tariffs.** Duties on imports which protect the development of industries in our own country.

its opportunity for development will be crippled by these laws. It agrees with Thomas Jefferson in saying, "That government is best which governs least."

Recent federal legislation has been enacted laying down new policies for banking and finance and insuring payment of bank deposits. Laws were passed limiting working hours, fixing minimum wages, and prohibiting certain kinds of child labor. Many types of public businesses, such as railroads and public utilities, are strictly regulated by government. Consequently the government's relation to business is becoming very important.

The United States government, until recently, has not attempted to regulate labor with the exception of its own federal employees. The Department of Labor has for years aided in bettering working conditions by its efforts to promote the welfare of wage earners, especially that of women and children.

In order to do away with the dangers of future unemployment conditions, Congress passed a national Social Security Act in 1935 providing old-age payments and unemployment insurance as well as other forms of assistance for the handicapped. In the same year, Congress passed the National Labor Relations Act providing for collective bargaining between employees and employers. It also provided for a National Labor Relations Board to enforce the provisions of this act. This board is given power to take testimony in labor disputes and decide which union is the proper bargaining agency. In 1938 Congress passed the Wages and Hours Act, making compulsory a minimum wage and limiting the number of hours a laborer may work each day in his employment.

Test and Study Exercises

Aids to Learning.

1. Recall the uses of money as a medium of exchange, a measure of value, and a standard of deferred payment.

2. Observe the differences between proprietorship, partnership, and corporation.

3. Notice the changing relations of government to business as a result of the recent economic depression.

Test Exercises.

Match items in the first list with corresponding items in the second list by putting together on a sheet of paper the numbers of the items which best go together.

1. Open shop	1. Business organized under government charter.
2. Wealth	2. The growing, making, or preparation of goods.
3. Partnership	3. Institution organized to deal in money or credit.
4. Consumption	4. Sale of goods.
5. Distribution	5. Material possessions valued in money.
6. Proprietorship	6. Single ownership of business.
7. Bank	7. Employment of any kind of labor.
8. Production	8. Organization of labor crafts.
9. Corporation	9. Business shared by two or more equally.
10. Profits	10. Use of products to satisfy our needs.
11. Social Security	11. Payment for use of capital.
12. Collective bargaining	12. Division of profits or wages.
13. Exchange	13. Old age and unemployment compensation.
14. Labor union	14. Trade agreement of employers with a union.
15. Interest	15. Payment to managers for their ability and knowledge.

Suggested Activities.

1. In your United States History read the accounts given about the invention of the spinning jenny, the cotton gin, and the steam engine. How did these pave the way for the industrial revolution?

2. In your Ancient History or in an encyclopedia read the story of the first use of money as "cow tokens." What does this name mean? Look up the origin of the word "pecuniary" in the dictionary.

3. With the help of your librarian, locate some popular magazine articles dealing with the recent financial depression. What do you think contributed most to cause this depression?

4. Look in your library for recent articles regarding Social Security legislation. How is the act of 1935 being financed?

5. *Group Activity:* The teacher may assign students to write to the U. S. Department of Agriculture, Washington, D. C., for free samples of *Consumers' Guide,* a biweekly publication. Get information here on prices and quality of commodities in which you are interested.

CHAPTER XVI

THE COMMUNITY MELTING POT

PREPARATORY NOTE: You are all immigrants or descendants of immigrants, as you see in the following chapter. Even the American Indian is said to have come here originally from Asia. Our newer immigrants are of various kinds, of all nations and races, all religions and creeds. They have contributed both good and bad influences to America. It is necessary that immigrants become real Americans. We cannot have large masses of people following only the customs of the lands from which they come, if we are to keep our country a democracy of all the people.

Our Ancestors. Of all civilized nations, the United States is one of the youngest, largest, wealthiest, and most progressive. Its population is made up of immigrants from many other nations. It is called the "Land of the Free" because of its form of government. It is a government "of the people, by the people, and for the people." Before we consider the government of our country, let us see who our ancestors were, what were the problems of immigrants to our country, how they were educated, and how they secured citizenship.

First Settlers. Although the Indians were in America long before the white men settled here, they were not the founders of the America of today. The settlement of Virginia in 1607 and the landing of the Pilgrims in 1620 on the shores of what is now Massachusetts were among the first permanent white settlements. By their courage, fortitude, and zeal, these pioneers won for themselves homes in the American wilderness. These first immigrants came to the American wilderness for religious, political, or economic reasons—that they might have a free and independent home life. Since that time, other immigrants have been coming to these shores for the same reasons, and the ideals fostered and the independence sought by the early settlers developed into the very foundation of American liberty and democracy.

Early Immigrants. At the time of the Declaration of Independence several million people lived here, about ninety per cent of whom were of English descent. However, there were settlers of other countries found here and there throughout the colonies. These were made up of various nationalities. The Swedes, Dutch, Germans, Scotch-Irish, and Welsh came to Pennsylvania; the Dutch settled also in New York; and the Germans, Scotch-Irish, Swiss, and French Huguenots settled in the Carolinas and in Georgia. Other later settlers came from Ireland, Norway, Sweden, and Denmark. During the Revolutionary War, immigration was practically at a standstill because during wartimes people are not allowed to move from one country to another. Then after peace was restored and the United States was organized under its own constitution as an independent nation, the French Revolution broke out and immigration still was limited. The French Revolution caused a general political and social upheaval throughout Europe lasting for over twenty years.

The number of immigrants to the United States previous to 1820 is not known accurately but it is estimated at about five or six thousand a year. During the next decade it increased slowly, but in the period between 1830 and 1840, it jumped to sixty thousand a year, and in the next decade, to one hundred seventy thousand a year. The potato famine in Ireland in 1847 and the revolution in Germany in 1848 produced a great tide of migration to America, reaching three or four hundred thousand annually for the next thirty years. Up to 1880 immigrants had come almost entirely from northern and western Europe. We sometimes refer to these as the "Old Immigrants."

Later Immigrants. Those who came after 1880 are sometimes called the "New Immigrants." They came mostly from southern and eastern Europe: Italy, Russia, Poland, Austria-Hungary, and Greece. These later immigrants were mostly unmarried men who belonged to the uneducated classes and so did not appreciate the value of becoming Americanized. Because of their poverty they grouped themselves together in city slums where they were easily led by corrupt politicians and became a problem to our democratic form of government.

The greatest number of immigrants came in the decade following 1905, reaching over a million for each of several years. Up to 1917 there had been little restriction placed upon the number of white immigrants. The first restriction prohibited illiterates from entering this country. In 1921 emergency legislation limited those coming from each country to a definite percentage share of the number that had been previously sent from that country. In 1924 and again

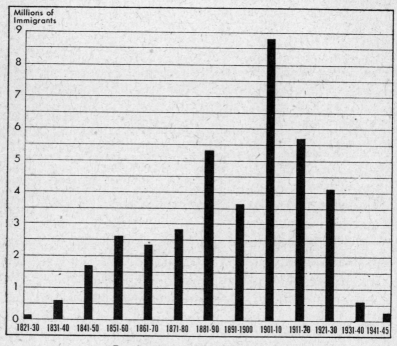

Immigration to the United States

in 1927 this was modified so as to keep the total annual immigration down to about one hundred fifty thousand. A summary of these figures is given in the foregoing graph.

Contrast of "Old" and "New" Immigrants. In contrasting the early and late immigrants, you will notice

certain differences which are shown in the following
table regarding these two groups.

Immigrants	Early or "Old"	Later or "New"
Birthplace	Northern and North-western Europe.	Southern and South-eastern Europe.
Education	Mostly well educated; intelligent.	Not well educated; frequently unable to read and write.
Occupation	Merchants, farmers, skilled workmen, professional men.	Unskilled laborers, few merchants.
Location in which they settled	Rural communities and small towns.	Cities in slum areas.
Purpose in coming	To establish a permanent home; to escape religious persecution or harsh government control.	To gather wealth; to escape training in the army; to return later to Europe.
Kind of groups	Entire families.	Unmarried individuals; few families at first.
Number becoming citizens	Nearly all.	Small part.

Labor Problems. Because their ways of living were
so different, workers from southern and southeastern
Europe could live more cheaply than those from northern Europe. Nor did they require the same standards
of living as native Americans. Therefore they were
willing to work for much lower wages than the native
Americans, whom they began to replace in industry.
This created an employment problem of grave importance which resulted in a great deal of dissatisfaction.

This was especially true in cities on the Atlantic coast where so many of these immigrants settled.

Employment. Obtaining satisfactory employment has always proved a difficult problem to the newer immigrants. Trained on the farms of Europe they found industrial life in the big cities wonderful but terrifying. Hard labor was usually all they could secure and that only as occasional demands occurred. In the large cities help was offered them by free employment bureaus which brought them into contact with those who needed workers. Various welfare organizations such as the Young Men's and Young Women's Christian Associations, the Knights of Columbus, the Young Men's Hebrew Association, or the Salvation Army also gave them help in obtaining work and in preparing them to hold these positions. However, with all this help, many of the newcomers were frequently unemployed.

Housing. As the newer immigrants flocked to the larger cities they grouped themselves together in colonies of their own kind. The "Little Italy" or "Little Russia" in many of our cities almost duplicated the European standards of living. As a rule only foreign newspapers were read and the English language was hardly heard in places of worship or other spots where they gathered. For these reasons American ideals of government were of little importance in their daily lives. These immigrants did not intend to become a part of the new country but continued to think of themselves as Europeans transplanted for a time into America.

As they were ignorant and poorly paid, they lived wherever they could. The poorest dwellings were all that they could afford. Because they did not understand American conditions of living they accepted the tenements as necessary. The unsanitary conditions, to which we referred before (See page 185.), also caused

Immigrants from Eastern and Southern Europe

dissatisfaction. Their children had no place to play except in the streets, where they learned defiance of the law rather than respect for American ideals.

Congestion. This crowding together in these unsightly districts, called slums, had a serious influence on American city life. Although the immigrants themselves were obviously not to blame, yet their presence in such large numbers produced these slums in the cities. The very fact that the immigrants retained their European customs and languages and that they were unable to read and write English made it difficult for them to secure employment and kept them poor. Their poverty made crime desirable, so that gangs grew and crime prospered. Often, boys in gangs turned to petty stealing so as to appear heroes in the eyes of their leaders. Their success in stealing frequently led to more serious crimes.

We must not think that a large part of these immigrants turned to crime. Fortunately this was true of only a small part of the whole group. Many foreigners have added greatly to our cultural values in music, art, literature, and science. The Hungarian, Michael Pupin, as a youth of sixteen was almost penniless when he landed at Ellis Island over sixty years ago, and yet he became a professor at Columbia University and one of the great inventors of his day. The German, Walter Damrosch, came to America at the age of nine and has been a great leader in the musical life of our country. The little Russian girl, Mary Antin, learned her first lesson of America in the slums of Boston under conditions that would have seemed very bad to many of us. But America became the *Promised Land* which she wrote about years afterward.

Education of Immigrants. The education of immigrant children is not very different from that of native-born children. Some time is spent in learning the new language but after this has been accomplished they fit readily into the new environment. Soon it is difficult to distinguish them from the others.

But this is not the case with their parents. Their education in Europe, as a rule, has been very brief and they have no desire to face the terrors of school in a foreign land. But Americanization classes have been held out to them as an opportunity to better their living and working conditions. Here they gradually learn to read and write the English language. Here they can prepare for citizenship and in addition they can learn the American ideals of freedom and co-operation, respect for law and order, and also reliance on their own abilities.

Knowledge of the new language helps them to obtain work and shows them how to avoid dangers in the use of machinery while working. The new language enables them to deal with those who do not speak their native language. It also gives them a chance to improve their methods of living and even to learn new kinds of employment. Finally their knowledge of our language and customs improves their relations with their growing children and helps the children to look upon their parents as "Americans" rather than as "foreigners."

The public libraries of most villages and cities offer immigrants who are becoming Americanized a great amount of free information. Books, magazines, and newspapers may be read daily in the reading room of the libraries at no cost. Books may also be borrowed and taken home for a week or two. The library is one of the best adult education institutions in our country. In towns with evening schools, and also where no evening schools exist, the public library offers an op-

portunity for the uneducated to improve themselves
in many different ways.

Assimilation of Immigrants. It is necessary to make
the immigrants feel that they are a part of our community, rather than of their own foreign commmunity,
if they are to be content and happy with their lot.
America is constantly striving to do this. Nearly forty
million immigrants have been welcomed to the United
States since its beginning. The poverty, unhappiness,
and oppression which caused them to come here have
been decreased. Many of them have found peace and
happiness and have prospered. They should respect
America and its institutions, obey its laws, be peaceful, honest, and industrious, and become naturalized
Americans.

Advantages of Citizenship. A naturalized citizen
of the United States has many advantages over an
alien. He may help to select the officials of the local,
state, and national governments, by voting at all elections. He may be elected to any public office in the
United States except the office of President or Vice-
President. He may obtain passports to travel abroad
under the protection of the United States flag. He
may obtain public land from the government in un-
developed parts of the West, upon which to build a
permanent house for himself. He may apply for any
position he chooses, enter into business for himself,
and own his own property. He may serve on juries
in the courts. He is entitled to all the other guarantees
and privileges given by the Constitution of the United
States.

Immigration Laws. It is the duty of a nation to protect its citizens and to preserve itself and its form of government. America does not welcome those who would interfere with her liberty, happiness, and prosperity. Our immigration laws provide that such persons as anarchists, who plot to overthrow all forms of government, be excluded from this country and sent back to their own country.

Our immigration laws provide also for a similar exclusion and deportation, at any time, of those who are a danger to our country through disease, crime, or immorality. To admit to this country, without restriction, all who desire to come, would be harmful both to this country and to its citizens.

Securing Citizenship. The fourteenth amendment states that, "All persons born or naturalized in the United States, and subject to the jurisdiction thereof, are citizens of the United States and of the state wherein they reside." Also foreign-born children under twenty-one become naturalized when their parents become citizens.

The alien of white or African race may file his intention of naturalization as soon after his arrival as he wishes, if he is eighteen years of age or over. Two years after these first papers have been filed, and after five years of continuous residence in this country, he may take his second step and file his petition for citizenship. He must do this, however, not more than seven years after he has declared his intention to become a citizen. This petition must be signed by the applicant and he must be able to speak English.

Thirty days later he may appear before the court to take the oath of allegiance to support the Constitution of the United States.

American citizenship is too high an honor to be given away thoughtlessly, and for this reason careful restrictions are placed on those who desire our citizenship. However, America welcomes to her shores those who are sound and healthy in mind and body, those who have unquestioned character, and who are honest, thrifty, and industrious. America welcomes such who want to be naturalized and to make this country their home.

Test and Study Exercises

Aids to Learning.

1. Distinguish between the old and the new immigrants in matters of birthplace, education, occupation, and purpose in coming to America.
2. Remember that many immigrants have added greatly to our cultural values in music, art, literature, and science.
3. Observe the many helps that adult education has been to the immigrant in the necessary process of Americanization.

Test Exercises.

On a separate sheet of paper give the letter for the correct answer for each statement.

1. Prominent among the early settlers in New York were the (*a*) Swedes, (*b*) French Huguenots, (*c*) Dutch, (*d*) Welsh.
2. The largest number of immigrants came to this country in the decade (*a*) 1880-1890, (*b*) 1905-1915, (*c*) 1830-1840, (*d*) 1890-1900.
3. One of the most valuable Adult Education Agencies is the (*a*) Public Library, (*b*) Free Employment Office, (*c*) Salvation Army, (*d*) Public Parks.
4. An immigrant who became influential both in the business and cultural life of America was (*a*) Walter Damrosch, (*b*) Michael Pupin, (*c*) Mary Antin, (*d*) Edward Bok.

5. The most important privilege of citizenship is (*a*) use of public libraries, (*b*) owning of property, (*c*) right to vote, (*d*) jury service.

6. Before an immigrant may become a citizen he must live in the United States (*a*) five consecutive years, (*b*) five years, (*c*) two years, (*d*) seven years.

Suggested Activities.

1. With the help of your librarian, study the biographies of such immigrants as Mary Antin, Edward Bok, Michael Pupin, John Muir, Edward Steiner, Andrew Carnegie, or Jacob Riis and discover the characteristics which contributed to their success.

2. (*a*) Consult a world almanac or encyclopedia regarding the change in immigration flow into the United States. (b) Make a table showing the changes in United States immigration and emigration by decades from 1820 to 1940.

3. On an outline map of the United States indicate by different colors the nations which were most frequently represented in the original settlements. Some states may require more than one color.

4. How many different nationalities are suggested by the first thirty names in your telephone directory?

5. *Group Activity:* The teacher may ask each pupil to inquire from his parents the different nationalities represented in his own family for the past four generations. What nations are represented by the largest number of the ancestors of all pupils?

6. *Group Activity:* If you live near a city, the teacher may take the class on a trip to a social-settlement house to study their Americanization work.

PART IV

YOUR GOVERNMENT AND ITS CITIZENS

The word "citizenship" used in the title of this book is very important because it shows you that we are all citizens of our government. In discussing the foundations of citizenship, we have pointed out the part you have in the family, the school, the church, and the community. But in these discussions we have referred to the importance of government and law in every detail of our lives.

You have learned that our government is a democracy, that it is a government "of the people, by the people, and for the people," and that it will be your duty to vote and to do your part in the government as a citizen. But you have not learned much about the government itself. In part four you will learn about your government: *the structure of your government, how you finance your government,* and *how you uphold your government.*

You will find that, instead of one government, you really have several governments; that the powers are

divided among these various governments; and that written constitutions were adopted which provided for the governments and which assigned to each their powers.

In general we have three governments in which all of us are citizens and to which we owe allegiance. These are our *local governments,* our *state government,* and our *national government.* You notice that the word government is singular when used with the term national and state, but plural when used with the term local. That is because any one of us may be a citizen of several local governments at the same time. There is but one national government and while we have forty-eight state governments no one can be a citizen of more than one of these state governments at the same time. We shall describe these governments in the order in which they developed rather than in the order of their power. That means that we shall describe first our local governments, secondly our state government, and thirdly our national government. Also, we shall attempt to make clear the device or organization which enables us to have a part in each of the governments to which we belong. These organizations are known as political parties.

CHAPTER XVII

THE STRUCTURE OF YOUR GOVERNMENT

PREPARATORY NOTE: The following chapter brings you to the consideration of our government and its citizens. The nation consists of communities, the community of families, and the family of individuals. So the government of the nation depends on its communities, its families, and the individual citizens. Governments are necessary for civilized nations. The foundation of our government was very unusual and very interesting for us to follow. There were various attempts at government made before the Constitution was finally adopted. Our nation is what it is today as a result of this Constitution and the laws that have grown out of it.

Importance of Government. The word "government" means the exercise of authority, or control. Thus when we speak of home government we mean local authority or control of the affairs in the community; when we speak of state government we mean the control of public affairs in the state. It is evident that you should be able to control yourself before you attempt to control a community or a state.

You may not realize the ways in which government influences your life. It is so important in fact that you could not live peacefully without it. To play the

simplest games you need rules to govern them. Imagine a football or baseball game without rules. Just as it is necessary to have rules to conduct a game of any kind, so is it necessary to have certain rules or authority to maintain and operate a home, school, church, or a community of any size. An institution of any kind must have good government if it is to be operated successfully. Government protects and safeguards your life and property at home and abroad, thus enabling you to live more happily.

Government is one of the most important social institutions. It helps to maintain peace, security, and justice. From your birth to your death, you are affected by the government under which you live. You are continually receiving benefits and services from the government which you could not receive from private agencies such as the home, school, or church.

Under a democracy, such as we have in the United States, the government is the instrument or agency through which the will of the people is carried out. The people rule themselves through the representatives whom they elect. It is therefore necessary that laws passed by the representatives of the people be obeyed.

The Duties of Government. Every government, whatever its nature, performs certain duties of which the following are the most important.

Providing protection is perhaps the most essential work of government and was one of the principal reasons why government came into existence. People cannot live and do business without protection—local,

national, and international. Government is the only organization that can provide such protection.

It is also necessary that some organization be responsible for *enforcing the laws* and maintaining order. There are many causes of disagreement and conflict among groups of people. Through the courts the government is able to settle these quarrels and to see that justice is secured.

There are many other duties performed by governments such as *securing social betterment,* which could not be done as successfully by private agencies. For example, institutions for the care of the sick, the insane, the aged, the poor, and the criminal as a rule are maintained and administered by the government. Education also has become one of the principal tasks of government. The safeguarding of public health, the passing of laws to protect labor, the building of roads and dams,—all these highly important duties are performed by your government. The ever-expanding nature of governmental functions brings up the interesting question of just how far the government should go in caring for its citizens and just how much should be left to private agencies.

Foundation of Your Government. The people who settled here, in what is now the United States, but what was then a land uninhabited by civilized men, did so because they wanted freedom. They wanted to worship God according to their own conscience and in their own way. They wanted to have a voice in the government. They were willing to sacrifice. They had strong will power and the courage to carry out their

plans. It is due to a great extent to the honest motives, wise plans, and courage of our forefathers that the United States is a leading nation today.

Declaration of Independence. After much struggling, suffering, and sacrificing, our ancestors were

© *Underwood & Underwood*

Signing the Declaration of Independence

determined to fight, if necessary, for freedom and their rights. The first Continental Congress, which met September 5, 1774, was composed of great American leaders. The course of action recommended at this first congress was safe but determined. At the second Continental Congress, which met in May, 1775, plans for independence at any cost were decided upon. Ac-

cordingly, after debate and deliberation, the Declaration of Independence was formally adopted July 4, 1776. This date, which commemorates the birth of our nation, is accordingly celebrated with great enthusiasm every fourth day of July.

Articles of Confederation. The Declaration of Independence proclaimed the colonies a free nation. Many problems of a serious nature now confronted this newborn nation. A set of rules or laws was necessary to govern and guide the people. A national government was accordingly formed by adopting the Articles of Confederation. The same congress that drew up the Declaration of Independence appointed a committee to draw up these articles. It required five years, from 1776 to 1781, to secure the signatures of all the colonies and to adjust matters finally, since transportation and communication consumed so much time in those days. During these five years the only central government for the colonies was the weak government of the Continental Congress. The country was governed by these Articles of Confederation from 1781 to 1789.

Weakness of the Confederacy. When we remember that the early colonists came from different countries, that they had different customs, languages, methods of doing things, and different viewpoints of life, it is only natural that they had considerable difficulty in organizing the first national government.

Congress consisted of but one house which represented the states as such, rather than the people. The small states with but a few inhabitants had just as

many votes in congress as the large states. The government had no president, as it was a body without a head or executive officer. There were no national courts. Congress could make treaties, but could not compel the states to obey them. It could borrow money, but could not guarantee its payment. Each state levied its own taxes, and it often happened that congress had no money and could not pay its obligations. It could recommend taxation for the support of the central government, but could not enforce the collection of taxes. In general, congress lacked power to enforce the laws it passed.

The United States Constitution. The American leaders of that day recognized the weaknesses of the existing government and possessed a strong desire to strengthen it. As a result of the influence of such men as Hamilton, Madison, Franklin, and Washington, delegates from twelve states met in a constitutional convention at Philadelphia in 1787 to revise the Articles of Confederation. George Washington was chosen president of the convention. The meeting occurred in Independence Hall shown in the following photograph.

Nothing was said in the instructions to the convention delegates about framing a constitution. Their sole work was to remodel the old Articles of Confederation. When the convention assembled, however, it was soon realized by such leaders as Madison and Hamilton that what was needed was an entirely different and new framework of government which would correct the errors and remedy the evils of the Articles.

They realized that it was impossible to change the Articles sufficiently to satisfy these urgent needs.

Independence Hall, Philadelphia

Although many differences of opinion developed, yet they felt the need for an entirely new constitution.

Therefore the Articles were discarded and the convention set about to draft a constitution.

At first there were two plans presented. The one which gained their attention was known as the Virginia plan. The Virginia delegation was composed of men of high intellectual ability who were well informed on the fundamental principles of government. They had made a plan as drawn up by Madison and presented by Randolph. This proposed a complete change in the governmental structure of the new national government from that provided for in the Articles of Confederation. One of its most important features was that the individual citizen should be directly responsible to the central government. There were to be three measurably independent but co-operating branches of the government: a legislative or lawmaking department, an executive or law-enforcing department, and a judicial or law-interpreting department.

In this plan there was to be a congress composed of two houses. This body was to have power to legislate on all matters of national concern and to have authority over the states in these matters. Representation in both of these houses was to be based on population. All major offices of the executive and judicial departments of government were to be filled by appointments of the congress. It was clear that the congress would have the final control of the government and consequently the populous, larger states would be in control of the central government. There was a reaction among the smaller states because of their fear that

they would not have a fair share of authority. This resulted in a small state plan introduced by Paterson of New Jersey and consequently called the New Jersey plan. In this plan it was provided that there should be but one house in congress, and that all states should have equal representation.

For a time there was danger of deadlock and a failure of the convention to form any government whatever. However, after much discussion and many compromises, a plan was agreed upon which took care of the interests of both the large and the small states. The Connecticut delegation made the suggestion which brought this about. It was agreed that there be an upper house called the Senate, in which the representation of all the states should be equal, and a lower house, known as the House of Representatives, in which representation was to be based on population.

The problem of ratification, or approval, of the Constitution was an important one. It was provided that the Constitution should be considered for ratification in each of the states by a state convention elected by the voters for that purpose. The Constitution was to go into effect as soon as it was ratified by nine of the thirteen states. The issue of ratification brought about the first political parties in the United States. Those who favored the adoption of the Constitution were called Federalists and those opposed, Antifederalists.

Division of Powers. The United States Constitution provides for a federal form of government. Powers are divided between the national government

and the states. This principle of the division of powers is an underlying principle of our Constitution.

In the United States system, the national government is supreme over the states. This principle is stated in the Constitution in the following provision in Article VI: "This Constitution, and the laws of the United States which shall be made in pursuance thereof, and all treaties made, or which shall be made, under the authority of the United States, shall be the supreme law of the land; and the judges in every state shall be bound thereby, anything in the Constitution or laws of any state to the contrary notwithstanding." This means that if a state law conflicts with a treaty, the judges of that state must enforce the law affected by the treaty. Moreover, the federal courts have the power to decide, when a case is brought, whether or not a certain state law conflicts with the national law.

The Constitution provides that governmental powers shall be distributed in the following way:

Powers given exclusively to the national government are enumerated in the Constitution. They affect the country as a whole, since they include conduct of foreign affairs, regulation of foreign and interstate commerce, declaration of war, making of treaties, coinage of money, and regulation of weights and measures.

Powers given exclusively to the states are not enumerated. They include all those powers which are not given to the national government and are not prohibited by the Constitution to the states. (Tenth Amendment.)

Powers given to both the national and state governments are said to be concurrent powers because they both have the right to exercise authority in the same field. Such a power, for example, is that of taxation.

Powers forbidden to the national government include taxing exports, or levying direct taxes except those which are levied in proportion to population. Congress is also forbidden to make such laws as may interfere with freedom of speech or the press, or with the right of the people to keep and bear arms.

Powers forbidden to the state government include making treaties or alliances, coining money, laying import or export taxes, keeping troops or ships of war in time of peace (except with the consent of congress), or engaging in war except when invaded.

Powers forbidden to both national and state governments include passing an *ex post facto* law[1] or a bill of attainder[2] or granting a title of nobility. The fifteenth amendment forbids both the national and the state governments to deny or abridge the rights of citizens of the United States to vote, on account of race, color, or previous condition of servitude. The nineteenth amendment forbids discrimination in this respect on account of sex.

Significance of the Constitution. The Constitution of the United States is worthy of study because it is the framework of the government under which we

---

[1] **ex post facto law.** A law providing punishment for acts committed before the law existed.

[2] **bill of attainder.** A legislative act which inflicts punishment without a judicial trial.

live. All of us, because of our participation in government, may some day influence this government. We should study the Constitution because it is one of the best in the world and because it has exerted widespread influence upon the constitutions of the South American republics and the new democracies of Europe. Gladstone, a famous British statesman, once remarked, "The American constitution is the most wonderful work ever struck off at a given time by the brain and purpose of man." James Bryce, another British statesman, said of this document, "It ranks above every other written constitution for the intrinsic excellence of its scheme; its adaptation to the circumstances of the people; the simplicity, brevity, and precision of its language; its judicious mixture of definition in principle with elasticity in details."

Summary of the United States Constitution. A national constitution is a document containing the law or laws which explain the form of a nation's government and which point out the powers that may be exercised by that government. Considered as a whole, a constitution has four fundamental characteristics. First, it explains the source of authority; second, it provides for the organization of the government; third, it provides for making its own amendments; and fourth, it defines the field of individual liberty. We find these characteristics in the Constitution of the United States as summarized below.

First, the Preamble to our Constitution explains that the supreme authority lies with the people. It does this by saying, "We, the people of the United

States, . . . do ordain and establish this Constitution for the United States of America.''

Second, the organization of our government is provided for. Article One outlines in detail the legislative department of government, Article Two deals with the executive department, and Article Three provides for the judicial department. In the organization of our government the Constitution divides all governmental powers between the two governments. One is the central government, now located at Washington, D. C., and the other is the local or state government centered at the state capitol in each state. Article Four explains this division of powers between the two governments and guarantees every state a republican form of government.

Third, Article Five provides for making amendments to the Constitution.

Fourth, a part of our field of individual liberty is found in Article One on legislative power. A field of individual liberty is one in which the government has no power to control the action of an individual or to punish him for any act specified. In Article One it is stated that the privilege of the writ of *habeas corpus*[3] cannot be suspended, and that the use of a bill of attainder, or the use of *ex post facto* laws are forbidden. However, the field of individual liberty is especially guaranteed in the the first ten amendments. Here the government of the United States is forbidden

---

[3] **writ of habeas corpus.** A court order requiring that a person be brought immediately before a civil court to learn the reason for his imprisonment or detention.

to interfere with the freedom of speech, or of the press, or of religious worship, to search homes without a warrant, or to quarter soldiers in homes of the people in times of peace without their consent. These amendments also provide for trial by jury and prohibit the national government from doing many other things which might be unjust. The thirteenth amendment prohibits the existence of slavery within the United States. Other amendments concern the organization and management of the government.

Amendments to the Constitution. The methods by which the Constitution of the United State is amended are more difficult than those of any other nation. An amendment may be proposed by a two-thirds vote of the two houses of Congress. An amendment may also be proposed at a national convention, called by Congress, at the request of the legislatures of two-thirds of the states. In either case the amendment must be ratified by the legislatures of three-fourths of the states, or by special conventions in three-fourths of the states.

The Unwritten Constitution. The Constitution alone gives us an incomplete knowledge of the operation of our government. To understand our governmental system completely, we must study those political customs and practices which are known as the "unwritten constitution."

For example, political parties were not provided for in the Constitution, but they are, nevertheless, among the most significant influences in the operation of the United States government. The part played by polit-

ical parties in the nomination of the president is one
instance of the importance which they have assumed.
Another body authorized by custom rather than by
the Constitution is the president's cabinet. We find
no mention of such a body in the Constitution, but it
has become an extremely important institution of our
government.

The Development of Political Parties. There were
no political parties as we know them, until our Constitution was ratified. The Federalists and the Antifederalists were just coming into being then. People
disagreed with one another on important governmental questions, but there was no organization of
those who favored some particular policy. For example, Jefferson was very much against a strong
national government and Hamilton was very much in
favor of a strong national government. Both men
urged their views but neither was backed by any definite organization. Washington appointed both men to
important offices in his cabinet.

Washington did not believe in political parties. He
thought of any organization of that kind as a troublesome faction. However, he was not able to get Jefferson and Hamilton to work together. Both men re-
signed several times but Washington would not accept
the resignation of either. Finally Jefferson began organizing his supporters. Washington decided that he
could not follow the principle of having those holding
opposite views on public questions represented in his
administration. As he agreed with Hamilton rather
than Jefferson, he accepted Jefferson's resignation.

Jefferson, freed from his obligations as a member of the government, organized our first active political party. It was called the Democratic-Republican party, and later the Democratic party. Those in power

Washington and His Cabinet
Washington, Hamilton, Knox, Jefferson, and Randolph

in the government were called Federalists. However, the Federalists had very little party organization.

The Uses of Political Parties. A political party may be defined as a voluntary organization whose members believe in certain principles and policies of government and who nominate and try to elect men to public office who will carry out these principles and policies. In our government, since Jefferson's organization, we have always had two major parties. One or the other has always controlled the government. Sometimes a

major party dies out and is succeeded by a new party
as was the case between 1850 and 1860 when the Republican party replaced the Whigs as one of the major
parties. The important work of a party is the nomination and election of its candidates for public office and
the selection of its own party leaders.

In a democracy, political parties seem necessary.
There is no other way that people can influence government except through organizations which elect the
officials who carry out the policies of government. In
an absolute monarchy or a dictatorship, parties are not
necessary because the people have no voice in the government. In fact, a political party in opposition to
such a government is considered treasonable and its
members are punished or driven out of the country.
Sometimes men by dishonest and unfair methods get
control of a political party of a city or a state, and use
that control for private gain for themselves and their
friends and supporters. These men are called *bosses*.
They are interested in governmental contracts, the control of purchasing agents, and many kinds of petty
graft. In reality they are enemies of good government
and a great handicap to the party to which they attach
themselves, just as leeches and parasites attach themselves to living bodies. Too many of such bosses will
cause any party to die.

The Organization of Political Parties. Our political
parties are highly organized working bodies. The national party organizations are based upon the party
organizations in the states. In most states these organizations are now controlled by law and, therefore,

are much alike. The important unit in the organization is the county committee or city committee. These committees are composed of representatives from the townships or wards. The chairman of the county or city committee is the official leader of the party. Each party has a state committee usually composed of representatives from the congressional districts of the state. The chairman of the state committee is the leader of the party in the state. In each state there is also a national committeeman and a national committeewoman. These representatives of the party, when called together by the national chairman, form the national committee of the party.

Such in brief is the organization of our two major political parties. The political party is the agency through which every citizen may express himself on the questions of government. Membership in a political party is the only practical way a citizen can have a voice in his government. That does not mean that he must vote for every man his party nominates for office. Sometimes a unit like a county or city is controlled by a politician who names men for nominees on the party ticket. In such cases it becomes the duty of the good citizen to disregard the party ticket and vote for those who will make honest, efficient officers. New issues may arise. The party he has been connected with may take what he thinks is the wrong side on a new issue. If the issue is of great importance it may become his duty to change parties in order that he may exert an influence for what he thinks is the right solution of the new question.

"A"

OFFICIAL BALLOT

If you desire to vote an entire party ticket for state, congressional, legislative and county offices make a cross (X) or other mark in the circle (O) under the party designation at the head of the ballot. If you desire to vote for particular persons without regard to party, mark in the square at the right of the name of the candidate for whom you desire to vote if it be there, or write any name that you wish to vote for, in the proper place.

DEMOCRAT ○	PROHIBITION ○	REPUBLICAN ○	SOCIALIST ○	INDEPENDENT
For Governor— JOHN DOE ☐	For Governor— JOHN DOE ☐	For Governor— JOHN DOE ☐	For Governor— JOHN DOE ☐	For Governor—
Lieutenant Governor— JOHN DOE ☐	Lieutenant Governor— JOHN DOE ☐	Lieutenant Governor— JOHN DOE ☐	Lieutenant Governor— JOHN DOE ☐	Lieutenant Governor—
Secretary of State— JOHN DOE ☐	Secretary of State— JOHN DOE ☐	Secretary of State— JOHN DOE ☐	Secretary of State— JOHN DOE ☐	Secretary of State—
State Treasurer— JOHN DOE ☐	State Treasurer— JOHN DOE ☐	State Treasurer— JOHN DOE ☐	State Treasurer— JOHN DOE ☐	State Treasurer—
Attorney-General— JOHN DOE ☐	Attorney-General— JOHN DOE ☐	Attorney-General— JOHN DOE ☐	Attorney-General— JOHN DOE ☐	Attorney-General—
United States Senator— JOHN DOE ☐	United States Senator— JOHN DOE ☐	United States Senator— JOHN DOE ☐	United States Senator— JOHN DOE ☐	United States Senator—

A Sample Ballot

The Australian Ballot. One of the most important reforms required by party organizations was the ballot. At first, voting was done by voice but later it was necessary to indicate on paper the choice between candidates. The *Australian Ballot* is a form which has come into use in most states. The names of all candidates for each party are printed in one column. This arrangement makes it easy to vote a straight party ticket by placing a mark at the top of a column under the heading of the voter's party.

Along with the Australian Ballot came secret voting. Laws require polling places to be equipped with booths. The voter is given his ballot and goes into a booth alone, where he prepares it for the ballot box. Provisions are made for allowing election officials to mark the ballot of any voter who cannot mark his own.

Test and Study Exercises

Aids to Learning.

1. Remember that the fundamental duties of government are protection, law and order, and social betterment.

2. Note how all government has grown out of attempts to solve common problems.

3. Observe that the division of powers between the national government and the states is an underlying principle of our constitution.

4. Be sure you understand why political parties play an important part in our government.

Test Exercises.

On a separate sheet of paper write the following sentences including the missing words.

1. "Government" means the exercise of ____ or ____.

2. A government which is the instrument through which the will of the people is carried out is called a ____.

3. The early settlers of our country wanted ____, ____, and ____ freedom in their new home.

4. The United States was governed from 1781 to 1789 under the ____ of ____.

5 The United States Constitution divides power between the ____ government and the ____.

6. The Preamble to the Constitution indicates that the supreme authority lies with the ____.

7. Among the political practices of the "unwritten constitution" are the formation of ____ ____ and the ____ ____.

8. In the ____ ____ the names of all candidates for each party are printed in one column.

Suggested Activities.

1. With the help of your librarian, locate magazine articles describing the last presidential election. Write in parallel columns the most important planks or principles in the party platforms of the Republicans and Democrats and decide which of these have been carried out thus far.

2. In the same way locate the political addresses made by the successful candidate for the presidency at the last presidential election. How far have these statements been adhered to by the President?

3. Make a list of the leading statesmen who favored the new Constitution in 1787 and those who opposed it.

4. Memorize the Preamble of the Constitution. What are the features in it which make it so valuable an introduction?

5. Write a series of arguments for continuing the two-party system of elections for our national government.

6. *Group Activity:* With the help of your teacher, nominate and elect a class president, vice-president, and secretary. See that all voters have first registered. Use the Australian Ballot.

7. *Group Activity:* The teacher may appoint sides for a debate on the subject, Resolved: That the radio is more influential than the newspaper in the national elections.

CHAPTER XVIII

HOW YOU FINANCE YOUR GOVERNMENT

PREPARATORY NOTE: The financing of a family or a community or a nation is a more serious problem today than ever before. It is difficult enough for our government to secure the money necessary to run it, but it seems even more difficult to decide how to spend this money. The amounts dealt with by our government are in the millions or billions of dollars. The World War has added to the expenses directly and indirectly with the result that a heavily mounting debt is facing us. How to handle this is one of our most pressing problems treated in this chapter.

Incoming Money. The finances of the government, whether local, state, or national, will be discussed here under three divisions: Incoming Money, Outgoing Money, and the Management of Public Funds.

Governments have many sources of income. The most important sources are: taxes, fees, licenses, fines, and loans. There are many other minor sources of income, but of all sources of income for government maintenance, taxes are the most important.

Taxes. A tax is a required payment to the government by a person or group of persons for the purpose of contributing to the maintenance and operation of the government for the benefit of all.

From the beginning of our government to the War between the States, our national income came mostly from tariff duties, or *customs,* on imported goods. From the War between the States to the First World War, the chief sources of our national income shifted, although customs still supplied a heavy source during the first twenty years of that period. Taxes or *excises* were placed on products like liquor and tobacco produced in this country. The income thus collected is known as *internal revenue.* Since the Sixteenth Amendment was adopted (1913), the *income tax,* a tax on individual earnings, has supplied an increasing part of our national income.

Income tax is a payment of a certain percentage of a person's net receipts during a specified period of time, usually a year. It is considered one of the fairest taxes because it falls upon those best able to pay. In recent years it has been adopted by most of the state governments as well as by the United States government.

The total regular income of our national government in 1945 was approximately forty-eight billion dollars. About seventy-five per cent of this amount came from taxes on incomes of individuals and corporations. These taxes greatly increased during the war years. The amount of income derived from these tax sources in 1945 was about seventeen times as much as in 1940. The balance of national income came from excise taxes, customs, miscellaneous internal revenue, charges for public service, various fees and fines, and income from the sale of government property. The

Social Security tax contributes a considerable amount to national income. Some of these sources of income are also used by the state or local governments. The graph below indicates the largest sources of contribution to the national income.

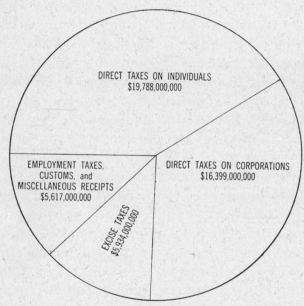

DIRECT TAXES ON INDIVIDUALS
$19,788,000,000

DIRECT TAXES ON CORPORATIONS
$16,399,000,000

EMPLOYMENT TAXES,
CUSTOMS, and
MISCELLANEOUS RECEIPTS
$5,617,000,000

EXCISE TAXES
$5,934,000,000

Federal Income for 1945

General *property taxes* constitute more than half of all state and local revenue in the majority of the states. Some states are now substituting sales tax and income tax for the general property tax. There are taxes on real estate and on personal property. Real estate is land, a house, or any permanent improvements on the land. It is not movable property as a rule. Personal property consists of such items as furniture, cattle,

automobiles, stocks, and bonds. It is movable property. The rate of general property tax varies from a few cents on each hundred dollars' worth of property in some rural communities to several dollars on the same amount of property in some cities. Special property taxes include inheritance taxes, which are paid when a person receives money from some relative or friend who has died, and also taxes on stocks, bonds, and mortgages.

Corporation taxes are large amounts of money collected by the government from taxes on industrial earnings. The federal income includes taxes on the earnings of telephone, telegraph, and express companies; mining, oil, and railway companies; insurance companies; and manufacturing companies. The state income includes taxes upon corporations for their privilege of engaging in business within the state and also taxes on the earnings of public service enterprises such as docks and wharves, ferries, toll bridges, canals, irrigation systems, and land settlements. The city income from this source includes taxes on water, gas, electric systems, markets, cemeteries, and many others.

Sales tax is a tax levied on various kinds of sales. Nearly half of the states have enacted a general sales tax of two or three per cent of the total sales of every retail merchant. A tax on each gallon of gasoline sold for automobiles also is assessed by all of the states.

Fees and Licenses. A fee is a payment by a person to the government either in return for some service rendered by the government or in connection with a government service rendered for the common good of

all. For example, the recording of a deed, or owner-
ship of property, requires the payment of a fee to the
county government.

A license is a privilege granted by the government
which permits one to engage in a certain business or to
perform a certain act. For granting such a privilege
the government receives a sum of money. For example, the merchant obtains a license from the city
to operate his store. Hunting, fishing, and automobile
licenses are obtained by paying an amount of money
to the state government, and marriage licenses are
obtained from the county government. Rents are paid
for public school lands and public works which are
owned by the city or state and which are rented and
operated by a private person.

Fines and Loans. Fines have always been collected
by the government as penalties for various offenses.
In times of peace and normal prosperity, the government's funds from ordinary taxes are sufficient. In
times of war, however, or during any other special
and unexpected emergency, it may be necessary for
the government to borrow money. The World Wars
were an example. When the government borrows
money, it gives bonds to which are attached coupons
that call for the payment of interest at stated times,
usually twice a year. Because of the strength of our
country, government bonds are among the safest kinds
of bonds to buy.

Local governments may, and often do, borrow
money by selling bonds for public improvements.
When a water system is to be installed in a city, or

when state highways are to be constructed, or a county sanitarium to be built, money is usually borrowed.

Such borrowing by the government—whether local, state, or national—is justifiable only when the money borrowed is put to a use that will provide permanent good. It must be remembered that money borrowed by the government can be paid back only from the government's income in later years. Therefore, money borrowed for use today will be paid by the taxpayers of tomorrow, and it is only fair that they should receive benefit from their tax money.

Need for Taxation. An enormous amount of money is needed to maintain and operate a government as vast as ours. Thousands of officials must be paid for their services. Problems of road building and maintenance, provisions for education, protection from criminals, and many other problems must be solved by our government. The money required for such expenditures must be raised for the most part by taxation. It is right for citizens to demand that public funds be raised economically and spent wisely. Paying taxes is a patriotic duty which is more willingly performed when each person knows that he is paying his just share toward the support of his government.

Outgoing Money. The total normal cost of government in the United States for one year has exceeded fifteen billion dollars. Over half of this amount has been spent for federal government, about one-third for local government, city, township, and county, and one-sixth for state government. Some of the main items of government expenditures will now be given.

War Expenditures. The budgets for national expenditures for the past several years have shown obvious changes. National defense consumed a billion and a half dollars of the total budget of approximately nine billion dollars in 1940. This expenditure increased

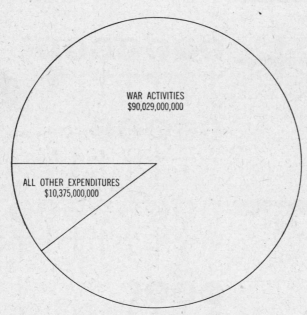

Federal Expenses for 1945

to six billion dollars in 1941, and to twenty-six billion in 1942. The above graph shows that in 1945 war expenses consumed practically nine tenths of the total budget. The total costs for this war are not yet known. The War between the States cost over three billion dollars. Although this sum shocked the nation at that time, it is a relatively small amount compared

with our share of the cost of the First World War, said to range from twenty to forty billion dollars, de-

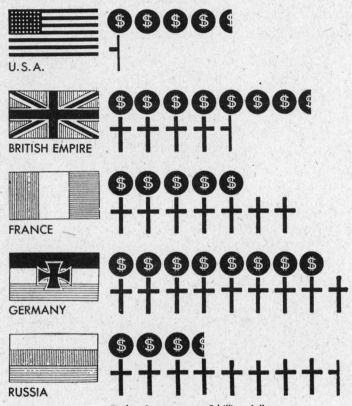

U.S.A.

BRITISH EMPIRE

FRANCE

GERMANY

RUSSIA

Each coin represents 5 billion dollars
Each cross represents 200,000 lives lost

Pictorial Statistics, Inc., for Harper and Brothers

Relative Costs of the First World War to Some
of the Leading Nations

pending on how many indirect costs are included. The pictograph shows how our share of this cost compares

with that of other nations which played an important part in the First World War.

Education. Most of the money expended for public education comes from the local and state governments. The federal government, however, has been appropriating more money in recent years to help reduce illiteracy and to provide to some extent for vocational education. The American people spend more money for education than do any other people on earth. That is one of the reasons for the rapid development and growth of the United States. The great cost of education is a necessity in a democracy, since an uneducated people cannot rule themselves wisely. The people of the United States realize that money spent for education is money wisely invested. Over two billion dollars is spent for public school education each year.

Highways and Waterways. Money expended for highways in this country comes from local, state, and national governments. Several national highways extend from coast to coast. Many state highways have been constructed by the different states. Counties and cities are paving roads and meeting the expense involved with money from their own treasuries. There has also been a continuous development of waterways. The most important inland waterways today are the Great Lakes—St. Lawrence system, and the Mississippi River system. These are connected through the Illinois Waterway system at Chicago by various rivers and canals from Lake Michigan to the Mississippi River. Over one billion dollars is being spent every year on highways and waterways.

Protection of Life and Property. Expenditures for the protection of life and property include the wages and equipment for firemen and policemen. The money expended on this item comes from local, state, and national taxation. However payment of the wages of policemen does not cover all the expenditures caused by lawlessness. Loss of life and property resulting from lawlessness must be borne by the individual. The cost of a trial alone includes such items as feeding the criminal before, during, and after the trial; judges' salaries; jurymen's wages and housing; and many other items. The total cost of crime for one year is estimated at fifteen billion dollars. This is such an immense sum that we cannot understand it except by comparisons. It is about the same amount that is spent by all our forms of government in the United States each year. It is equivalent to one hundred fifteen dollars spent by every man, woman, and child in the whole country—for the purpose of preventing, punishing and paying for crime. A great deal more money is spent on account of lawlessness than for health and sanitation, and far more than for hospitals, asylums, sanitariums, and similar institutions.

Health and Sanitation. Every department of the government is spending money to improve health conditions. This money is well spent. The theory and efforts in the field of medicine today are to prevent disease as well as to cure it. Much progress has been made in this direction. Through legislation concerning the labor of children and women, inspection of factories, safety devices in mines and mills, quarantining

of disease, and inspection of food, health conditions have been greatly improved.

Recreation facilities financed by public money provide an important element in improving health conditions throughout the country. The American people are realizing the value of play. Park systems and public playgrounds are maintained almost everywhere.

Hospitals and sanitariums are necessary and must be provided for. They include all general hospitals and also special hospitals, such as those for the care of tuberculosis or contagious diseases, those for the mentally sick or for children, and those for cripples or for those having special diseases. The state carries the greatest burden for the support of hospitals, but the local and national governments are also concerned to a lesser extent. After the World War, our nation discovered that it must support hospitals to care for the disabled soldiers of that war. This is certainly a worthy cause, as these veterans deserve the best care the government can give.

Salaries of Government Officials. Every unit of government must pay its officials and employees. This is a considerable item of expense. The great army of government employees ranges in position from the street sweeper and garbage collector working for the small village to the Chief Justice of the United States Supreme Court and the President of the United States. The salaries of federal employees range up to seventy-five thousand dollars for the President.

Public Debt. Practically every unit of government has had a public debt at one time or another. A large

part of the national public debt is usually caused by war. In 1938 the national public debt exceeded thirty-eight billion dollars, much of it, in one way or another, as a result of the First World War. A large part of this,

FEDERAL DEBT OF U.S.

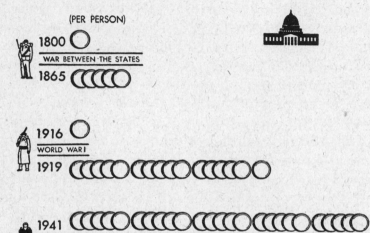

(PER PERSON)

1800

WAR BETWEEN·THE STATES

1865

1916

WORLD WAR I

1919

1941

WORLD WAR II

1944

Pictorial Statistics, I..c., for Modern Age Books, Inc.

Each disc represents 15 dollars

termed "war debts" resulted from lending money to other countries during and after the war. In 1943, the national public debt rose to the unprecedented total of $136,696,000,000 to pay the huge war costs. It seems likely that this will surpass $200,000,000,000. This im-

mense public debt is also beyond our ability to appreciate unless we break it down into our own shares. In the pictograph we see that the share of each person in our national debt increased from fifteen dollars in 1916 to over one thousand dollars in 1943.

State governments have public debts caused by borrowing money for state public improvements, such as highways and waterways. The total debt of all the states is between two and three billion dollars.

Cities and counties install public improvements and borrow money to pay for them. In all cases when money is borrowed by any unit of government, bonds are sold. Interest must be paid by the government just as an individual pays interest when he borrows money. This paying of interest is usually extended over a long period of years. These local debts are much larger in total than are all the state debts. The total of state and local debts is about twenty billion dollars.

Management of Public Funds. The misuse of public money reached its high mark some years ago in city governments. Reform of city business became a necessity and students of public finance proposed a plan known as the budget system.

A budget, as we saw on page 41, is an estimate of probable expenses arranged item by item for a year, with a similar estimate of probable incoming revenue to meet these expenses. Sometimes a loan must be made, if the revenue to be collected does not equal the probable expenses. Sometimes the tax rate or the assessed valuation of property has to be increased in order to increase the receipts. The important part of

the procedure is to be certain that all groups which spend the public money have turned in a careful estimate of expenses and income which they will agree not to exceed.

The rapidly increasing expenditure in national, state, and city government has caused a strong demand for the introduction of the budget system. As the greatest abuses in spending public money developed in city government, so the first progress in reform in public expenditures came in cities. Better methods of accounting and provisions for budgets are contained in charters adopted in recent years, and most cities which have the commission or the council-manager types of government[1] have a budget system. More than half of the states have adopted plans for more efficient estimating and recording of expenses. Much progress has recently been made by the national government in the direction of budget legislation.

Test and Study Exercises

Aids to Learning.

1. Observe that the rapid increase in public expenditures has resulted from the fact that the government is constantly undertaking new work.

2. Note the increasing importance attached to the income tax as a source of government revenue.

3. You see that a budget is necessary as a control for wise expenditures.

Test Exercises.

Match items in the first list with corresponding items in the second list by putting together on a sheet of paper the numbers of the two items

[1] **commission or council-manager types of government.** Forms of city government in which a few elective officers exercise all legislative and executive powers. The manager corresponds to the general manager of a business firm.

which best go together according to your own judgment.

1. The income tax	1. are found in nearly half of the states.
2. A budget	2. are usually exempt from the payment of property taxes.
3. Local governmental debts	3. is approximately five billion dollars a year.
4. Sales taxes	4. spends more than the state and local governments together.
5. Schools and churches	5. is approximately thirty-eight billion dollars.
6. Our present federal debt	6. corresponds to the general manager of a business firm.
7. The council-manager	7. is an important source of governmental income.
8. The total federal income	8. is an itemized estimate of probable income and expense.
9. The federal government	9. are much larger in total than state debts.

Suggested Activities.

1. (*a*) Inquire about the taxing system in your community. (*b*) Find out how much money is turned over for public education and what portion of the total local tax is spent for education.

2. Compile a list of the kinds of taxes which your own family has paid during the past year. Were they paid to the local, state, or federal government?

3. How much do you estimate your family would have to spend each year to provide fire and police protection, school facilities, street or road maintenance, and water supply if these were not covered by local taxes. Would you save or lose by this change?

4. With the help of your librarian, find some recent magazine article which will compare the amount of taxes our citizens pay and those paid in England or France. Are ours more or less than those paid in Europe?

5. *Group Activity:* With the help of your teacher, arrange a discussion on the relative merits of the property and sales taxes.

6. *Group Activity:* The teacher may appoint several pupils to inquire the tax rate used in your community for real-estate taxes. Is the assessed value the same as that for which you would be willing to sell your property?

CHAPTER XIX

HOW YOU UPHOLD YOUR GOVERNMENT

PREPARATORY NOTE: In the hurry of modern life we are more concerned with our privileges and our rights than with our duties. We have many guaranties of rights given to us by our forefathers but we must not overlook the duties placed upon us because of these rights. The good citizen distinguishes carefully between those privileges which came to him as a definite right, and those duties which he owes to his community and to his nation. You will see their differences in this chapter.

American Ideals. American ideals are dramatically expressed by the pledge to the flag.

"I pledge allegiance to the Flag of the United States of America and to the Republic for which it stands; one nation, indivisible, with liberty and justice for all."

The flag is used here as a symbol for the government itself. This flag becomes the ideal for the citizen and in pledging allegiance to it, he pledges himself to do his duty to all his fellow countrymen and not merely to those who are his friends; he promises to do his part to keep his country up to the highest standards of achievement and not to let its officers stoop to do any wrong; he vows that he will be unselfish in his citizenship and not seek merely that which will benefit him alone.

CONTENTS

THE POLITICAL HISTORY OF ILLINOIS

As You Read This Chapter

Be sure you understand how the present system of government in Illinois developed.

Illinois in Colonial Times. *Under the French.* The first white settlers in Illinois came from France and Canada. The settlements grew very slowly, but by the time of the French and Indian War there were six settlements and a number of fur-trading posts in the Illinois country.

Under the English. In 1763 France ceded all her rights in the Illinois region to Great Britain. The French settlers were given time to decide whether they wished to become English citizens or to remove from the territory.

If they stayed, the French people were required to take an oath of allegiance to the English king. Colonel Wilkins acted for the king in establishing the English system of common law by setting up a court of seven justices and introducing jury trial at Fort Chartres. This was the first attempt in Illinois at "living and working together" under our present legal system.

The new government was not very successful. There were few English inhabitants. The king discouraged the immigration of English settlers from the eastern colonies by adding the Illinois country to the Indian lands west of the Appalachian Mountains and refusing to grant any more land titles. Many of the French settlers refused to take the oath of loyalty to England and moved across the river to the French settlement at St. Louis. Fort Chartres was almost destroyed

5

by Mississippi floods in 1772. The French inhabitants who
remained in the territory complained bitterly about the use
of English law and trial by jury. It was partly in response
to their complaints that England finally added the region to
the Province of Quebec and gave back to the people the
French laws and customs. Thus ended the first attempt to
establish the English law and civil system in Illinois.

Early History of Illinois Under the United States Government. *Illinois During the Revolution.* During the Revolutionary War General George Rogers Clark drove the British
forces out of the northwest region. The French settlers aided
him in his campaigns, as France had joined the colonies in
their war against England. This was important because it
made it easier for the old French inhabitants and new American settlers to work together in building the state of Illinois.

Illinois as a County of Virginia. As soon as the news of
General Clark's success reached Virginia, Governor Patrick
Henry declared that Illinois was a county of Virginia. Colonel
John Todd, who had fought with Clark, was appointed as
Governor Henry's representative in the new country. He
arrived in Kaskaskia in May, 1779. English laws and customs were again introduced. Authority was vested in an appointed executive who cultivated the good will of the French
people.

Illinois as Part of the Northwest Territory. After a few
years Virginia ceded her claims to the County of Illinois to
the government of the United States. The Congress of the
Confederation incorporated it as part of the Northwest Territory.

In the Ordinance of 1787, under which the territory was
organized, there were several provisions which had a direct
effect upon our way of working together in Illinois today.

The Ordinance had a provision against slavery. This did much to prevent Illinois from becoming a slave state during the stormy Missouri Compromise days. It contained a provision which made all children of a family equal before the law instead of giving the family estate to the first-born son. It made provisions for public support of education and for popular control of government as soon as there were a sufficient number of people. It gave the boundaries of the Illinois country as the Wabash, Ohio, and Mississippi rivers.

Illinois as a Territory. *Separation from Ohio and Indiana.* From the beginning the United States government recognized two kinds of territories. A territory of the first class had a small population and was ruled by a governor and by judges appointed by the President. As soon as a sufficient number of people were present, a territory would be raised to the second class, which gave it an elected legislature. Thus the people could make their own laws. Illinois changed from one to the other class several times before the people finally achieved the dignity of statehood.

In 1790 Governor St. Clair was appointed by President Washington to rule the Northwest Territory. He came to Illinois and created St. Clair County and Knox County in the Wabash Valley.

In 1795 the southern third of St. Clair County was cut off and organized as Randolph County. Thus started the division of counties into smaller and more serviceable units. This continued until the present number (102) was reached in 1859.

In 1799 each of the three counties in the Illinois region sent elected representatives to the territorial legislature at Cincinnati. In 1800 Ohio was cut off to become a state. This made the Indiana-Illinois district again a territory of the first class. Its governor was General William Henry Harrison. He

did some good work, but he was very unpopular among the settlers of St. Clair and Randolph counties, who felt that he favored the Indiana district.

By 1805 the territory had enough people to be given again a representative government. The legislature met at Vincennes. The representatives from St. Clair and Randolph counties complained of the great distances they were compelled to travel and proposed the separation of Illinois from the Indiana territory. A bitter quarrel ensued, which led to the creation of Illinois and Indiana as separate territories. In 1809 Illinois Territory was created with its capital at Kaskaskia. Again Illinois was a territory of the first class.

For three years Governor Edwards with a group of judges and sheriffs labored to speed the growth of Illinois. In spite of the Indian outrages under Tecumseh and the War of 1812 the population grew steadily. New counties were organized, and in 1812 the territory was raised to the second class. A representative government was again established in Illinois.

The Laws of Illinois Territory. The territorial legislature adopted a set of laws taken from the older states, especially Indiana and Kentucky. Many of these laws were very harsh according to our present way of thinking. Penalties and fines were heavy. The pillory was in common use. The creditor was favored over the debtor, who could be imprisoned for inability to pay. For certain offences persons could be publicly whipped. Not until the great movement for popular rights under the leadership of Andrew Jackson were these old customs swept away.

The Problem of Land Sales. When the government began selling public land in 1789, it was sold in large tracts to wealthy men or companies, who in turn sold it at retail to actual settlers. The poverty of the settlers kept many from

buying the land they settled on. The tracts were too large and the price was too high.

Largely through the efforts of William Henry Harrison, territorial delegate in Congress, the size of the tract was reduced to 640 acres. The price was reduced to $2.00 per acre with a cash payment of one-fourth the amount. In a later act the size of the tract and the price were still further reduced. In 1804 land offices were opened at Vincennes and Kaskaskia, enabling the people to deal directly with the government. As a result of these provisions many settlers were attracted to Illinois.

Much trouble had been caused in these frontier communities by the sale of government land upon which settlers had built cabins and made clearings. The land was often bought by speculators who forced the settlers to leave without paying them for the improvements made on the land. Thus the settlers lost the fruits of their toil. In 1812 the Illinois delegate in Congress, Shadrack Bond, secured the passage of the *preemption law*. This protected a squatter upon public land against the loss of the improvements he had made, through the sale of the land to some other purchaser. The pre-emption law also gave the squatter first claim to the land he lived on. This was a just and much-needed rule in the new country.

Illinois as a State. *How Illinois Became a State in 1818.* In 1818 the Illinois representative, Nathaniel Pope, presented to Congress a petition asking for an enabling act. This is the official permission to the people of a territory to take steps to become a state. Pope persuaded Congress to fix the number of people needed at only 40,000 and to move the boundary of the new state about fifty miles to the northward. Through this change Chicago and the counties to the north and west of the city were included in the state.

As the census was taken, it became obvious that Illinois did not have quite 40,000 people. Immigrants and travelers were counted until the enumerators turned in 40,000 names. Delegates from the fifteen counties were elected to draw up a constitution. The constitution was accepted by Congress, and Illinois became a state December 3, 1818.

The first constitution was not submitted to the people for ratification. It went into force on its acceptance by Congress. It gave the right to vote to all white male inhabitants after six months' residence. The legislature was given almost unlimited power. It appointed all judges and justices. The governor had no veto power. The provision of the Ordinance of 1787 against slavery was weakened enough to allow slavery to remain in Illinois. The process of amending the document was made very difficult.

Anyone studying this document and the acts of the first legislature must marvel at the gains made by the people in the art of self-government since that time.

Early Problems of the State. The first great political battle in the newly created state was over *slavery*. It should be remembered that many slaves had been introduced into Illinois in the days of the old French settlers, and that the early English-speaking settlers came from states where slavery existed. The Treaty of 1763 with the French had guaranteed the slave owners full protection in their property rights, thus keeping slavery. The slave state of Virginia had made a similar provision in ceding her claims to the Congress of the Confederation. Nevertheless, the Ordinance of 1787 forbade slavery in the territory. In 1790 Governor St. Clair had avoided a decision of the question by allowing slavery to remain but forbidding further introduction of slaves. The

constitution of 1818 had a carefully worded provision which left the matter open for debate and state action.

The quarrel over the Missouri Compromise in 1819-1820 brought the slavery question to a decision in Illinois. The proslavery party made slavery the chief issue in the election of 1822. The antislavery candidate for governor was Edward Coles, who had been a slaveholder in Virginia. He had freed his slaves and brought them to Illinois in 1819 and helped them to establish themselves as free men. Coles was elected governor, but the slavery party secured a majority in the Assembly. A resolution was passed by a majority of one vote calling for a convention which should draw up a slavery constitution for the state.

The campaign which followed was long and bitter. Interest in the slavery question overshadowed everything else. The old French counties near the Mississippi and the southern counties generally were proslavery. The northern counties, which were filled by more recent settlers from the free states, were equally strong against slavery. In the final vote the Coles party won by a vote of 6,640 against 4,972. Thus Illinois was prevented from becoming one of the slave states in America. One hesitates to think what might have happened had this first great political battle been decided differently.

Its decision against slavery allowed Illinois to become the center for the movement against slavery in the period shortly before the Civil War. A new party set against the further spread of slavery in the nation was born at Bloomington, Illinois. Abraham Lincoln was the candidate of this party for United States Senator in 1858. His opponent was Stephen A. Douglas. Although Lincoln was defeated, this campaign placed him before the country as the great antislavery candidate for the presidency in 1860.

The *money* question was another problem faced by the new state. During the first few years of statehood times were very hard in Illinois. There was little commerce down the Mississippi River. Banks in Ohio, Indiana, and Kentucky had failed. Money had all but disappeared from circulation. If any Spanish silver dollars came up the river from New Orleans in payment for flatboat produce, they were immediately shipped out to the eastern states in payment for loans and supplies furnished to the new settlements. Many people in the state were in debt to the business men of the older sections of the nation. Many were in debt to the government for their lands.

It was felt that the only way to secure money for carrying on trade was to create a state bank and issue paper money. The second General Assembly, accordingly, chartered a state bank with a nominal capital of $500,000. The legislature selected the directors and pledged the credit and honor of the state to redeem the paper money. The results were discouraging. The paper money of Illinois soon became almost worthless. A legislative investigation disclosed incompetent and corrupt management. The affairs of this first bank were finally closed in 1831, the state borrowing $100,000 in Cincinnati with which to pay its losses. A later state bank ended even more disastrously.

We should not censure Illinois too severely for this "wild cat banking practice." In those early days many of the other states set up banks that had nothing but the credit of the state to stand back of them; but the people suffered severely as the result of their unsound financial policy. The losses in the banking business plus those in internal improvements almost bankrupted the state. The situation was saved by the able management of Governor Ford. Under his administra-

tion the debt was reduced, confidence was restored, and Illinois was saved the humiliation of repudiating her debts.

As a result of their experiences, the people included in their next constitution a provision which forbade the state government to go into the banking business except after a popular vote approving the plan. This provision is still in force. In 1851 the legislature proposed a banking system copied somewhat from the state of New York. Under this plan the state granted the charter and regulated the business but held no direct interest. State banks of this type are serving us today.

Crime and punishment were dealt with more humanely by the new state laws than by the territorial laws of earlier days. Imprisonment began to take the place of the extreme punishments of older times. Ten years after Illinois became a state the General Assembly voted to build a penitentiary. This is an important event as it marks the passing of the cruel, inhuman punishments of the earlier days. During the hundred years since Illinois built its first penitentiary the ideas of our citizens in regard to the treatment of criminals have become more and more enlightened.

The problem of *transportation* was an important element in the prosperity of early Illinois. The need for better transportation led to the building of the Illinois and Michigan Canal. When the Erie Canal was completed (1825) from the Hudson River to Buffalo on Lake Erie, Illinois saw her opportunity. The legislature decided to connect the Illinois River with Lake Michigan by cutting a canal from LaSalle to Chicago. In 1836 the work was begun, and after twelve years it was completed at a cost of $6,500,000.

The canal was a successful undertaking, although it added to the heavy state debt. Goods from the Illinois Valley began

to "flow uphill" toward the markets of the East. Chicago began its rapid growth. Power and political influence shifted to the northward in Illinois. The canal was paid for in part by the sale of land and town lots owned by the government in the cities along the way. People were eager to buy and values rose rapidly. Within ten years after the completion of the Illinois and Michigan Canal the railroads began to carry much of the goods formerly transported by waterways.

In 1890 the Sanitary District of Chicago began a second canal connecting the Illinois River and Lake Michigan by way of the Chicago River. The new waterway, which was called the Chicago Drainage Canal, joined the Illinois and Michigan Canal at Joliet. While the canal provided a means of transportation, it was primarily built for purposes of sanitation. As the city of Chicago grew, its industries produced more and more waste materials which polluted the water in Lake Michigan. The new drainage canal was made by reversing the flow of the Chicago River. Instead of flowing into Lake Michigan, it was made to flow from Lake Michigan into the Illinois River. The sewage from Chicago was diverted into the canal, and the waters were gradually purified by nature.

Changing the Constitution. After many attempts to secure a new constitution had failed, a bill to call a convention was passed in 1846. The work of the convention was done during the next year. In 1848 the people ratified the new constitution, and Illinois entered a new era of political development. Many lessons learned by the people since 1818 were embodied in the new law.

1. The state was forbidden to go into the banking business.

2. The legislature was prohibited from incurring state debts beyond $50,000 without a vote of the people.

3. The Governor was given the veto power.

4. Many offices formerly filled through appointments by the legislature were made elective.

5. Counties were given the right to adopt a township organization.

All of these provisions have been kept until today.

The present constitution of Illinois is the third constitution of the state. In the election of 1868 the people declared themselves in favor of another constitutional convention. A very able convention was elected. Its members drew up the constitution of 1870, which was a great improvement over the constitution of 1848.

The constitution of 1870 increased the power of the Governor, improved the judicial system, and made certain duties compulsory on the legislature. Special legislation on twenty-three different subjects was prohibited. Counties, cities, and towns were forbidden to subscribe for the stock of any railroad or private corporation. Their power to borrow was limited to five per cent of their taxable property. The action of the legislature in amending the constitution was limited to one article at a session.

The unusual scheme of minority representation now in use in Illinois was adopted to break down the growing sectionalism in the state. The southern part of the state was Democratic, and the northern part was Republican. It was thought desirable to have the minority Republicans of the south and the minority Democrats of the north represented and thus form bonds of common interest through the political parties. The state was divided into fifty-one districts, each one to elect one senator and three representatives. Each voter was given three votes for representatives. He might give one vote to each of three candidates, all three votes to one candidate, or one and a half votes to each of two candidates.

Twentieth-Century Problems in Illinois. *Transportation.*
Beginning under Governor Dunne (1913-1917), Illinois became a great road-building state. Automobile license fees were
placed in a good roads fund, and state bonds were sold to
provide additional funds for the construction of hard-surfaced
roads. Later a gasoline tax was levied for the same purpose.
Today Illinois has a fine system of modern hard roads and is
rapidly improving her county and local roads.

The people of the state have shown an increasing interest
in the development of the Chicago Drainage Canal into a
connecting link in a great waterway for barge transportation
from Lake Michigan to the Gulf of Mexico. The canal has
ceased to be the sole channel for the disposal of waste from
Chicago. The continued growth of the city has led the state
and the nation to require the Chicago Sanitary District to solve
part of its sanitation problem by installing great sewage-treat-
ment plants. The drainage canal is now an important part
of the sanitary system of Chicago; moreover, it is a useful
branch of the water transportation system of the state. This
drainage canal has become nationally important as a waterway since the proposed waterway from Chicago to New Orleans
has been completed.

Proposed Changes in the Machinery of State Government.
Under the leadership of Governor Lowden in 1917 a much-
needed reorganization of the machinery of state government
in Illinois was effected by means of the Civil Administrative
Code. By its provisions more than one hundred separate
boards and other government agencies were united under the
leadership and control of the Governor. The detailed work
of administration was assigned to nine departments, to which
one more has recently been added. This centralization of
power and responsibility has brought better service to the

citizens at greatly reduced cost. Several other states have followed the example of Illinois in this direction.

The need for a revision of the state constitution has been generally recognized for some time. Rapid changes in economic, social, and political life make changes in government very necessary. The constitution of 1870 had served for fifty years when a constitutional convention met to draft a new state constitution in 1920. The convention had a stormy career. The interests of the city of Chicago and the downstate section had become very different. Efforts to agree on compromises acceptable to both sides continued for more than two years. Finally a constitution was drafted and submitted to the people for ratification. It was rejected by an overwhelming vote. Pressing problems now remain unsolved.

Since they must be solved sooner or later, the more important proposals of the convention are worthy of our attention.

1. A more flexible and modern system of taxation was proposed.

2. The court system was to be reorganized, giving the Supreme Court the power to make rules for all court practice and procedure.

3. Large powers of home rule were to be given to Chicago.

4. The system of minority representation in the General Assembly was to be abolished.

5. The number of senators from Cook County was to be limited to one-third the number of members in the state Senate.

6. Cook County was to have less than one-half the members in any future constitutional convention.

The state government has tried to solve its important problems by other means since the failure to adopt a new constitution, but its attempts have not been very successful thus

far. A bill providing for the reapportionment of members of Congress elected from the various districts of the state was passed by the legislature in 1931. A bill to reapportion the members elected to the state legislature failed because it was impossible to unite the city and rural sections of the state on the question. The General Assembly passed and submitted to the voters the *Gateway Amendment* designed to make easier any change in the provisions of the state constitution. At the referendum election the vote was 1,080,541 for the amendment and 275,329 against. The total vote at the election was 3,465,927. As an amendment must have a majority of all votes cast, the proposal failed.

The Governor appointed representative committees to study the tax situation, the improvement of our school system, the parole system for criminals, and the conservation of natural resources. At present (1937), plans are being worked out from which much progress is expected.

In 1936 a *Permanent Registration Law* was passed and tried out at the presidential election. If enforced, this law will improve the honesty of elections in our large cities.

The present session of the legislature has the task of enacting a state *Unemployment Insurance Law*. The Federal Government is now collecting assessments from employers and employees to build up funds out of which small wages will be paid during future periods of unemployment. The only way to get this money back into the state is to operate a state unemployment system. At present the systems of other states are being studied so that we may adopt a system of insurance that will have the good points worked out elsewhere and that will also fit Illinois conditions.

The government needs the intelligent co-operation of its citizens for the solution of the complex and difficult questions

which it faces. Our junior citizens should cultivate the spirit of co-operation and should interest themselves in the study of public affairs. They are the ones who must deal with the future crises and solve the future problems of our state.

Test and Study Exercises

Aids to Learning

1. Notice that the government of Illinois has been influenced by the Ordinance of 1787; also by the experiences from 1818-1870.

2. Observe that the existence of a great city population in the northern part of Illinois and of a rural population in the southern part creates a serious problem in state government.

Test Exercises

On a separate sheet of paper write the numbers of the following statements. After each number write the word or words which belong in the blank spaces.

1. The first white settlers in Illinois were _____ people.

2. English law and government were first introduced in _____.

3. Illinois was first organized as a county of _____.

4. The Ordinance of 1787 forbade _____, provided for public support of _____, and established the idea of _____ government.

5. The most important legislation by Congress for Illinois during the time it was a territory dealt with the sale of _____.

6. Illinois became a state in _____.

7. The first great political conflict in Illinois was over _____.

8. The Illinois-Michigan Canal was completed in _____.

9. The present constitution of Illinois has been in effect since _____.

10. An important present-day issue in Illinois public affairs is _____.

Suggested Activities

1. Draw a map of Illinois and locate on it the ten largest cities in the state.

2. Find in a newspaper or periodical discussions of some of the present problems in Illinois public affairs.

3. Find out what proportion of the population lives in Cook County.

4. Make a list of counties that have lost population since 1900.

LOCAL GOVERNMENT IN ILLINOIS—THE COUNTY

As You Read This Chapter

Learn how county and township governments in Illinois serve the people.

Units of Government. Earlier in this book we have learned that our government operates through a number of units, each of which has the power to make rules, levy taxes, and to take land needed for buildings, parks, highways, water reservoirs, and other purposes. In some states the units of local government are simple and few in number. In Illinois we find a greater variety than in any other state. We have counties, townships, road districts, incorporated towns, cities, villages, and a great variety of districts organized for special purposes, such as schools, parks, health, and drainage.

This great variety of local units in Illinois is due to two reasons. First, the early settlers came from two different sections of the nation having different types of local government. In the beginning the early pioneers from Kentucky and Virginia planted the simple county system in the southern part of our state. About fifty years later people from the New England section introduced the township system in the central and northern parts of the state. Second, varying conditions in different parts of the state led to variations in local government. The increasing difference in the density of our population, the uneven distribution of our taxable wealth, and the wide difference in the occupations and interests of our people led them to create local units to fit their different local needs.

The County in Illinois. The county is the oldest unit of

government through which we "work together" in Illinois. St. Clair County is twenty-eight years older than the state.

The county is rural in character and exercises little authority in the cities or villages. At present there are one hundred two counties in Illinois. Ford County, the youngest, was organized in 1859. The constitution makes it difficult to organize new counties or to change the boundaries of existing counties.

In Illinois the county serves three purposes. It is a unit of local government; it serves the state as a tax collector and as a judicial unit in the enforcement of state laws; and it is used as a convenient unit for grouping citizens in judicial, senatorial, and congressional districts for election purposes.

For the purpose of regulating fees and salaries, the counties are divided into three classes, according to the population of the census of 1900. Those counties with less than 25,000 people are in the first class; those with between 25,000 and 100,-000 people are in the second class; and those with more than 100,000 people are in the third class. This division is made to insure to the people good civil service at a reasonable cost. The size of fees and salaries depends upon the class in which the county is listed. In the smaller, poorer counties rigid economy is necessary, and lower salaries and fees are paid than in the larger counties.

The County Board. Every county has a county board. There are three different types of governing boards in use today. Under the constitution of 1818 all counties were organized with a board of three commissioners elected, one each year, by voters of the county at large. In seventeen counties of southern Illinois the people have preserved this simple form of county government, and it works satisfactorily and economically at the present day.

Cook County was given a special form of organization by
the constitution of 1870. Its board consists of fifteen members, ten elected from Chicago and five from the rest of the
county. The president of the board is elected separately and
is given much power. His powers are comparable to those of
a mayor in a large city or a governor in a small state.

The remaining eighty-four counties have availed themselves
of the permission granted in the constitution of 1848 to divide
themselves into smaller units of local government called civil
towns, or townships. Under this system some of the work of
the county is given over to the townships. The chief officer of
each township is the supervisor. He represents his township
on the county board. Populous townships elect assistant supervisors whose only duty is to act as additional representatives
on the county board. If this were not done, a township of
one hundred people would have as much authority in county
affairs as a township of two thousand people. This would be
unfair. Boards of supervisors vary in size from five to more
than fifty members.

Any county desiring this form of government may adopt it
by a majority vote of the people. Cass County made this
change in 1922.

The county board organizes at the first regular meeting of
the year. The new members present their certificates of election. A member is elected as chairman, except in Cook County,
where a president is elected by the people. Committees are
organized, and the board is ready for work. A majority constitutes a quorum. All meetings of the board are open to the
public.

The county board levies taxes for county purposes, pays out
the county funds, fixes the salaries and provides office space
in the court house for the county officials, provides a county

jail, provides assistance to the township supervisors for out-door relief, operates the poor farm and other institutions, builds roads and bridges, and attends to all county business not given to some other county officer. It may also create a county board of health.

Other County Officers. All counties have the following elected officers: county judge, county clerk, sheriff, state's attorney, county treasurer, coroner, clerk of the circuit court, and county superintendent of schools. Each officer serves for a term of four years. Each must take a prescribed oath and furnish a bond before he takes office. Formerly the bonds were given by friends. Now they are usually given by a security company, the costs being paid by the county.

The *county judge* presides over the county court. He has jurisdiction in civil suits in which the amount is $2,000 or less. He also has jurisdiction over minor criminal offenses. He orders the levy of special assessments for pavements, sewers, and other local improvements. He enters judgments on suits filed by the county clerk for the sale of property upon which taxes have not been paid. He directs the settlement of estates and looks after the affairs of the insane, spendthrifts, and children who are under age.

In counties of more than 85,000 people the work of the county court is divided, and a special *probate judge* is elected. He attends to the settlement of estates and looks after all the work connected with wills, trusteeships, and guardianships. Counties having between 70,000 and 85,000 people may do this also, subject to a referendum election.

The *county clerk* keeps the records of the county board and the county court. He receives from all the taxing authorities a statement of the amount of taxes levied and computes the amount of taxes to be paid by every taxpayer in the county.

He canvasses the vote of the county in all general and special elections. Upon payment of a prescribed fee, he issues marriage licenses and makes copies of any paper in his office. In the seventeen commission-governed counties he also acts as clerk of the circuit court.

The *sheriff* is the guardian of the peace. He has full power to exercise his authority anywhere in the county. He has the authority to draft any citizen who is near when he needs assistance to enforce the law. In emergencies he may ask the Governor for the aid of the state militia. Usually the sheriff does not exercise his police power in cities and villages but leaves that work to the local police forces. In case of serious trouble, however, it is his duty to take charge of the situation.

The sheriff is the strong arm of the court. He must serve, execute, and return warrants, orders, and decrees that are legally given to him in his county. He or his deputy must attend all sessions of the courts of record in his county. His deputy is known as the bailiff. In the commission-governed counties the sheriff also serves as county collector.

The *state's attorney* has the duty of prosecuting all criminal offenders. He is the legal adviser of the county board and of all other county officers. He represents the county in all lawsuits and aids the grand jury in its work.

The *county treasurer* keeps the funds of the county and pays its bills when ordered to do so by the proper authorities. He must make regular reports of all money received and paid out. In counties of less than 100,000 people the treasurer collects the taxes. He cannot succeed himself in office.

In all counties having more than 75,000 and less than 300,-000 people, a *county auditor* is elected. It is his duty to audit all claims against the county.

The *coroner* inquires into the cause of the death of any

person who has died suddenly or who has been found dead under suspicious circumstances. He selects a jury, usually of six persons, to aid him at the inquest. He may arrest and hold for trial any person implicated in the crime. In all cases in which it would not be proper for the sheriff to act, the coroner acts in his place.

The *clerk of the circuit court* keeps the records of the circuit court and issues subpoenas, summonses, citations, executions, and other legal papers. He assists the circuit judge in the conduct of trials. In the smaller counties he is also the recorder of deeds.

In counties of more than 60,000 people a separate *recorder of deeds* is elected. His duty is to copy into large record books all deeds, mortgages, and other valuable legal papers.

The *surveyor* makes surveys of the real estate in the county. He makes plats and records of these surveys and keeps them available for the use of the public. The method of choosing the surveyor was changed in 1936 from election to appointment by the county board.

The *county superintendent of schools* is elected at the *off-year* elections. This is done to keep the office out of politics. The county superintendent serves a term of four years, beginning on the first Monday in August following his election.

The county superintendent is the chief executive officer in the public-school system and attends to a large number of very important duties. He visits each public school and observes the methods of instruction and the textbooks used. He notes the general condition of the schools and gives advice to teachers and school boards. He holds teachers' institutes, gives examinations, gathers school information, and reports the information to the state superintendent. He distributes the money received from the state for school support in the

county. He audits the accounts of all school treasurers and accounts to the county board for all money received, loaned, or expended. He assumes leadership in school affairs and works to improve school conditions and standards of teaching.

A *superintendent of highways* is appointed in counties having highways under the state-aid system. The appointment of this officer must have the approval of the State Department of Public Works and Buildings. The superintendent of highways prepares plans and specifications for bridges, is in charge of the construction and maintenance of roads in which the county is interested, inspects the highways and bridges, and directs the repair of all state roads in his county.

The *county board of review* usually consists of the chairman of the board of supervisors and two members appointed by the county judge. In counties of more than 250,000 the members of the board are elected by the people. In the commission-governed counties the commissioners act as the board of review. The board assesses property not listed by the assessors, hears complaints against the work of the assessors, and sometimes changes the assessment of whole townships in order to equalize the tax burden. For many years this board did little work, but the breakdown in our general property tax system has recently increased the amount and importance of its work.

Subdivisions of the County. *(1) The Township.* In the eighty-four counties under boards of supervisors we find the only political unit in Illinois that has any semblance of pure democracy. This is the township with its annual town meeting. This assembly is held the first Tuesday in April, which is the day of the regular township election.

Many of these meetings are attended by only a few interested persons. Sometimes the interest is so slight that the

officials have to go out and bring in enough people to perform the work of the meeting. In some townships, on the other hand, the old New England spirit and interest in direct government is still strong enough to make the town meeting an important event.

At 2:00 P.M., the balloting in the township election is stopped temporarily, and the town meeting is called. The clerk takes charge until a moderator is chosen and qualified. The business of the annual meeting is then transacted. All our young citizens should attend such a meeting if possible and note how the work is done.

The town meeting levies the annual taxes for township purposes. This includes the costs of printing, elections, salaries, promotion of good health, cutting obnoxious weeds, and care of township cemeteries. The meeting makes rules concerning stray animals and provides for the establishment and maintenance of pounds and the abatement of nuisances. It has the power to buy, sell, and regulate the use of township property. It makes provision for needed roads and bridges and directs the town clerk to certify the total tax levy to the county clerk. After the necessary business is completed, the town meeting is adjourned; and the annual election is resumed.

Township Officers. The officers chosen are: a supervisor and, if needed, assistant supervisors; a town clerk; an assessor; justices of the peace; constables; and a highway commissioner.

The *supervisor* serves for four years. He is treasurer of all funds except the money raised for roads and bridges and the township library. His reports are posted at the annual town meeting. He is overseer of the poor and distributes the county and township poor-relief funds. In this work the supervisor is allowed considerable discretionary power. The Gen-

eral Assembly made some important additions to his duties by putting pauper relief in the hands of the township.

The supervisor is prosecutor and defender in lawsuits involving his township. He is a member of the township election and health boards. He represents his township on the county board. In populous townships assistant supervisors are chosen. These assistants are paid by the day and have no other duties than to act as members of the county board. The purpose is to insure fair representation to the people of the different townships in the decision of county matters.

The *town clerk* keeps all records of the township and acts as clerk at the town meeting. He is registrar of births and deaths, the record of which he sends to the county clerk. He is clerk at elections and is a member of the auditing and health boards. For a small fee he makes copies of official records.

The *assessor* annually places a value for taxing purposes on all personal property in the township. He places a value on all real estate every four years. All general property taxes are based on this assessed valuation. Assessors and their methods of work have been severely criticized lately in some parts of the state. As a result, assessments are now closely supervised by county authorities. The assessor is also a member of the board of health.

Each township elects at least two *justices of the peace*. Populous townships may have as many as five. Since the courts enforce state law, the justices of the peace are commissioned by the Governor after filing their bonds with the county clerk. Failure to file bond within a specified time disqualifies the one elected.

Each township elects two or more *constables*.

The *highway commissioner* serves for four years. He makes his estimates of the expenses for building and maintaining

local public highways, and from this estimate the tax rate is determined. The amount may be altered by the county clerk for tax levying. The township highway commissioner usually acts in co-operation with the county superintendent of highways, but in the spending of small amounts for local roads he acts independently.

The *township board of auditors* audits all the accounts of the supervisor, checking the entries with the canceled checks and the orders from the town clerk. This work is done during the week preceding the town meeting. The audited report is posted for public inspection.

The *township board of health* seldom does any work except to prevent the spread of disease. Two or more townships or road districts may join to create a unified health district. A special tax may be levied; and a trained health officer, approved by the State Board of Health, may be chosen. The authority of the health board of this new district is the same as the authority in matters of health formerly vested in the township board.

(2) The Road District. The seventeen commission-governed counties have a very simple, easily understood organization. The county is divided into road districts, the lines generally corresponding to the survey townships. Each road district elects a road commissioner. A district clerk is also elected by each of these road districts.

One justice of the peace is made overseer of the poor by action of the county board. The county treasurer acts as assessor, the sheriff as collector, and the county clerk as recorder. The treasurer and the sheriff have local assistants. There are no local auditing boards. The three commissioners constitute the board of health. They may employ a physician as health officer.

Test and Study Exercises

Aids to Learning

1. Remember that the purpose of our local governments is to give better service to the people in matters of local concern.

2. Note that the county in Illinois serves three chief purposes.

3. Note that townships and road districts are subdivisions of counties.

Test Exercises

Match the items in the first column with the items in the second column by putting together on a piece of paper the numbers of the two items which make a true statement.

1.	Township assessor	1.	Levies the county taxes
2.	Township supervisor	2.	Values property for taxation
3.	Town clerk	3.	Prosecutes criminals for the county
4.	State's attorney	4.	Prevents the spread of disease
5.	County superintendent of schools	5.	Represents the township on the county board
6.	Township board of health	6.	Keeps register of births and deaths
7.	County board	7.	Presides over the county court
8.	County clerk	8.	Gives teachers' examinations
9.	Sheriff	9.	Issues marriage licenses
10.	County judge	10.	Serves and executes warrants

Suggested Activities

1. Draw a map of your county. Show the townships or road districts. Locate the county seat, the important towns, and your school.

2. Is your county in the first, second, or third class?

3. Make a complete list of your county and local officers.

4. Find out how the taxes are collected in your county.

LOCAL GOVERNMENT IN ILLINOIS—CITIES AND VILLAGES

As You Read This Chapter

Find out how the people of Illinois are served by their city and village governments.

Growth of Cities. In 1818 Illinois had no cities. All local needs were satisfied by the county government. Today over two-thirds of our people live in cities and villages. This change brought with it great changes in our local government. New forms of "working together" had to be developed.

When people live in close and frequent contact with each other, it is necessary to have many rules of conduct not needed in farm life. Some people must be compelled to do or not to do certain things. Experience has also shown that many things can be done better, more quickly, and at a lower cost by working together than when each person does them for himself. In very densely settled areas there is what firemen call "exposure." On a farm, buildings are set far apart to check the spread of fire. In a city a fire must be put out promptly or adjoining buildings will be destroyed. A similar "exposure" exists in the fields of crime and disease.

Municipal governments need the power to tax, to police, and to take land for public purposes as much as county, state, and national governments do. The chief difference is that the cities are limited in the use of these powers to the purposes enumerated by the state law.

Special Charters. Until 1870 Illinois delegated powers to newly created cities and villages by special acts of the legislature. Whenever a group of citizens wished to incorporate,

they wrote their own charter and introduced it in the General
Assembly. This method produced variety in the types of municipal governments. Each charter fitted the needs of the community and gave a large amount of "home rule." The incorporated town of Normal, which grew up around the first
Teachers' College, had a provision against the sale of liquor a
half century before the nation adopted prohibition. With the
repeal of the Eighteenth Amendment this provision became active again. Citizens living in a city operating under a special
charter should get their charter and study it carefully.[1]

Cities Since 1872. The lack of uniformity in city government and the abuses of some powers granted became a serious
matter after the Civil War. To remedy the evils, the constitution of 1870 forbade the granting of more special charters.
Since July 1, 1872, new cities and villages have been incorporated under a general law which insures uniformity—the *Cities
and Villages Act*. It describes the government to be set up
in a village or city of a given size. It delegates power to the
officers to discharge certain duties. Fifty or more voters of
any contiguous territory, not exceeding four square miles
and having not less than 1,000 inhabitants, may sign a petition to organize a city. This petition is filed with the clerk
of the county court and addressed to the county judge, who
calls an election. The petition is granted if a majority vote
in favor of it.

City Government. Most cities in Illinois operate under
the *mayor and council type* of government.

---

[1] On July 1, 1936, these towns and cities were still operating under charters
obtained before 1872: Annawan, Astoria, Atkinson, Belle Prairie, Bentley, Cen-
tral City, Chatsworth, Chenoa, Cortland, Dakota, Elkhart, Fayetteville, Galatia,
LaHarpe, Lake Forest, LaPrairie, Lena, Mason, Minooka, Naples, New Boston,
New Salem, Nilwood, Normal, Oneida, Otterville, Palatine, Palestine, Rushville,
Shipman, Sigel, Spring Bay, Toledo, Topeka, Winnetka.

The Executive Officers. The *mayor* is the executive head of the city government. He serves a term of four years. However, by a special vote in any regular election the people may adopt a two-year term for the mayor and all other elected administrative officers. The mayor of Chicago has a four-year term by a special act of the legislature. In case of a vacancy occurring less than one year before the regular election, the office is filled by the city council from its membership; but if the unexpired term is more than one year, a special election is held to fill the vacancy.

The mayor is responsible for the maintenance of law and order and has the power to appoint and remove a number of lesser administrative officers. In the larger cities this is an important function and gives the mayor great influence. He presides over the city council but votes only in case of a tie. He may veto ordinances. Annually and from time to time he gives information to the city council on conditions in the city. It is his duty to see that all ordinances are executed. He may draft anyone over eighteen years of age to help suppress riots, and he may ask the Governor for the aid of the state militia. He may be brought to trial for incompetence or misconduct. If convicted, he may be fined or removed from office, or both.

In the larger cities the administrative work is done by departments created by the council. The department heads are appointed by the mayor. These provisions are in the general state law under which our cities now operate. Other provisions apply to the work of all the other officers.

The *city clerk* keeps a record of the proceedings of the city council and keeps the bonds of other city officials. He receives petitions and is the keeper of the city seal. He is ex officio city comptroller and city collector where no such special offices are created by the council. He has the duty of keeping the

record of births and deaths in the city and of reporting them
to the county clerk.

The *city treasurer* cannot succeed himself. It is his duty to
receive, keep, and pay out on order all the money of the
city and to keep a record of the same. Where separate funds
are created, he must keep separate accounts. He must account
for interest earned by public funds and make a monthly report
and an annual financial statement. Special assessment money
must be kept in a separate fund and must be used only for the
purpose for which is was collected, except to reimburse the
city for money advanced for the special purpose.

The *city attorney* is appointed by the mayor with the assent
of the council. His chief duty is to advise the city officials
in their official capacity. He attends to all legal business and
represents the city in its lawsuits.

A number of other officials are found in the larger cities.
The state law provides that all cities may have a *superintendent of streets* and a *city engineer*. All cities of over 50,000
population must have a *commissioner of public works, a superintendent of special assessments*, and a *superintendent of sew-
ers*. Other offices, such as collector, comptroller, corporation
counsel, etc., may be created by the city if needed. Large
discretion is given to our cities in perfecting the details of
their organizations. The list of offices and boards in Chicago
is too long to enumerate. It may be obtained from the special
laws passed for Chicago or from officers at the city hall.

The City Council. This body is made up of aldermen, two
from each ward, elected by wards of fairly equal population.
The aldermen serve for four years, one being elected every two
years. Thus the city has a council in which a majority of the
members are experienced. Cities of less than 3,000 people have
three wards and six aldermen; those of 3,000 to 5,000 people

have four wards and eight aldermen; those of 5,000 to 10,000 people have ten aldermen; those of 10,000 to 30,000 people have fourteen aldermen; and in larger cities there are two additional aldermen for each additional 20,000 inhabitants. In Chicago there are fifty wards, this number being fixed by a state law passed in 1919.

The council is the judge of its own members and makes its own rules of procedure. An alderman must be a qualified elector and a resident of his ward. He must not be interested in any city contract or hold any other lucrative city office. A majority of aldermen elected is a quorum. The council sets the time and place of meeting by ordinance. It may call special meetings. In larger cities the council organizes itself into committees for the study of special problems. These committees make recommendations to the council.

A record of the proceedings is kept in a journal. The majority of the aldermen present—provided there is a quorum— can pass or reject ordinary proposals. The affirmative vote of a majority of all aldermen elected is necessary for the passage of ordinances and the appropriation of money. The assent of two-thirds of the aldermen is necessary for the sale of any city property. The vote of each alderman is recorded on all important proposals.

After an ordinance is passed, it is submitted to the mayor, who may approve it or veto it. If he fails to act within a specified time, the ordinance becomes a law without his approval. He has power to approve part of an ordinance and to veto items. The council can pass an ordinance over the mayor's veto by a two-thirds vote.

A complete list of the powers granted to our cities and vested in the council runs to more than one hundred items. The list is growing steadily as new needs are constantly arising in our

rapidly changing city life. Thirteen items are given below to show the nature of this work. The council has power:

1. To control the property belonging to the city.
2. To levy taxes for general and special purposes.
3. To appropriate money.
4. To borrow money and to issue bonds payable in twenty years. (Bonds cannot be issued in excess of five per cent of the equalized assessed valuation or without the consent of the people.)
5. To fix the terms and manner of issuing and revoking licenses.
6. To lay out, widen, grade, and pave streets and to vacate the same.
7. To regulate the use of streets and public grounds and to provide for their cleaning, lighting, and beautification.
8. To regulate the use of sidewalks and to force the owners to keep them free from snow and other obstructions.
9. To name or change the names of streets and to provide for the numbering of houses and lots.
10. To build, repair, and operate gas, water, and other utility plants and to provide for the disposal of sewage, garbage, ashes, and rubbish.
11. To require railroads to fence their property, place flagmen at crossings, and change grades and crossings.
12. To construct and repair bridges, viaducts, tunnels, drainage channels, and canals for commerce.
13. To organize the administrative work of the city into departments such as law, finance, fire, police, and public works, and also to make the rules for the conduct of these departments.

The City Judiciary. In Illinois the city is not important as a judicial unit. Each city, except those that are under special

acts, elects a *police magistrate* every four years. He holds
court at the city hall and has the same powers as a justice of
the peace. He is not a part of the police system, as many
people assume. The *justice of the peace,* although elected from
the township or highway district, has jurisdiction in the city.
Generally the more important part of the judicial business in
our cities is transacted in the county and circuit courts.

By an act of 1901 any city may, by a majority vote, have a
city court which has the same rank as the circuit court. The
judges and the clerk are elected in the same manner, but not
at the same time, as the other city officials. In cities of less
than 5,000 people the salary is $800 and is paid out of the
city treasury. In larger cities the judges are paid by the state.
Salaries range from $1,800 to $4,500. About twenty-five cities
have such courts.[1]

In Chicago the *municipal court* takes the place of the justice
courts, the police magistrates' courts, and the city courts created by the act of 1901. The municipal court deals with cases
enumerated in the act creating it. It consists of a chief justice
and thirty-five justices elected for a term of six years. It
has several branches dealing with particular types of cases,
such as the *court of domestic relations,* the *morals court,* and
the *traffic court.*

The Commission Type of Government. An act of 1910
makes possible the adoption of the commission form of government in any city or village under 200,000 population. To
change to the commission form, a petition must be signed by
one-tenth of the legal voters. It is then presented to the county

[1] Cities having a city court are Alton, Aurora, Beardstown, Benton, Calumet
City, Canton, Carbondale, Charleston, Chicago Heights, DeKalb, DuQuoin, East
St. Louis, Eldorado, Elgin, Granite City, Harrisburg, Herrin, Johnston City,
Kewanee, Litchfield, Marion, Mattoon, Moline, Pana, Spring Valley, Sterling,
West Frankfort, and Zion.

judge, who submits it to a vote of the people. About seventy
cities in Illinois are operating under commissions. Mattoon
made this change in January, 1937.

Under this form of government the council consists of a
mayor and *four other commissioners*. The work of the city
is divided into five departments; namely, *public affairs, accounts and finances, public health and safety, streets and improvements,* and *public property*. The mayor is head of the
department of public affairs. The other four commissioners
are assigned as heads of the other departments.

The council determines the powers and duties of each department, thus fitting the work to the needs of each particular
city. The council meets once a week. Three members constitute a quorum. The mayor is the presiding officer but has
no power of veto. The officers are subject to recall by a
special election. There is also a limited use of the initiative
and the referendum.

After two years' trial one-fourth of the electors of a city
may file a petition asking that an election be held to determine
whether the commission form is to be continued. If the majority of the votes cast are against continuing it, the city goes
back to the general plan provided for by the state law.

The City Manager Type of Government. An act of 1921
provides that cities and villages under 5,000 population may
adopt a city manager type of organization. To adopt this
form of government, a petition signed by ten per cent of the
voters asking for an election must be presented to the county
judge, who calls an election. If a majority of the votes cast
favor the petition, the plan is adopted. This form of government is growing rapidly in many states, but little has been done
with it in Illinois.

Villages. Village government is simple and inexpensive,

yet meets the needs of a small group living together. Towns
under special charters may change to the village form of government. Also, any one hundred people in Illinois, living
in an unincorporated area not exceeding two square miles,
may organize themselves into an incorporated village by a
majority vote. Fifteen legal voters may call an election by a
petition to the county judge.

The elected officers of a village are: a *president* of the village board, six *trustees,* and a *village clerk;* and there may
be a *police magistrate.* The annual election is held on the third
Tuesday in April of the odd-numbered years. Salaries are determined by a vote of the board of trustees. For villages above
20,000 people definite limits are prescribed for salaries by state
law. Other officers, such as *public engineer, treasurer, street
commissioner, attorney,* and *village marshal,* may be appointed
if needed.

A village may have adjacent areas added to it; it may be
united with a neighboring city or village; it may have outlying
areas cut off from it; or it may be dissolved and become an
unincorporated area. Any village that contains one thousand
people may by a majority vote change its organization to
that of a city.

Boards of Local Improvement. One of the most difficult
problems that had to be solved when we began to "work together" in cities and villages was finding a way to compel
our citizens to make local improvements. An improvement is
local when the benefits go largely to those living near the
improvement and when the value of the near-by property is
increased. It is not a local improvement when the benefits
are distributed generally.

If a street is paved, the value of every lot on the street is
actually increased; but the value of lots elsewhere in the city

may be actually decreased. It is fair, therefore, that the adjoining property owners should pay a large share of the cost. If a new city hall or a water plant or a centrally located park is built, the benefits are not local; and the city as a whole should pay the cost.

It is always easy to get a majority to favor improvements, but those who must pay often object and appeal to the courts. To settle these troublesome questions, the General Assembly passed an act in 1897 creating boards of local improvement in our cities and villages. These boards are made up in different ways, but the board in each community wields a great deal of power. The system has worked so well that today it is definitely established.

An improvement may be started by petition of interested citizens or by action of the board itself. All owners of property to be assessed are notified that a hearing is to be held. At this meeting arguments for and against the proposal are heard. The board then decides the question.

The power of the board is limited in two ways only. The contract for any improvement costing more than $500 must be awarded to the lowest responsible bidder. Also, property owners may convince the court that their assessments are greater than the benefits they would receive from the improvement. In such a case the court would cut down the assessment, making it impossible for the board to raise enough money to proceed. It is a general principle that the cost of a local improvement must not be greater than the benefits accruing to the property owners who pay the special assessment.

Even with these two checks on their power, boards of local improvement have become effective instruments for the gradual transformation of our cities into finer and safer places in which to live.

Test and Study Exercises

Aids to Learning

1. Observe that the purpose of organizing cities and villages is to give better service to the people.

2. Note that cities and villages are organized by the state independently of county and township government.

Test Exercises

On a separate sheet of paper write the words which have been omitted from the sentences below.

1. City and village governments are limited in their powers by the provisions of their _____ and by _____ law.

2. Most cities in Illinois operate under the _____ type of government.

3. In the _____ type of government a city or village government is divided into five departments.

4. Under the city _____ type of government a city or village is managed by an expert in city government.

5. In the larger cities the _____ has great influence because he has the power to appoint and dismiss many officers and may veto city ordinances.

6. In most cities in Illinois important judicial business is transacted in the _____ and _____ courts.

Suggested Activities

1. Choose sides and debate the question: Resolved, That the city manager type of government gives the people more efficient service than the mayor and council type of city government.

2. If you live in a village or city, make a list of the names of the chief executive officer and the members of the council or board.

3. Make a list of different kinds of local improvements and compare your list with those of your classmates.

4. What kind of judicial officers does your city or village have?

CHAPTER IV

STATE GOVERNMENT IN ILLINOIS

As You Read This Chapter

Learn how you are served by your state government.

Distinctive Features of Illinois State Government. The state government of Illinois differs from that of most states in several important particulars. Senators and representatives are elected from the same districts, the one by plurality election, the other by a system of *cumulative voting*. This is not done in any other state. Our executive department is being developed along lines resembling our national executive department. Our judiciary is very complex. Our Supreme Court judges are elected from seven state judicial districts.

The Legislative Department. The state legislature, which is called the General Assembly, has two houses, the Senate and the House of Representatives.

The *Senate* has fifty-one members. A senator must be twenty-five years of age, a citizen of the United States, a resident of the state for five years and of his senatorial district for two years. He must not hold any other lucrative public office, and his record must be free from "conviction of bribery, perjury, or other infamous crime." His term of office is four years. His salary is $5,000 per session, plus expenses at the rate of five cents per mile necessarily traveled in going to and from the sessions.

The senators from even-numbered districts are chosen in the November elections of 1936, 1940, and so on. Those from odd-numbered districts are chosen in 1938, 1942, and so on. They begin their service in January following the election.

Through this arrangement a majority of the Senate always consists of members experienced in the work of lawmaking.

The *House of Representatives* consists of one hundred fifty-three members. The qualifications for representatives are the same as those for senators, except that the minimum age is twenty-one years. The salary is $5,000 per term, plus five cents per mile necessarily traveled. Representatives are elected in November of even-numbered years and take office in January following. They are elected in each senatorial district by the cumulative voting plan.

Under this plan each voter has three votes. He may give his three votes to any one candidate; he may give one and one-half votes to each of two candidates; or he may give one vote to each of three candidates. The purpose of this system is to enable a strong minority in a senatorial district to elect one of the three representatives and thus secure representation. In many districts the political parties have made agreements about the number of candidates to be nominated. Usually the stronger party in the district names two candidates, and the weaker party only one. This plan assures results as the party chiefs wish them. In the Constitutional Convention of 1922 an attempt was made to abolish this system, but without success.

The Work of the General Assembly. The legislature meets in regular session from January to June in odd-numbered years. Special sessions are held when called by the Governor. During the early part of the session little work is done except by the leaders. The members usually go home over the week ends. Toward the end of the session night meetings are held to get the necessary work done.

Each house elects its own officers, except that the Lieutenant Governor presides over the Senate. Each house makes its own rules and organizes its committees. A majority of the members

is a quorum. Twenty-six votes are necessary in the Senate and seventy-seven in the House of Representatives to enact laws in regular manner.

A two-thirds vote in each house is necessary to pass an emergency measure which would go into effect at once, or to pass a bill over the Governor's veto, or to propose an amendment to the constitution.

Bills are introduced in typewritten form, with a sentence at the top which states the purpose of the bill. This sentence is called the title of the bill. Bills begin with, "Be it enacted by the people of the State of Illinois represented in the General Assembly." Any member may introduce a bill. The bill is read by title only and referred to the proper committee for consideration. It is then printed for the use of the legislators and for distribution among interested citizens. Sometimes "hearings" are held by the committee, thus giving an opportunity for friends and opponents of the bill to present their ideas. If the committee approves of the bill, it is reported back to the house, with or without amendments, with the recommendation "that it do pass." It is then taken up in regular order for second reading, at which time amendments are proposed and voted on. The bill is then read a third time and put to a vote.

If the bill receives a majority vote on the third reading, it is sent to the other house. Here a similar course of action is followed. If the bill passes both houses, it is sent to the Governor for his signature. If he signs the bill, it becomes a law. If the Governor vetoes a bill, it is dead unless both houses pass it over his veto by a two-thirds majority vote.

If the bill is passed by the second house with some changes, it must go back to the first house, which may agree, disagree, or make further changes. Whenever a deadlock on a bill oc-

curs, a "conference committee" with members from both houses is appointed. If it can reach an agreement, both houses usually vote to accept the compromise worked out by the committee. The bill then goes to the Governor, who signs it, vetoes it, or allows it to become a law without his signature.

The most important work is the appropriation of money with which to operate the state government. In all money bills the legislature must list the items and their purposes in order to give the Governor the opportunity of approving the bill after striking out the items he wishes to veto.

The Executive Department. The state constitution provides for seven elective officers in the executive department: Governor, Lieutenant Governor, Secretary of State, Attorney General, Auditor, Treasurer, and Superintendent of Public Instruction. These officials have many appointed subordinates. All the elective officers are chosen at the time of the presidential election, except the Superintendent of Public Instruction. He is chosen at the *off-year* election to keep the office as free from political influence as possible.

A new Treasurer is chosen at each regular election. He serves a term of two years. The provision that he cannot succeed himself acts as a check on the handling of state money. At each change both the outgoing and the incoming Treasurer make sure that all funds are correctly accounted for.

The Governor. The constitution provides that "the supreme executive power shall be vested in the Governor." He has some legislative authority in that he prepares the biennial budget and may veto bills passed by the General Assembly. He has some judicial authority in that he may postpone, shorten, or set aside entirely the sentences for crime imposed by the courts. This power is called the power "to reprieve, to commute, or to pardon."

In order to give him the power of law enforcement, the Governor is made commander-in-chief of the state militia. He fills by appointment state offices for which no other method of selection has been provided. He has large powers of removal. He is ex officio member of the Tax Levy Board, the Canvassing Board, the Legislative Reference Bureau, and the Board of Library Commissioners. His compensation is $12,000 per year. He also has free use of the executive mansion and an allowance for traveling expenses.

The activities of the state government have increased very rapidly in the last few years. This increase has built up the power and influence of the Governor, who, under the Civil Administrative Code of 1917, has become the head of a group of officers comparable to the cabinet of the President of the United States.

The *Lieutenant Governor* is a governor in reserve. He takes the place of the Governor whenever that officer is out of the state, or in case of a vacancy. When the General Assembly is in session, he presides over the Senate. His salary is $5,000.

The *Attorney General* is the legal adviser of all state officers. Changes in the law often lead to doubt as to what an administrative officer can legally do. In such cases the officer applies to the Attorney General for an "opinion." The Attorney General's opinion may later be set aside by the Supreme Court, but in the meantime any action that he advises is regarded as legal action. He represents Illinois in lawsuits and directs the state's attorneys in the different counties. His salary is $9,000 per year.

The *Secretary of State* is the keeper of the great seal of the State of Illinois. He affixes it to all important documents. He publishes the laws, is custodian of all state papers, and has charge of all state property at the capital. He issues automo-

bile licenses and gives charters to new corporations. His salary is $9,000 per year.

The *Auditor of Public Accounts* issues all warrants on the Treasurer for the payment of state bills. Jointly with the Governor and the Treasurer he determines the state tax rate whenever the state makes a levy on general property. At present (1937) no levy is being made. He guards the finances by balancing the accounts at least once a month with the Treasurer. His salary is $9,000 per year.

The *Treasurer* receives the state funds and pays them out on order from the Auditor. He turns into the treasury any interest money earned on surplus funds deposited in banks. He is under heavy bond, serves for two years, and cannot succeed himself. His salary is $9,000 per year.

The *Superintendent of Public Instruction* does not have great power, as our school system places the control of the schools largely in the hands of local boards of education. Indirectly, however, he wields a large influence in the improvement of education in the state. He gives addresses on educational subjects, compiles educational statistics, issues reports, and publishes much valuable material for the schools. He advises county superintendents and other school officials. School inspection is carried on from his office. He is secretary of the board that has charge of the five teachers' colleges of Illinois. His term is four years, his salary $9,000 per year.

Administrative Departments. There are ten departments of administration, each of which is provided with experts to render service in highly specialized fields. The salary of the director in each department is $6,000 per year. The nature of the activities of these departments and the wide variety of services rendered to the people can be seen from the duties listed for each department.

The *Department of Finance* examines all accounts and aids the Governor in preparing a budget for the legislature. A budget contains an estimate of the expected revenue and a list of the proposed appropriations. The department also studies the operation of all other departments and makes recommendations for reducing the cost of the services rendered. It superintends the state printing and purchases all supplies. The State Tax Commission is attached to this department. Its purpose is to study state and local tax problems. At present this is one of the most important questions before the people.

The *Department of Agriculture* is charged with the administration of all the state laws relative to foods and dairies, animal industry and veterinary science, apiary inspection, plant and seed industry, poultry husbandry, markets, and agricultural statistics. It also handles dairy extension work and manages the State Fair.

The *Department of Labor* was created in response to the demand of organized labor for aid in the improvement of labor conditions. It enforces the laws regulating factories, workshops, stores, and other industries employing labor. It has charge of all state free employment agencies. It collects, prints, and distributes valuable information relative to labor.

The *Department of Mines and Minerals* enforces all state laws that apply to the operation of mines, the conditions under which miners shall work, mine inspection, miners' examination, and the fighting of fire in mines. It investigates all accidents and plans to prevent their occurrence.

The *Department of Public Works and Buildings* has charge of all state construction, such as highways, parks, and public buildings. It is also the trustee for memorials.

The *Department of Public Welfare* manages the charitable and penal institutions of the state. It investigates and re-

ports to the Governor on all applications for pardon or commutation of sentence of convicted criminals. It studies the causes of moral, mental, and physical defects in an effort to find means of cure and prevention. It provides for humane and scientific care of our unfortunate fellow citizens in institutions built and supported by the state.

State hospitals for the mentally deficient are located at Elgin, Kankakee, Jacksonville, East Moline, Alton, Peoria, Chicago, Anna, Dixon, Menard, and Manteno. Other institutions and their locations are as follows: the Lincoln State School and Colony at Lincoln; the Illinois School for the Deaf and the Illinois School for the Blind at Jacksonville; the Industrial Home for the Blind at Chicago; the Soldiers' and Sailors' Home at Quincy; the Soldiers' Widows' Home at Wilmington; the Soldiers' and Sailors' Children's Home at Normal; the Illinois Eye and Ear Infirmary at Chicago; the State Training School for Girls at Geneva; the St. Charles School for Boys at St. Charles; the Illinois State Penitentiary with its three branches at Joliet, Menard, and Pontiac; the State Reformatory for Women at Dwight; the Illinois State Farm at Vandalia; and educational hospitals in Chicago. On February 1, 1936, the number of wards cared for by the state in these institutions was 49,103. In addition to these wards, there were 10,000 other persons receiving supervision outside the institutions.

The *Department of Public Health* is charged with the administration of all state health and sanitation laws. It has very broad and general powers in this field.

The *Department of Registration and Education* has charge of the five state teachers' colleges operating under a single Normal School Board. The director of the department is chairman of the board. This department also administers the

laws relating to the examination and registration of the regulated trades and professions in Illinois.

The *Department of Conservation* enforces the game laws of the state and encourages and promotes the interests of hunting and fishing. Prevention of stream pollution and the conservation of forests are also vested with this department. These two functions are likely to grow in importance in the future.

The *Department of Insurance* is the latest addition to the Governor's group of appointed, trained administrators. Its duties are to see that insurance companies, of all kinds, are financially sound and honestly managed and that companies from outside the state meet the requirements of Illinois law. Insurance contracts are inspected to see whether they are fair and reasonable. Small loan companies are licensed and their business supervised. The Division of Fire Prevention examines buildings and property to eliminate fire hazards.

The Judicial Department. The chief purpose of a court system is to establish justice in civil and criminal cases. *Civil cases* are lawsuits between private parties when personal or property rights are involved. *Criminal cases* are prosecutions by the state of persons accused of crime against society.

The court system of Illinois is rather complex, owing to the creation of many special courts. This was necessary to take care of the large amount of new court business in our rapidly growing cities. The state courts proper are: the Supreme Court, four appellate courts, eighteen circuit courts, and the Superior Court of Cook County.

The *Supreme Court* consists of seven justices. The state is divided into seven districts, from each of which one justice is elected. The term of office is nine years, and the salary is $15,000.

The Supreme Court policy is to try no cases that could

first be adequately tried in a lower court. This policy is necessary in order to avoid congestion of work in the Supreme Court and to insure speedy justice. The court studies written briefs submitted to it and hears the arguments of the attorneys representing the parties in dispute.

The Appellate Courts. Illinois is divided into four appellate districts, of which Cook County is one. The justices of this court are appointed by the Supreme Court from judges of the circuit courts or from the Superior Court of Cook County. Their duty is to hear and pass upon appeals coming up from the lower courts. Their chief duty, therefore, is to relieve the Supreme Court. It is regarded as an honor for a judge to be chosen by his superiors for this duty. In Cook County this court has three divisions with three judges for each division. Each of the other districts has three judges. The Appellate Courts sit at Chicago, Ottawa, Springfield, and Mt. Vernon.

The Circuit Courts. There are eighteen circuits in Illinois. Seventeen of them elect three judges, who hold court in every county in the circuit at least twice every year. They divide the work among themselves. In case of disagreement, the Supreme Court divides and assigns the work.

In the Cook County district the amount of judicial work is so great that the legislature has increased the number of circuit judges to twenty and has added a superior court with a large number of judges. A separate division has been created for criminal cases. The superior and circuit court judges alternate in presiding over the criminal court. The salaries of the circuit and superior judges are paid partly by the county and partly by the state. This is done to attract honest, capable men to these positions. The regular salary paid by the state would not be sufficient in the city to justify successful lawyers in giving up the practice of law.

Attorneys at Law. A function not usually thought of as judicial is the admission of persons to the practice of law. Attorneys in Illinois are officers of the court. Without well-trained, honest lawyers the courts are unable to function properly. Therefore, the Supreme Court makes rules regarding educational and other qualifications for admission to the bar. It holds examinations and issues licenses to those who are qualified. Occasionally it revokes the licenses of lawyers who have shown themselves unworthy of the profession.

Test and Study Exercises

Aids to Learning

    1. Note that the legislative, executive, and judicial departments have distinct functions to perform.

    2. Observe that there are six elective executive departments and ten appointive administrative departments in Illinois.

Test Exercises

    On a separate sheet of paper complete the following sentences.

    1. A bill may be _____ in either house. If it is passed by both houses, it is sent to the _____ for his signature.

    2. The Governor may sign a bill, veto it, or let it become a law without his _____.

    3. The chief duty of the _____ is to enforce the laws.

    4. The judiciary deals with two kinds of cases, _____ and _____.

    5. The legislature has increased the number of _____ courts in Cook County and has provided for _____ and _____ courts in Chicago because of the unusual amount of work in the city.

Suggested Activities

    1. Find out who represents you in the two houses of the General Assembly.

    2. Who are your probate, county, and circuit judges?

    3. Find out the differences between civil and criminal cases.

CHAPTER V

FILLING OUR OFFICES

As You Read This Chapter

Find out what an intelligent citizen should do to help select competent persons to fill government offices.

Three Methods of Selecting Officials. Offices in the various units of government in Illinois are filled in one of three ways. The most important officers are elected at general elections provided for by state law. Other important officers directing lines of work in which technical training is required are appointed by elected officers, such as the Governor or the Attorney-General of the state and the mayors of the cities. An increasing number of lesser clerical positions are filled with candidates who have passed competitive examinations given by civil service boards. Promotion to better positions in the civil service comes by competitive examinations and by good service records.

Formerly the minor positions as well as the more important positions not filled by elections were filled by appointments made by the successful party after election. Often people who were unfitted for government positions were appointed for political reasons. The result was poor service to the public until the new appointees had gained some experience in the discharge of their duties. The purpose of civil service examinations is to secure the selection of workers who are qualified for their positions.

Voting. *The Citizens' Duty.* Under our government citizens should be active in the public affairs of their community and state. They should take part in the nomination and election of good officers. They should observe the conduct of their

53

officers and inform themselves on public questions that are likely to come up for decision at the polls. The right to vote is not a mere privilege. It is a duty that must be exercised regularly if democratic government is to be a success.

Qualifications for Voting. The laws of Illinois require that a voter be a native-born or naturalized citizen of the United States. He must be twenty-one years of age. He must have been a resident of the state for one year, of the county for ninety days, and of his precinct thirty days next preceding the election.

Registration. The law makes provision for the registration of all voters in order to minimize fraud in the elections. Two methods of registration are now in use.

In the larger cities the conduct of all elections is under the control of a board of election commissioners. In these cities registration is compulsory under the provisions of the Permanent Registration Act passed in a special session and approved June 6, 1936. Anyone failing to register is barred from voting at the next election. The commission announces certain days on which the registry books will be open for voters to register their names and places of residence. Rigid provisions are in this law to insure proper identification of the voter and to prevent illegal and fraudulent voting.

In the smaller cities and towns where all voters are more or less known to the election judges and clerks of the precincts, the registry lists are made up from the voting lists of the last election. Any changes caused by removals, etc., are made after the voters have had an opportunity to see whether their names are properly entered. By this method any voter may swear in his vote at the election if his name was omitted from the list.

Nominations. *Why Nominations Are Important.* Under our system of government the nomination of good candidates is

essential to the election of good officers. The nominations determine whose names shall appear upon the ballots at elections. Unless honest and capable candidates are nominated, the voters will have no choice on election day but to decide which of the undesirable nominees shall be chosen for office. The majority of our citizens do not seem to be aware of this truth. There are a number of different methods of nomination in use in Illinois, in all of which every voter has a right to participate.

The Party Caucus. A political party may call a caucus of its members for the purpose of making nominations for office. The call for the caucus must come from the regularly chosen party officers. The caucus must not be held at an unusual time or place. The names of the candidates selected are certified to the election officials and printed on the ballot.

The Primary Election. A primary election may be held under the state law which provides for primary elections and specifies the manner in which they are to be held. The primary election is a party election at which a party ticket is nominated by the members of each party. The regular election officers and polling places are used. Under the primary law a political party is any group that has cast at least five per cent of the vote at the last regular election.

To participate in the primary election, a voter must declare himself a member of a party. Voting in a party primary makes him a member of that party for two years, which means that he cannot vote in any other party's primary election for that length of time. He may, of course, vote for members of whatever party he pleases in all but the primary elections.

In a primary election each party ticket usually contains several candidates for each office. The names are put on the party ticket upon the presentation of a petition signed by a

sufficient number of qualified voters. The candidate receiving the highest number of votes for each office is declared the nominee of the party. The names of the nominees for each party are then certified to the county clerk or the election commissioners, who print them on the ballot for the regular election. The primary is at present the most widely used method of nominating candidates.

Nomination by Petition. Any qualified citizen may have his name placed on the regular election ballot by filing a petition signed by a sufficient number of qualified voters. The number of signatures varies with the importance of the office. For a state office the petition must carry the names of at least 25,000 qualified voters, properly distributed over the state. For local offices the number must be between five and eight per cent of the number of votes cast at the last preceding election in the district. These petitions are filed with the clerk of the district, who places the names on the ballot.

Nominating Conventions. Formerly party conventions named all the candidates for the offices of the city, county, and state governments. This method has some good points, but it is very easily misused in the interest of party machines. For this reason, the primary election has taken the place of the party nominating convention to a large extent.

Party conventions still name the candidates for a number of important offices, chiefly those in which the party interest is not strong. The delegates to the nominating conventions are chosen from the active workers in the party by the central committees. A central committee is organized in each county and important city. In each voting precinct the party elects a precinct chairman. These precinct chairmen compose the county or city central committee which meets to elect officers and direct the affairs of the party. These central committees

play a part in managing all party affairs in the county or city and serve as links with the state central organization.

All circuit and Supreme Court judges are nominated by party conventions held in their judicial districts. The nominees for positions as trustees of the University of Illinois are named in the state conventions of the parties. Each party also nominates at its state convention a list of presidential electors. However, the names of the electors are no longer printed on the voter's ticket.

General Elections. General elections to fill county, state, and national offices are held in November of the even-numbered years. In commission-governed counties the election district is fixed and the judges are appointed by the commissioners. In other counties the judges of the election are appointed by the county board of supervisors. Only two of the three judges may belong to the same party. Each township is an election precinct unless it contains more than eight hundred voters, when it is divided. In cities the board of election commissioners makes all arrangements for, and conducts, the election.

Manner of Holding Elections. Every precaution is taken to insure the voters the right to cast a secret ballot and to guard against the casting of false ballots. The ballots are printed and distributed to the precincts by the county clerk at county expense. The county board furnishes the ballot boxes, which the election officials are required to open and publicly examine before any ballots are cast. The polls are opened in the morning at a specified hour and are closed in the evening at a specified hour. The arrangement of the furniture in the polling place is prescribed in the election law. The judges must allow one, but not more than two, challengers from each political party to be present at the voting place. As

the voter enters, he may be challenged by party representatives if they doubt his right to vote.

How to Vote. The voter gives his name to a judge, who calls it out in a loud voice to the election clerks. The clerks look for the name on the registered voting list. If the name is found, it is checked; and the voter receives from the judge an initialed ballot, or ballots if more than one is to be cast. In cities operating under the 1936 Permanent Registration Act the voter must comply with strict rules governing elections. Identification is by registration cards.

After receiving his ballot, the voter retires alone (except in cases of illiteracy or blindness) to a curtained booth and marks his ballot. The candidates for office are listed on the ballot by parties under the names of the offices they wish to fill. At the head of each column is a circle, and at the left of the name of each candidate is a square. The party that won the last general election and is in power takes the first, or left-hand, column.

A voter wishing to vote a straight party ticket places an X in the circle by the party name. He thus casts a vote for every candidate of his party.

A voter wishing to *split* his ticket may do so by placing an X in the square before the name of each candidate of his choice, no matter in what party column the name is listed. A voter wishing to support his party generally, but desiring to *scratch* certain names, may do so by placing an X in the party circle and then placing an X in the square to the left of the candidates of other parties for whom he wishes to vote. The careful voter will give each candidate for whom he votes separate consideration and will vote for the individuals who he thinks will make the best officers.

Marking the ballot in any way so that it may be identified

spoils the ballot. Voting individually for more candidates than are to be elected to an office disqualifies the vote for that office only. Putting crosses in the circles above two or more party columns spoils the entire ballot. If a spoiled ballot is dropped into the ballot box, it is not counted. If a voter spoils his ballot, he may return it and receive another.

When he has finished voting, the voter folds his ballot so that the judge's initials will show. He then hands it to the judge, who puts it into the ballot box.

Absent Voting. If a qualified voter is unable to be present and vote in person, he is allowed to vote by affidavit. He secures the necessary blanks from the county clerk or from the election commissioners not more than thirty, nor less than five, days before the election. He fills them out before a notary public and mails them so that they will reach the election officials on or before the day of the election.

Counting the Votes. The votes are counted immediately after the polls are closed on election day. The judges and clerks must not stop their work until they have counted all the ballots. First they count the straight votes and give all the candidates of each party the number of votes to which they are entitled by the number of straight party ballots. Then they check the ballots on which individual names are marked. One reads from the ballot each name before which the voter has made a cross, and each of the clerks gives the candidate a mark. After all the ballots are counted, the total votes for the candidates are recorded.

The counted ballots are filed with the proper clerk. They must be preserved until the time for contesting the vote has elapsed. The results of the election are published in the newspapers by the county board and are certified to the proper state officials.

Test and Study Exercises

Aids to Learning

1. Observe that Illinois has civil service regulations designed to secure competent public officers in the minor government positions.

2. Note that primary elections insure to the voter a chance to help nominate the candidates of his party for public office.

3. Remember that the careful and intelligent voter considers each candidate individually and votes for the one he thinks will fill the position efficiently.

Test Exercises

On a separate sheet of paper write short answers to the following questions.

1. Why do civil service regulations improve the quality of the service given by minor public officials?

2. What are the four ways of nominating officials in Illinois?

3. Why is it important that all citizens vote in primary elections?

4. How may a voter who is not at his home on registration day register so that he may vote?

5. What are the qualifications for voting in Illinois?

6. In what election are the names of candidates of each party printed on separate ballots?

7. When will the next general election be held in Illinois?

8. Why is registration required?

9. What three types of errors in marking a ballot invalidate the ballot?

10. What five precautions are taken to prevent fraud at general elections?

Suggested Activities

1. Choose sides and debate the following question: Resolved, That city elections should be free from the influence of national political parties.

2. Get a specimen ballot and learn how to mark it correctly.

CHAPTER VI

PAYING THE COST OF GOVERNMENT

As You Read This Chapter

Find out why it is necessary for citizens to pay taxes and why our present system of taxation is unsatisfactory.

Securing Money for Government Expenses. All the units of state and local government do work that is of benefit to the people living under them. Most of the services they render are indispensable. To do this work for us, the government must have money. The officers must be paid, and all the running expenses of this big business must be met. This money must come from the people who receive the benefits of the government.

Taxation. The government is given a dependable source of income in the right to levy and collect taxes. In Illinois this power is limited as to the kinds of taxes that may be levied. The General Assembly grants the power of taxation, with limitations, to all local units of government. Counties are limited to a levy of seventy-five cents per hundred dollars of property. Cities, villages, schools, park districts, sanitary districts, and all other districts are strictly limited in the amount of taxes they may levy. There is no tax limit placed on the township. It is assumed that voters in town meeting will not tax themselves too heavily.

Borrowing Money and Issuing Bonds. Whenever the amounts of money raised by taxation are insufficient to pay the current bills, the state and its local units must resort to borrowing in some form. This may be done by issuing tax anticipation warrants, by borrowing at the banks, or by selling interest-bearing bonds.

Illinois made use of this power quite early in its history. Through badly managed banking ventures and poorly planned internal improvement projects it accumulated a state debt of $16,700,000. This was a heavy burden, but it was gradually paid off by 1880. The experience thus gained taught the people a valuable lesson. In the constitution of 1848 they forbade the borrowing of more than $50,000 by the state unless the bond issue was authorized by a vote of the people. This provision was retained in the present constitution (1870) with the amount allowed increased to $250,000.

Illinois remained free from debt from 1880 to 1922 except for $17,500 of the old debt that was never called for. During the following ten years the people saw fit to pass favorably on several large bond issues. As a result, the state indebtedness grew to $190,286,500 by 1930. Emergency relief bonds raised this amount to $219,282,411 on January 1, 1936.

Kinds of Taxes. Illinois has a variety of sources from which it draws its revenue. Since early days the state has placed its main dependence on a general property tax. As the expenses of government grew, the state added other sources to its system of taxation.

The Illinois Central Railroad Tax. When the Illinois Central Railroad was built, it received valuable assistance from the state. The United States government granted to the state large tracts of land lying along the line of the railway. These tracts were turned over to the railroad company. In return, the Illinois Central agreed to pay to the state seven per cent of the gross receipts of its charter lines. In 1928 the payment was $3,300,000; in 1935 it was about $1,600,000. This source of revenue is falling off because of the rapid decline of railroad business. No other taxes are paid by this company on the parts of its system that are known as charter lines. This plan

works a hardship on the taxpayers in the local tax units along these lines.

Franchise Taxes. Illinois has not developed this profitable source of revenue so much as have some other states. Illinois levies a tax of two per cent on insurance premiums collected by companies which are chartered outside the state. It also levies a tax on some corporations. The income from these sources varies somewhat with business conditions. At present the yield is about $10,000,000 annually.

The Inheritance Tax. In 1895 the General Assembly added an inheritance tax to our taxing system. This is a form of taxation that is growing in favor in many of our states. It is a tax on the right to inherit property. It is levied on all inherited property above certain small amounts known as exemptions. Exemptions are free from the payment of this tax. The exemptions vary in amount with the degree of relationship between the person or persons who inherit the property and the person from whom the inheritance comes. The rate is graduated. For a child, widow, father, or mother it ranges from two per cent on amounts up to $50,000 to fourteen per cent on amounts over $350,000. This tax is administered by the county judge in co-operation with the Attorney General. The highest yield in any one year was $15,666,000; the lowest $3,739,000.

Fees. The state has some income from fees charged for charters of incorporation and licenses to practice certain professions. There is also some interest earned on state money deposited in banks.

The *Motor Vehicle License Tax* has been in use since 1907 and is now our third largest source of revenue. In 1935 it amounted to $18,585,401. The rates were then slightly reduced to yield an estimated $17,000,000 annually. This money is

put into the Road Fund. About one-half is used to retire
outstanding road bonds; the other half pays for road repairs
and new construction.

The Gasoline Tax. Illinois was one of the last states in the
Union to avail itself of this profitable source of revenue. This
delay was due to the opposition of the oil companies and
the dissension among the friends of the tax. It was difficult to
agree on a rate per gallon, methods of collection, and a fair
division of the proceeds between the state and the locality in
which the tax was collected.

Next to the Sales Tax this is the largest source of state
revenue. The rate is three cents per gallon; the yield is about
$30,000,000 annually and is divided equally among the state,
the county, and the cities. The state uses its share for highways. The local governments use their shares partly for
streets and highways and partly for the payment of bonds
issued to meet the demands for relief during the depression.

Liquor Taxes. The state is now issuing licenses for the sale
of alcoholic liquors. This tax yields over $8,000,000 a year
and goes into the General Revenue Fund for general purposes.

The *Retailers' Occupation Tax* is commonly known as the
Sales Tax and is the largest producer of state revenue. It
is a "tax upon the business of selling tangible personal property
at retail." At present the rate is three per cent but is likely
to be changed frequently according to business conditions and
the changing revenue needs of the state. The amount yielded
is over $65,000,000. This tax was the chief reliance of Illinois
for funds to meet relief needs, to support schools, to pay pensions, to construct new buildings, and to pay interest on bonds
during the depression. As these needs will change, the uses
of the funds will no doubt be changed; or the tax may be
repealed.

The *Public Utility Tax* is the latest form of taxation to be adopted by Illinois. It was adopted to secure additional money to pay for unemployment relief. It imposes a three per cent tax upon the sales of utility companies. It is estimated that this tax will yield approximately $7,000,000 per year. It is paid into the Emergency Relief Fund.

After some months of operation the law was declared unconstitutional by the Supreme Court. However, the need for relief was still so great that the legislature passed another utility tax bill (March, 1937). In all probability Illinois will continue to use this dependable source of revenue.

The *General Property Tax* is the oldest part of our revenue system. It is a tax upon property of every kind. It is administered by locally elected officials. During the early years this tax worked well and supplied all the governments with needed revenue. In 1927 it yielded about $24,000,000 to the state and probably ten times this amount to the local governments. The general property tax is based on two assumptions: first, that the amount of property a person owns is a good measure of his ability to pay taxes; second, that all property can be found and assessed fairly. Both ideas were good when our state was young, but today they are questioned by most students of taxation.

During the depression, payments of property taxes fell into arrears. To meet this situation, the state adopted the forms of taxation described above, leaving the general property tax to the use of the local governments. It is today the chief source of tax income in all our local districts. In many, it is the only source.

Administration of the General Property Tax. There are four steps in the collection of property taxes in Illinois. The assessors place a value on all property, the boards of review

equalize all assessments, the county clerk computes the rate and extends the tax, and the collectors gather the money and turn it into the county treasury.

Assessing Property for Taxation. The work of assessing the property is done by the assessor in the township, by a special elected board of five assessors in Cook County and in St. Clair County, and by the treasurer or by assessors chosen by county boards in the commission-governed counties. The State Tax Commission makes the assessment of certain corporations and of the railroads and their rolling stock; the value of such property in each county is certified to the county clerk. Personal property is assessed where the owner resides, and real estate is assessed at its location.

The assessment of real estate is made every four years. Improvements are added whenever they are made. Personal property is assessed every year.

The assessor places a value on property. The law requires that this be the fair cash value of the property. However, assessed valuations are far below that figure. The assessors have a code of their own. They keep values down in their tax districts, as that will reduce the amount of money that the "home folks" must pay toward the support of the county and all governments above the assessment districts.

The value placed on the property becomes the basis for all taxes levied against it by all the taxing units in which it lies. To make this plain, let us suppose that the farm of Mr. X lies in School District Number 1, that it is a part of a drainage district, that it is a part of a community high-school district. Mr. X would then pay taxes on the assessed value of his farm to all those units, as well as to the township and the county.

Equalizing Assessed Values. The next step is the equaliza-

tion of assessments. This work is assigned to the board of review, which hears complaints and may make changes in the assessed valuation of the property concerned. It may raise or lower the whole assessment of any township to equalize the tax load upon all the townships in the county.

During recent years the boards of review have experienced some stormy sessions because of the many complaints against the new valuations placed on real estate by the assessors. Their work at present indicates that these boards may become a valuable part of our local taxing machinery.

Computing the Rate and Extending the Tax. As soon as the assessed valuations are definitely determined, the county clerk begins his tedious work of computing rates and extending the tax. He now has the value of all the property in each district. He also has the total amount of money to be raised as given him by the various township, city, and village clerks. He *computes* the rate by dividing the total tax levy by the assessed valuation. For instance, if the total township tax levy is $3,000 and the assessed valuation is $500,000, the tax rate is .006, which may be expressed as six mills on the dollar or as sixty cents per hundred dollars.

The same process is followed for every taxing district, including the county. When the work is completed, a list of rates is printed and sent to the taxpayers with the tax bill. Such a rate slip from a central Illinois city for the year 1930 is shown below. The figures in the right-hand column are the rates for the same district in 1936.

State	$ .39	$ .00
County	.35	.58
Sanitary dist.	.26	.48
Township	.03	.41

School	1.37½	1.73
Corporate	.66⅔	.67
Bonds	.11	.15
Library	.1083	.12
Streets, bridges	.12	.17
Public benefits	.10	.05
Parks	.06	.06
Garbage	.10	.10
Police pension	.01½	.02
Fire pension	.02	.02
Band	.04	.04
Total Tax Rate	$3.74½	$4.60

After the rates are computed, the county clerk *extends* the tax. *Extending* means multiplying the value of the property by the rate and placing the product in the tax books opposite the name of the taxpayer. For example, if a man living in the city with the $3.74½ tax rate has a house valued at $3,000 and personal property assessed at $500, his taxes would be $112.35 (30 × 3.745) on real property and $18.73 (5 × 3.745) on personal property. These amounts are entered in the tax books which are given to the tax collectors.

Collecting the Taxes. After a sufficient time has been given for the payment of taxes, the collector files with the county clerk a list of the persons who are delinquent. It is then the duty of the clerk to file a suit in the county court to obtain a judgment against this delinquent property. The property is then put up for sale. The owner must be notified. He may at any time before the sale pay the taxes plus the costs caused by his delinquency. If he allows the property to be sold, he may redeem it at any time within two years by paying the taxes, all the costs, and a high rate of interest on the money advanced by the purchaser. The county clerk signs the certifi-

cate of sale. If the property is not redeemed at the end of two years, a tax title may be given to the purchaser.

When the collection is completed, the county officers are ready to make division to the various units of government. The state's share (if any) is sent to Springfield; the rest is placed to the credit of the school boards, district commissioners, township supervisors, and other taxing bodies. All the local governments are thus enabled to pay their bills.

The Tax Situation Today. The building of a dependable system of taxation that distributes the cost of government justly is one of the first duties of every group that wishes to live and work together for the common good. In the discharge of this duty Illinois has been rather backward, at great cost to herself.

Why is the general property tax now being so bitterly attacked by some people and so stoutly defended by others? The reasons will probably become clear if we look at the differences in government costs and forms of wealth in early Illinois and in the state today.

When Illinois was young, the amount of work done by its state and county governments was small, and the cost was very low. The upkeep of a small Statehouse and the payment of a small salary list constituted the only expenses of state government. The total disbursements in 1820 were only $35,665. The first institution that increased the expenses of the state was the first penitentiary in 1830. The cost of government in the counties was also very low. The court costs were paid largely by the losers of the lawsuits. Sheriffs and clerks had fees which were paid by those to whom services were rendered.

At that time practically the only forms of wealth were land, animals, tools, house furnishings, and crude products such

as salt, provisions, liquor, peltry, etc. Few people had bank
accounts, bonds, stocks, costly jewelry, etc. Under these conditions tangible property was the only basis for taxation. The
local assessors had little trouble finding it or placing a fair
value upon it. It was natural for Illinois to adopt this form
of taxation; in fact, it is difficult to think of anything else
that could have been done during the early years.

Today the people are demanding services of their government that were undreamed of when the general property tax
was adopted. With the increase in the number of services,
there came a rise in the cost of materials, a rapid rise in
wages and salaries, and finally a demand that services be of
a higher quality. As a result, the cost of government now runs
high into the millions. This phenomenal rise in costs is well
shown by the following table on state income and expenditures.

YEAR	RECEIPTS	DISBURSEMENTS
1820	$ 53,362	$ 35,665
1850	402,179	640,287
1870	8,514,000	5,458,000
1890	10,421,000	9,815,000
1900	14,483,000	14,028,000
1910	21,612,000	21,017,000
1920	60,883,000	54,451,000
1929	110,732,000	112,123,000
1935	171,271,000	169,528,000

A similar development has taken place in local government.
Cities and towns were incorporated to enable these more
densely settled areas to collect the money needed to carry
on the necessary work. Drainage, park, high-school, health,
and other districts have come in rapid succession.

While the costs of government were rising, great changes
were taking place in the nature of personal property. In-

tangible wealth was increasing rapidly. *Intangible* property is property that cannot be easily seen or touched. Stocks, bonds, mortgages, and money in a bank are examples.

This intangible wealth has largely escaped taxation. It is difficult to assess these forms of property. Stocks and bonds are hard to find. Watches, jewelry, musical instruments, and works of art are not so easily listed at fair cash value as are farm animals, grain, machinery, etc. The result is that such property is often not listed at all.

In order to provide money for our government in the future, our taxing system must be thoroughly revised. Efforts to do so are now under way. It will be a difficult piece of work, as there are many conflicting interests dividing our city and rural sections. Fortunately this is not a new problem. Other states have had similar problems and have tried out many different solutions. Some states have classified property for taxation; some have tried new forms of taxation, such as income, inheritance, utility, franchise, gasoline, poll, sales, corporation, severance, and occupation taxes.

Our young citizens who are now in school should study the merits and faults of these new proposals. They should try to judge how they would work in their home counties. A certain kind of tax might be just, productive, and easily collected in the Minnesota iron mines, but it might not fit the conditions of the southern Illinois coal fields. Should this greatest of all our present civic problems be solved before our young citizens can play an active part in its solution, they will at least have helped in forming an intelligent public opinion. This is one of the most important services a citizen can render in a democracy.

Test and Study Exercises

Aids to Learning

1. Observe that the cost of government increases as the services rendered by the government increase.
2. Note that our state needs to reorganize its taxation system to provide sufficient revenue on the basis of ability to pay.

Test Exercises

1. The chief source of revenue of our local governments is _____ tax.
2. The _____ tax is the most productive tax in Illinois.
3. The gasoline tax is divided among _____, _____, and _____.
4. The Illinois Central pays _____ per cent of its gross receipts for its _____ lines.
5. The oldest form of taxation in Illinois is the _____ tax.
6. Illinois was free from debt from _____ to _____.
7. The most fluctuating tax in its yield is the _____ tax.

Suggested Activities

1. Make a list of the various purposes for which property is taxed in your community. Find out the tax for each purpose and the total tax rate.
2. Find out what proportion of taxes collected in your community is spent on education; road improvement; public welfare.

works for that flag. It represents every individual who has contributed to your country in the past. It will continue to represent in the future all those individuals who respect and honor it. By your work and life you help to make your flag, and thus your country, loved and respected the world over.

Patriotism. It is not enough to repeat a pledge or creed. You must believe in it and live up to its ideals. Merely to display the flag on national holidays or to salute it, is not patriotism. To become excited when the band goes marching by, playing the national anthem, is only a part of patriotism. To be patriotic, you must support your government by obeying the laws, whether you approve of them or not. Being patriotic only in times of excitement is like loving your family only when they provide you with a good time. The real test of your patriotism for country and affection for family comes in the everyday experiences you have, both pleasant and unpleasant.

In a democracy the majority rules. Your laws have become laws because the majority of your representatives' votes were cast for them. Therefore, you must accept them and uphold them. Patriotism means service. It means courage in the face of difficulties, loyalty to truth, sympathy with your fellow men, honor and generosity. These, with a love of country and a spirit of service, are most valuable.

Patriotism is not a wartime emotion. The true patriot hates war because war destroys the things for which he works. Unfortunately, there have been times in the past when war was resorted to, as the last available method of upholding the principles for which our forefathers stood and which had become a vital part of our national spirit.

To be a truly patriotic citizen, you must do your part in aiding your government to maintain and to promote its ideals. When these ideals are carried and developed far enough, perhaps we can do away with that barbaric method of settling disputes that we call war. You owe patriotism and daily service to your government in remembrance of your national heroes of all kinds who have died in its cause. You owe it to those who come after you to pass on to them a government at least as good, and if possible, even better than the one that was given to you.

Freedom. To say that the people in the United States have freedom does not mean that a person here can do as he pleases under any or all conditions. If this were true, many individuals would choose to do things that would interfere with the freedom of other people. Therefore, we must define real freedom as that condition which allows equal opportunities for all. As long as the laws are not violated, you are free to do as you desire. If you choose to violate rules, you are taking freedom away from someone else, and the law must take steps to enforce freedom for all.

So you can see that freedom involves self-control. You must be sure that you control yourself to the point of not interfering with other people's freedom. If you do not, your government will have to exercise control, or force you to abide by the law. It is the same in life as it is in games. There are rules about interfer-

ence with other players in all group games. These rules
are necessary. Some people pay too little attention to
the rights of others, and rules protect those who want
to see fair treatment for all.

No other country has sung with so much truth politically, "sweet land of liberty." Freedom of the
press and of speech are guaranteed by the Constitution. Liberal postal laws have favored extensive circulation of magazines and newspapers. Political discussion has always been unrestricted; the people's
government has not been afraid to let people know too
much. The very foundation of our country was built
upon freedom of religion. It was written into the Constitution that we should always be free to worship as
we choose.

The march of civilization has been steadily in the
direction of universal education and freedom of discussion, and the United States has taken a leading
place in this advance. Universal, free, public education has been the ideal in the United States. All three
kinds of government which Americans conduct for
themselves—national, state, and local—are concerned
with the promotion of free education. This education
is for all, irrespective of wealth, race, sex, nationality,
or any other mark of difference.

The cost of public education in America is considerable, requiring at least one-third to one-half of all
money raised by local taxation. Elementary schools
are free today to nearly all citizens in European countries, but nowhere outside of the United States has the
attempt been made to furnish free high-school and

college education to everyone. "It costs too much," or "We should have too many educated people," other countries seem to say. We think such ideas wrong as we have shown by our own school system.

Guaranty of Life. The rights of "life, liberty, and the pursuit of happiness" were guaranteed to all citizens by the Declaration of Independence, and have been upheld ever since by the Constitution. To enjoy these rights is a just demand and is a rightful expectation of every citizen. To guarantee these rights is the chief duty of every government.

The Constitution of the United States guarantees the right of protection of life, liberty, and property to its law-abiding citizens. The government provides this protection through the police, the state militia, and the armed forces of the nation. Whether at home or abroad, citizens can usually expect protection from the government as long as they do not endanger themselves with unwise, illegal, or unreasonable acts. Of course, one guilty of crime may forfeit all claim to protection. The government may take away his property, put him in prison, and even destroy his life, if the courts so decide. On the other hand, many policemen have risked and lost their own lives by protecting a man accused of crime from the fury of the mob until he has had a fair trial.

The right to personal security means that you have protection from bodily harm, burglary, death, and even threatening statements. In the case where bodily harm is threatened, you have the right of self-defense. In the case of burglary (breaking into a house), the occupant of the house is legally justified in defending his family and himself. If anyone threatens harm or injury, you may have such a person brought before a magistrate to be bound with sureties[1] to remain within the law.

Guaranty of Liberty. Personal liberty is a most valuable right exercised by the freeman of today and is in startling contrast to the slavery permitted in past ages. You may move about from place to place without hindrance. You may establish a residence wherever you choose, and engage in whatever lawful occupation you select. You may accumulate wealth honestly and own property. You can defend yourself against unjust imprisonment by appeal to the court through the use of a writ of *habeas corpus*. (See page 240.)

One of the greatest personal liberties of a citizen of the United States is that of religious freedom. The Constitution of the United States declared that citizens should be free to worship God according to their own consciences. Thus the United States has always been a nation in which the people may enjoy freedom in religious matters. Religious liberty allows you to choose your own church and to pay toward its support as you see fit.

Freedom of speech means that as a citizen you are free to speak and write upon any subject as long as you do not violate the laws of libel[2] or slander[3]. The

[1] sureties. Bonds or guaranties for the performance of some act.
[2] libel. An unjust publication exposing another to public contempt.
[3] slander. A report circulated with malice, to injure another's reputation.

government defends your reputation as well as your property.

Freedom of press means that as a citizen you are free to have your views and sentiments printed and published as long as the laws are not violated. A person who publishes false and malicious statements about his neighbor commits the crime of libel, for which he may be punished by the government.

Freedom of assembly means that as citizens you are free to assemble and to discuss freely and fully any questions or issues worthy of discussion, as long as the public meetings are conducted in an orderly manner and without lawlessness.

Freedom of petition means that as a citizen you are free to express your desires and wants to any officer of the government. If you think a certain law should be passed, or repealed, you may ask your representative to try to accomplish either of these acts.

Guaranty of the Pursuit of Happiness. Perhaps the highest ambition you can have in life is to reach the goal of happiness. Happiness does not consist of riches and luxuries obtained at any price, but rather of a full appreciation and enjoyment of all that is beautiful and just—a full and well-rounded life.

One of the ways to bring about happiness is to have a permanent place to dwell and call your own—a home. That which makes a home more peaceful is its security against fire, burglary, and seizure. This is furnished you by your government.

Another way to bring about happiness is to have all people certain that justice will be given them by the government. This is guaranteed in the Constitution of the United States by a provision to "establish justice," which has been carried out by the judicial system. It is guaranteed that you will not "be deprived of life, liberty, or property, without due process of law."

Political Privileges. As a rule, a citizen over twenty-one years of age may vote and hold office. These two privileges are known as political privileges. Citizenship means membership in a governmental organization. The organization may be large or small. For our discussion here, we are thinking of citizenship as membership in an organization such as the city, county, state, or nation. Citizenship in this American nation is granted to a person who was born here and who has continued to live here even though his parents are of foreign birth. It is also granted to persons born of American parents living abroad, provided they return later to live in the United States. If they do not, the child must make his own choice when he becomes of age as to the country of which he desires to become a citizen.

Naturalization grants citizenship to those persons born in other countries who want to become citizens. There have been cases when the United States has extended citizenship to a large group of people in a body upon the annexation of a territory to our nation. This procedure was followed with the people of the Louisiana Territory and those of Texas, Alaska, and Hawaii. However, the people of the Philippines were not granted citizenship. Indians born within the

United States were admitted to the citizenship in 1924.

Exercise of the duty of voting is called suffrage. Voters are called *electors* because they elect officers to represent them. Each state regulates the voting laws for the citizens within its own state. There are two principle restrictions with regard to voting. These are age and residence. Any citizen with good character and right mind may vote providing he or she is at least twenty-one years of age and providing he or she has lived the required time in the city, county, and state in which he or she resides. The length of time of residence required for voting varies from six months to two years in the various states and from ten days to twelve months in the county or city.

All states require the voter to be a citizen of the United States, and some of them require the voter to have paid a tax. In some cases this is a poll tax;[4] in others it is a general property tax. However, the property and taxpaying qualifications have, for the most part, been abandoned. Some states have set up the ability to read and write as a qualification. Undoubtedly the ability to read is necessary before problems of government can be understood by the voter. There can be no intelligent voting when one cannot read or write. More states are coming to realize this fact. A detailed account of these requirements for voting will be found in the appendix, page 421. The illustration on page 246 shows the ballot form in general use in one of the states.

[4] **poll tax.** A uniform tax of a given amount for each person over a given age.

Citizens Not All Voters. While all people born in the United States, or naturalized here, are citizens, only about sixty per cent of the population of the United States are eligible to vote, and less than two-thirds of these actually choose to vote at any election. Boys and girls under twenty-one years of age are not entitled to vote because they are not mature enough

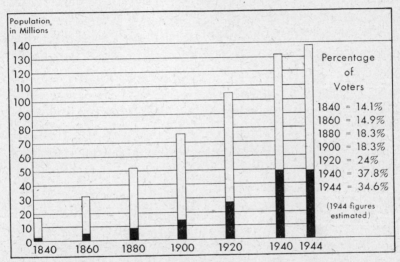

Percentage of the Population Voting at Certain Elections

in judgment and experience to share in government regulations. Others not entitled to vote are aliens, prisoners, and in some states, those people in institutions supported by the local, state, or national government. It is very unfortunate that so many qualified citizens fail to exercise this most important privilege. The foregoing graph will show the percentage

of the total population that actually voted at several
of the presidential elections.

The voters in a democracy control and direct the
government affairs. They do this by electing representatives, who in turn appoint others to help carry
out the wishes of the people. The officials selected by
the people usually determine the policy and plan its
execution, while minor officials, appointed by them,
carry out the plans and do the actual work.

There are only two offices in the United States that
a naturalized citizen may not hold: the Presidency
and the Vice-Presidency of the United States. Any
other office may be held by any citizen in good standing if his other qualifications are satisfactory, whether
he was born in this country or was naturalized.

Your Duties and Obligations. Your first duty as a
citizen is to know your country and its laws. This does
not mean that you should learn every law in detail;
that would be impossible. It does mean, however, that
you should know the spirit of the laws in order that
you may have a definite idea of right and wrong. With
this knowledge you will be able to conduct yourself
properly.

In order to respect the government of your country,
you must know what that government expects of you.
In a democratic government such as ours, you are
expected to keep informed on public questions and
issues so that you can act intelligently when called
upon to do so. You must know the needs of your
community and of your fellow men so that you may
serve them wisely and sincerely. You should seek with

an open mind to find out what is happening today, and work for whatever will do the greatest good to the greatest number of people.

Co-operation. If you expect your government to guarantee life, liberty, and the pursuit of happiness, you must be willing to co-operate with your government. To know the law is not enough. You must be willing to obey the law. Laws are not passed for the purpose of withholding your privileges; they are made in order that your actions may be guided into the right channels, rather than the wrong ones.

If you are tempted to overlook some rule or regulation, think of your fellow citizen. Is it fair to him for you to speed recklessly down the highway? Is it fair to him for you to drive through an intersection without stopping when there is no policeman near by, even though the traffic signal tells you to stop? Our busy life today demands that we work together. It is to your benefit to co-operate with your fellow citizen in obeying the laws of your nation.

Helping Others to Obey the Law. Have you ever tried to influence someone to do the right thing, when the wrong thing was about to be done? Did you ever try to show a boy or girl who was about to stay away from school his responsibility for being in school? Did you ever help another student resist the temptation to take something that did not belong to him? Your actions in such a situation might easily have shown the other pupil the responsibility of a citizen's playing fair and square in all matters, and the seriousness of even minor dishonest acts. It is surprising, sometimes, how a few good words may change a person's outlook on life, encourage him, and give him more self-respect.

Love and Honor for Your Country. Singing our national anthem, studying the Constitution, saluting the flag—all these may show love and honor paid to our nation if they are carried out with sincerity; but after all they are only outward expressions. To honor your nation truly and to show your love for her ideals, you must prove your loyalty to those ideals. Daily attention turned to the ordinary duties of citizenship are worth far more than applause at the display of the nation's military prowess.

Young citizens have as much opportunity to prove their loyalty as do the older ones. Your state and community have invested on the average between eight hundred and a thousand dollars on each pupil who completes a twelve-year course in the public schools. This expense is paid in order that you may be better prepared to serve your nation when you are out of school. You can show your loyalty by doing your best in school in order that you may be prepared to face the demands that the future will make of you.

Test and Study Exercises

Aids to Learning.

1. Remember that patriotism is belief in your country, living up to its ideals, supporting it at all cost, and serving it in every way.

2. Note that considerably less than half of the citizens of the United States actually vote at an election.

3. It is important to know that the guaranty of life, liberty, and the pursuit of happiness, made in the Declaration of Independence, has been upheld by the Constitution of the United States.

Test Exercises.

1. What are some of the qualities you should look for in considering a candidate for an important office?

2. What are the ways in which a patriotic citizen can be distinguished from one who is not patriotic?

3. Summarize the particular liberties which you enjoy in our country. Which of these are not available to boys and girls in countries under a dictatorship?

4. What is the meaning of the stars and the stripes in our national flag?

5. Why are all citizens not voters? Why do not all voters actually take part in every election?

6. (*a*) What rights are guaranteed to citizens by the Declaration of Independence? (*b*) What do you understand each of these rights to mean?

7. Are you free to write as you please about any citizen? How far may you go?

8. Are the political privileges of citizenship eagerly sought by most citizens?

9. To what extent must every citizen know the law to protect his own rights?

10. Why is it proper for a driver to stop his car at a stop sign at night when there is no traffic in either direction?

11. What qualifications should a state require to secure the best type of electors among its citizens?

12. What is the meaning of the sentence, "freedom ends where license begins"?

Suggested Activities.

1. Look up the qualifications for voting in your state: Are there requirements regarding payment of taxes; length of residence in the state, county, or town; educational qualifications; registration; age?.

2. Look up the meaning of the Latin motto—"ignorantia legis non excusat"—and explain its significance.

3. With the help of your librarian, locate articles in recent magazines describing the condition of school children in Germany, Italy, and Russia today. What opportunities do you possess which are now denied to them?

4. *Group Activity:* The teacher may select several pupils to discuss the question as to whether the intelligent nonvoter or the corrupt politician is the better citizen.

5. *Group Activity:* The teacher may appoint a committee to inquire of your local health department regarding the laws for vaccination, quarantine, and fumigation as preventive health measures. Do these interfere with your rights as citizens?

CHAPTER XX

YOUR LOCAL GOVERNMENTS

PREPARATORY NOTE: The most important part of our study of good citizenship is the government itself—local, state, and national. Your local government is based upon that which your forefathers had in Europe centuries ago. Its divisions and its officials concern all of us. We see its mistakes. We should also see how to correct these errors so that we shall have the best possible local government, such as this chapter describes.

Local Control. Have you ever seen the little mechanical device on a steam engine called the "governor"? It controls the speed of the engine and causes it to run regularly. You may have heard of a similar device which is placed on an automobile so that the car will not run more than a certain number of miles per hour. The word governor means control; and local government means local control or the control of the locality. Local governments are county, town, county-township, city, village, and some others such as school-district or road-district governments.

Colonial Government. Long before the English colonies were established, local governments of various kinds had been developed in England. The largest local government in England was the *shire*. Probably

281

the next in importance was the *borough,* or town. In addition, in some places, there was a different kind of local government called the *manor*.

Thus the people who came to America to settle were already familiar with several types of local government and when there appeared need for working together for any purpose, they drew upon their past experience in England and organized the kind of local government that seemed to fit their needs best.

Because the Pilgrims on board the Mayflower found that their ship had reached America far to the north of the place granted to them by the Virginia Company, they called a meeting and drew up a compact which made provisions for their government. In this company, each person agreed to obey the laws of the local government that was to be organized.

Establishment of Towns. When the Pilgrims landed they established towns similar to those they had known in England. By 1643 the towns in Plymouth Colony had increased to ten. In Massachusetts Bay Colony there were eight towns established by the end of 1630. In these New England towns all matters of importance were handled by the town governments. Churches were established and maintained in the towns. Soon schools were established in each Massachusetts town. As soon as a few towns were established both in the Plymouth and in the Massachusetts Bay Colonies, delegates were elected in each town to attend a colonial assembly. The assembly with the governor formed the colonial governments. The local town governments in New England levied taxes, passed laws regulating

Signing the Mayflower Compact

the conduct of the citizens of the town, and provided courts for enforcing the laws.

Establishment of Counties. In the colony of Virginia there were few towns of any size. The people there lived on large plantations. A number of these plantations in the same locality associated together for the establishment of such local government as was needed. These large communities were much like the shires of England but they came to be called *counties*. In each county several justices of the peace were provided. These justices held regular meetings called the county court and not only tried cases of law violation but transacted other local business for the county. Thus there were established two kinds of local government in America: (1) town government in the New England towns, and (2) county government in Virginia. In both cases these governments were established under the authority of the governors of the colonies. In the New England towns the officials were elected by the colonists; in Virginia they were selected by the stockholders of the London Company.

Before the United States became a nation, all of the thirteen colonies had local governments like those of the town-government plan of the New England towns, or those of the county-government plan of Virginia, or a combination of the two types.

State Control. When the colonies declared their independence of Great Britain in 1776, the Continental Congress recommended that each of the colonies adopt a constitution to take the place of the charters or the royal authority of the King under which they had been governed. In these constitutions, which declared that the people of the state were sovereign instead of the King of England, provisions were made for local governments such as had existed.

As new states were formed and admitted into the Union, provisions were made for local governments. In some cases the constitution contained detailed outlines of the local governments, but in others the legislature was given authority to create any local governments needed. Thus all the states of the country now have local governments existing under either constitutional or legislative state authority.

You have seen that under modern conditions people work together more than they formerly did. A great deal of this co-operative work is carried on through local governments. School districts, road districts, and drainage districts are examples of local governments that have a special kind of work to do.

The County. At the present time, local governments may be classified as follows: the county, the town, the county-township, and the municipality consisting of the village, borough, town, or city.

In general, the county government is the most important of local governments. There are more than three thousand counties in the United States. They vary greatly in size, population, and importance. County governments are found in every state, except in Louisiana where they are called parishes. Counties vary in size from over twenty-two thousand square miles for San Bernardino County, California, to twenty-two square miles for New York County, New

York. In population they range from about two hundred in Loving County, Texas, to about four million in Cook County, Illinois. Even in the same state the counties differ in size. Counties five times the size of another county in the same state are not uncommon. The number of counties in a state run from three in Delaware to two hundred fifty-four in Texas.

There are three types of counties: the southern type which performs most of the functions of local government; the New England type which is limited largely to judicial work; and the county of the middle states in which the functions of local government are not so important as in the South, but more important than in New England. In New England most of the local government is in the hands of the towns. In the middle states it is divided between the counties and the townships. This accounts for the fact that counties of other states are less important than those in the South.

The county, except in New England, has two distinct functions. (1) The county serves as an agent of the state for the administration of state law, for the assessing of property, and for the collection of taxes. (2) A more important function of the county is to serve as a unit for local government.

In most states the county is the unit for representation in the lower house of the state legislature. Ordinarily it serves as the basic unit in the organization of political parties. It usually takes care of the poor and unfortunate and performs the necessary charitable and welfare activities. It keeps the necessary records such as legal documents and marriage, birth, and death statistics. In many states the county is important in the administration of the schools, the building of roads and bridges, and the support of public libraries.

County Government. In the early settlement of the colonies, the county in the South was the unit for the administration of justice through the courts. The local judicial officer was the *justice of the peace.* There were several of these throughout the county in convenient places. At certain times all the justices of a county met at some central point, called the county seat, and held court for the trial of important cases. In addition to holding court, the justices of the peace constituted a board for governing the county. Thus in the early southern states the governing board was called the *county court.*

In some of the states settled later by settlers from Virginia and the older southern states the governing board was a small commission. However, it retained the name county court and the individual members were called judges, although the board to which they belonged did not have the functions of a court.

Today in Pennsylvania the county is governed by the *county commissioners* elected at large from the county. This commissioner system has spread westward to many of the states in the central part of the country, as Ohio, Indiana, Illinois, Missouri, Kansas, and others. However, in Missouri the three commissioners are called judges. Thus Missouri gets its system of county government from Pennsylvania, but the name for the governing body comes from Virginia.

In New York the early law provided that a commissioner be elected from each township to be a member of the *county board*. Thus the county board consisted of as many commissioners as there were townships in the county. This New York type of government spread westward to many of the northern states of the country. Michigan, Wisconsin, Minnesota, and other states are examples of the New York system of county government.

Besides the county board, which supervises the official work of the county and under the state law acts as both a lawmaking and a law-enforcing body for the county, there are two other groups of officers. There are six or more elective officers in every county in the country. In addition to the elective officers the county board appoints such officers as the law of the state may provide. In recent years the increase in the amount of government work of all kinds has caused a large increase in the number of appointive officers in most counties.

The work of the county board depends upon the state law governing counties. Therefore it varies in the different states. But in general the county board fixes the rate of taxation; levies taxes; appropriates the county money; authorizes county loans; sees that assessments are fair and equal; constructs and maintains public works such as highways, bridges, and public buildings; and issues warrants[1] for the county

---

[1] **warrants.** Orders which authorize the payment of money.

expenses. It also cares for the poor and in some cases the insane; in many cases it has charge of county, state, and national elections; it appoints many minor county officials; and it has a great many other duties.

The county officials having to do with the courts are the *sheriff,* the *prosecuting attorney,* the *coroner,*[2] and the clerk of the court. In some cases a *judge* of the court is elected by the people of the district which he serves. In addition to the officials named above the people of the county usually elect a *county clerk, recorder,*[3] *auditor,*[4] *treasurer, assessor, superintendent of public schools,* and occasionally other officials.

In most counties the county board appoints the minor officials. At times even some of the officials mentioned above are appointed. The officials whose duties require professional training such as the *county physician* and the *county engineer* are, as a rule, appointed. When new work is given the county, the officials required for the extra work are usually appointed. The tendency at the present time seems to be toward appointing county officials.

Weaknesses of County Government. The importance of county government, the fact that it directly affects practically every American citizen, the heavy expenses connected with it, and the taxation made necessary to support the county government and its many officials make it a major problem that must be dealt with in the near future. There are a number of weaknesses in our present system of county gov-

---

[2] **coroner.** An official who inquires into accidental deaths.
[3] **recorder.** An official who keeps the official copy of transactions.
[4] **auditor.** An official who examines the public accounts.

ernment. In the first place, it is very expensive and often wasteful. In some cases men are elected at high salaries to offices in which all the work is done by a few clerks getting very low pay.

In the second place, corrupt courthouse groups develop in many county seats. The members of these groups, by shrewd political activity, keep themselves and their friends in profitable offices for years, to the injury of the good government of the county. In some cases open corruption in contracts and in the purchase of supplies brings large profits to private individuals. Such groups often develop great political power and control all the work of the county.

In the third place, there are altogether too many counties. County government existed long before modern methods of travel and communication. Distances that took a long time to cover now take a short time. The size of many counties was determined by the distance one could travel in one day to the court held at the county seat, which was usually near the center of the county. Now that same distance can usually be traveled in an automobile or train in a very short time. Yet counties have changed in government but little and not at all in size. It has been stated that one-fourth the number of counties we now have would be ample for all needs of local government. But so many people have a fixed interest in the form of county government that it will probably be difficult to reduce the number of counties.

The New England Town. The word *town* has different meanings in different sections of the country.

In New England it is the term used to denote the unit of local government which includes both village and country population. In some sections it is used in the sense of township, denoting an area six miles square, which is the unit of our land survey system. In other places a town is a village or a community larger than a village and smaller than a city. In still other places there is a unit of local government known as a municipal township to distinguish it from the township of the land survey system. In this section we shall discuss the New England town which is the unit of local government in those states.

The town is frequently irregular in outline and varies greatly in size and population. Some towns are small rural settlements probably a square mile or even less in area and have a population fewer than one hundred. Others are forty or more square miles in area with a population running well up into the thousands.

The work done by the New England town government is very much the same as that done by the counties of the South and West. It consists of the organization and support of the public schools, the construction and maintenance of the public roads, and the care of the poor. In the larger and more populous towns, the paving of streets, police and fire protection, and other work which cities find necessary, are carried on by the town government. The town, like the county in other states, is an agent of the state for assessing property, collecting taxes, and administering and enforcing state law. The government of the town consists of the town meeting and the selectmen elected by the town meeting.

The *town meeting* is the legislative and policy-forming part of the town government. It is composed of all those residing in the town and qualified to vote for state officials. It meets annually and may be called at any time by the selectmen. The duties of the town

A New England Town Meeting in Colonial Times

meeting include the election of selectmen and other officers, the passing of laws or ordinances, the voting of tax levies or bond issues,[5] and the approval of the reports of officials and committees. Any citizen may speak, propose measures, ask questions, and criticize the officials. The New England town meeting is said to be the best example of pure democracy that has ever existed.

The most important officers of the town are the

[5] **bond issues.** Interest-bearing certificates authorized by a public or private body for the purpose of borrowing money.

selectmen. They number from three to nine, and form a governing board for the town. They issue calls for the town meetings, both regular and special, select the names for the jury, build and repair roads and streets, have control of the town property, conduct elections, appoint minor officials and do all the things necessary in the government of the town that are not otherwise provided for.

In addition to the selectmen the town meeting also elects a number of other officers whose titles indicate their official duties. These other elective officers usually include the clerk, assessor, treasurer, constable, justices of the peace, the school committee, and many minor officials.

In the developments of modern life many conditions make it more and more difficult for local government by town meeting to work well. Industrial development has caused factories to be located in many towns. A factory introduces two new elements into the population of a town—the factory owners or managers, and the factory laborers. Neither of these groups has a great deal in common with the rural people who form the basis of the population. With the coming of a factory, sometimes foreign people come in who are not familiar with democracy and know nothing of the duties of a citizen of a democratic town. With the increasing population the caucus[6] has developed in many towns. Slates, or lists of political candidates, are prepared and pushed through with little consideration.

[6] **caucus.** A meeting of the leaders of a party or faction to decide on their policies or candidates for office.

Finally the changes of modern society have made it cheaper and better to do the work of government in larger units than the town. Road building will illustrate this fact. Fifty years ago roads were built with picks and shovels and horse-drawn plows and scrapers. The tools were cheap and a small town of five to twenty square miles could own its own road tools and keep them in use most of the time. Now roads are built by high-powered motorized road machinery which costs large sums of money. No small town can afford to buy expensive tractors, graders, and other modern machines such as those shown in the photograph of modern road-building machinery on page 315. So road building today is frequently controlled by larger units of government. Private contractors, who make this their business, do the actual work. For these various reasons the trends of our time seem to be definitely against the successful operation of small units of government.

The County-Township. In the growth of the great Middle West, there has developed a kind of local government sometimes called the county-township. In this type there is a division of local government between the county and the township. There is a town meeting in the township which elects the commissioners or members of the township board. Such local work as assessing property, collecting taxes, and managing the school is done by the township government. In some cases the township is the unit of representation for the county board.

In some of the states, government by townships may

be adopted or discontinued by a majority of the voters of the county. The county-township type is somewhat confusing as there is frequently divided responsibility. But where township organization is adopted it is very seldom discontinued.

The Municipality. The word municipality comes from the Latin *municipium* which means "a free town having the right of a Roman citizenship, but governed by its own laws." Today the word urban, from the Latin *urbs* meaning city, refers to city life, especially in speaking of something that is different from country or rural life. The word city is used in a general sense to refer to a comparatively small area with definite boundaries and having a large number of inhabitants. In some states the words village and town are also used to refer to cities with but few inhabitants.

As you have already learned, cities have grown rapidly in recent years. The problems which arose as a result of city growth and the crowding of people together required solution. The local county and township governments could not furnish the services needed in the growing villages, towns, and cities. The sheriff and constables were not able to furnish protection for life and property under the new conditions. There were no agencies for building sidewalks, fighting fire, or maintaining streets in the rural local government. The new needs of these growing communities led the state to provide for local village, borough, town, and city government. The term municipal government is usually applied to such local governments.

When people move into a community and crowd

together around such necessary institutions as a school,
a church, a store, a garage, and a filling station, there
soon arises the need for working together in order to
do things that are of benefit to everyone in the growing community. The laws are different in the various
states, but they are alike in many ways. The new
community is given certain definite boundaries. It
is given a name and is usually known as a *village,
borough,*[7] *town,* or *city.* A certain population is required for such a municipal incorporation[8] but this
varies greatly in the different states. The name given
to the incorporated place also varies. For example,
all places having fewer than five hundred people are
called villages in Missouri. In Kansas, places of two
hundred or more may become cities. In a number of
states a place must have ten thousand or more inhabitants to become a city. In most of these states, places
may become incorporated as villages, boroughs, or
towns.

The municipal government in an incorporated place
provides for officers and agencies to do the work and
to render the services made necessary by people living
close together in a small community. The chief officer
is called the *mayor,* or sometimes the *president.* There
is usually a city council composed of representatives
elected from sub-divisions called *wards.* The Council
passes local laws usually called *ordinances,* provides
for necessary minor officials, levies taxes within the

---

[7] **borough.** A form of municipal corporation, used in several states, corresponding to the incorporated town or village.

[8] **incorporation.** A legal body constituting a corporation recognized by
law.

limits of taxation provided by the state, and in general determines policies of the village or town government. Usually the mayor appoints minor officers. In some places he is the judge of the village court, and is frequently the leading man of the village, town, or city.

Cities have always been a measure of civilization. Trade, the use of money, banking, and manufacturing all grew up with cities. In each of the great ancient empires some great city like Nineveh, Babylon, or Athens was the center. When the city fell or was captured, the empire came to an end. The Roman Empire, which developed the greatest civilization of antiquity, was an empire of city life. Everything of importance was done near the cities. The agricultural products necessary for city life were raised by slave labor. The cities had great buildings, theaters, crowds of unemployed, political machines, vice and crime, and relief rolls much as the cities of our modern civilization have. With the gradual decline of the cities both the Roman Empire and ancient civilization also declined. The following Dark Ages of superstition and ignorance had only a few small cities. With the gradual development of modern civilization cities have grown and increased in number until we now have more large cities than the world ever had before.

Will our cities continue to grow? Will they enforce higher standards of living? Will they clean up the slums and put the racketeers[9] and criminals behind

---

[9] **racketeers.** Those who secure money or advantages by threats of violence or by unlawful interference with business.

the bars? Will they destroy the political bosses and
machines that scoff and mock at the honesty of elections, and a fair ballot? Will they be able to solve the
many problems that appear as the result of crowding
great numbers of people and vast masses of wealth
into our cities? The answer to these questions will
determine whether our cities will decline and decay,
abandoning our wonderful civilization for another
period of dark ages, or whether they will advance to
still higher standards of living where justice will be
maintained and every man will get his fair share of
the products of our modern civilization.

Forms of Municipal Government. On the basis of
form, municipal government in this country may be
divided into three classes: that having the mayor,
sometimes called the mayor-council type; that having
the commission type; and that having the council-
manager type.

The *mayor-council type of city government* is an
imitation of our national and state governments and
like them is based on the theory of the separation of
powers. In a way the mayor corresponds to the governor, or the president, and is the chief executive of
the city. Likewise the council corresponds to congress
or the state legislature and is the lawmaking body
for the city.

The *mayor* is elected by the people. His term is
usually two years but in some cases it is one year and
in others as much as four years. His salary ranges
from very little to as much as twenty-five thousand
dollars a year in New York City. He is the chief

executive of such cities and is for the most part independent of the control of the council.

The *council* is usually a body of one house, although a few cities still retain the two houses. The councilmen are elected by the people, usually by wards or precincts, for a term varying from one to four years. Councils range in size from four or five members in small cities to fifty in Chicago and seventy-one in New York.

The city government has only such powers as are granted to it by the state constitution, the state law, or the charter which some states permit cities to adopt. These powers are exercised by the city council through ordinances or laws which it passes. Ordinances may be divided into two classes: contract ordinances by which the city grants franchises or rights to use public property to public utility corporations such as telephone, light, water, or street railway companies; and legislative ordinances which relate to the organization of the city government, to health, public safety, traffic, public improvements, and other important matters.

The *commission type of municipal government* originated in Galveston, Texas, after the very destructive tidal wave of 1900 had killed six thousand people and caused immense property losses. That city, like so many other cities, had been very poorly governed by the mayor-council plan and was heavily in debt. At a meeting of the leading citizens it was decided to adopt a simpler and more efficient form of government. Having secured the permission of the legislature of the state, they planned a government for the city

much as the stockholders of a company plan a governing body for the business of the company. Stockholders usually elect a board of directors. Galveston
elected five men and called them *commissioners*. These
five, one of whom was called the mayor, divided the
work of governing the city into five departments and
each commissioner took a department and became
responsible for the good government of his department. Each commissioner was responsible to the commission as a whole. The change that took place in
Galveston was remarkable. The debt was soon paid
off and a sea wall was built to protect the city from
tidal waves in the future. The plan worked so well
that it was not long before other cities were adopting
it. Many states gave their cities the privilege of adopting the commission plan if they desired to do so.
About one-sixth of the larger cities of the country
now have the commission form of government.

The general features of the commission plan as
now used are as follows: First, the legislative and
executive powers of city government are exercised by
a commission of from three to seven men elected by
the qualified voters of the city. Second, the work of
the city government is divided into as many departments as there are commissioners, and each commissioner is made responsible for the work of his department. Third, the commissioners are elected for a
definite term, usually four years; they receive a salary
of from a few hundred dollars to seventy-five hundred
dollars according to the size of the city and the work
of the commission. One commissioner is designated

mayor and presides at meetings of the commission and represents the city at public functions. Fourth, many cities having the commission form of government provide for the initiative[10] and referendum[11] of ordinances and the recall[12] of commissioners. Fifth, the tendency is toward nonpartisan primaries[13] and elections and the increased use of the merit system in the civil service of the city.

About thirty years ago, a few years after the value of the commission plan had been demonstrated, some cities tried a further adaptation of the methods of a large corporation. They elected a council of from three to seventeen men who were given the important duty of selecting a manager to carry on the business of the city, just as the stockholders of a company select the manager to carry on the business of the company. The manager is paid a salary from twelve hundred dollars to as high as twenty-five thousand, as in Cincinnati, and is the chief executive officer to carry on the business of the city. About four hundred seventy-five cities, in the class over one thousand population, now have this *council-manager form of government*. About one fourth of all the cities with more than fifty thousand population are included in this number.

In most council-manager cities the council provides for a civil service commission which gives examina-.

[10] **initiative.** A plan by which a small percentage of voters may present a law for acceptance or rejection by all the voters.
[11] **referendum.** A plan by which laws may be referred to popular vote for approval or rejection.
[12] **recall.** The right of voters to remove unsatisfactory officials.
[13] **primaries.** Preliminary elections to select candidates for final elections.

tions for the city service. A list of persons qualified by training, ability, and experience for the various types of work is kept from which the manager may find suitable persons to employ. The person employed for the city manager need not be a citizen of the city employing him. Frequently a city manager who has been very successful in a small city is employed in a larger city at a marked increase in salary. The council-manager type of government has proven to be the least expensive of the three types.

Important features of the council-manager plan are as follows: First, all governmental power of the city is placed in the hands of a small body of men, a council, or a commission, elected by the people. Second, the administrative power is exercised by a *city manager* appointed by the council. All department heads and subordinate employees are appointed by the manager. This manager is subject to the council and may be discharged by it for certain reasons. Third, the council-manager plan causes a short non-partisan ballot. Only the few men serving on the council are voted for at the polls.

Problems of Local Government. In summary of some of the topics discussed in previous chapters let us list here a few of the important tasks of city government usually handled by different boards or departments.

Perhaps the most important problem of a city of any size is maintaining good health. The work of the *health department* is largely preventive. Quarantine of contagious diseases, inspection of foods of all kinds, inspection of tenement houses, and enforcement of state health laws are the chief duties. Satisfactory water supply is closely associated with good health. Because of its importance it cannot be left in the hands of a private company but must be under the control of the people themselves.

The *fire department* and the *police department* usually enroll scores, hundreds, or even thousands of firemen and policemen in each city. The use of expensive, modern equipment and the training of skillful men are great aids in combating fire and crime—two enemies of society. The efficient, honest, and brave fireman or policeman is a very valuable citizen of any community. The proper care of streets and traffic is a great aid in keeping down fire and crime. The use of the best modern mechanisms, such as subways and traffic signals, does much to handle this problem.

Other Responsibilities. The lighting of cities by electricity is still largely in the hands of private companies organized for profit, but municipal plants are being constructed in an effort to keep down the costs of electricity and to extend its uses. Likewise, gas plants for heating and cooking, transportation lines, and telephone and telegraph facilities are, for the most part, in the hands of private companies.

The care of the poor and unfortunate has reached such a size that it is no longer merely a local problem. Certain responsibilities, however, still remain with the city government although the state and federal governments have to expend large sums for this purpose.

Finally city planning and zoning require constant

attention of city officials so as to keep down excessive crowding, to eliminate the outworn tenement buildings, and to aid civic beauty. Zoning laws are becoming very common, and villages and small cities are thus able to plan satisfactorily for their gradual increase in size.

Test and Study Exercises

Aids to Learning.

1. Notice the reason for the establishment of towns in New England and of counties in Virginia.
2. Note the importance of the New England town meeting, as the best example of pure democracy that ever existed.
3. Observe that there are three kinds of city government: the mayor-council, the commission, and the council-manager types.

Test Exercises.

On a separate sheet of paper give the letters for the correct answer for each question.

1. Counties were first established in this country in (a) New England, (b) Virginia, (c) New York, (d) Illinois, (e) Missouri.
2. The present number of counties in the United States is approximately (a) 2000, (b) 1000, (c) 3000, (d) 4000, (e) 500.
3. The first form of local government established by the colonists was the (a) county, (b) parish, (c) town, (d) village, (e) municipality.
4. The best example of pure democracy is the (a) city council, (b) county-township, (c) commission plan, (d) town meeting, (e) council-manager plan.
5. The chief obstruction to the use of the town meeting is (a) political graft, (b) unemployment, (c) modern conveniences of living, (d) high cost of living, (e) industrial development.
6. The council-manager form of government is valuable primarily because of (a) a smaller salary for the manager, (b) its widespread use, (c) greater efficiency in management, (d) the training secured by the manager, (e) the large number of elective positions.

Suggested Activities.

1. Review your history of the early Virginia colony to see why the county form of government was used there rather than the town.

2. Find out how many counties there are in your own state and see how large and how small they are in size and in population. How long would it take the average automobile to go across the largest of these counties?

3. Inquire from your local government as to the officials who are elected, their term of office, their salaries, and their duties.

4. *Group Activity:* The teacher may conduct a discussion on the advantages of the town meeting as an example of pure democracy.

5. *Group Activity:* The teacher may appoint a committee to write to the International City Managers' Association in Chicago to learn the history and progress of this movement.

6. *Group Activity:* The teacher may take a group of the class to visit the local council to learn the way in which the government is being conducted.

CHAPTER XXI

YOUR STATE GOVERNMENT

PREPARATORY NOTE: Your state government grew up as a combination of three main divisions of responsibility—the lawmaking, the law enforcing, and the law interpreting branches of government. These groups have changed in their methods along with the changes found in all other activities of our lives. You should understand what the duties are of all of these. The following chapter will help you to do this.

The Development of the State Government. You will remember that the colonists who came to America brought the idea of both town and county with them from England. But there is nothing like our state in the English system of government. The state as we know it is a development of American political experience.

When the English settled America they came as colonists under the authority of the king. They were to be ruled by some company or individual known as a proprietor who had been given a charter to settle and rule a certain territory having definite boundaries described in the charter. The governing power of the company or proprietor was also limited by the charter. For example, the charter of the London Company declared that the colonists who settled in Virginia should have all the rights of Englishmen. That made the Magna Charta and all the English common law apply to the people of Virginia just as it applied to the people of England. Thus the colonists were protected from tyranny of the colonial government just as Englishmen were protected from the tyranny of their government at home.

Colonial Government. The executive power in the colony was vested in a governor appointed by the company, by the proprietor, or later, in the Royal provinces, by the king. In the case of a few of the charter colonies like Massachusetts, the governor was elected by the qualified voters who were required to be church members and have some property.

In 1619 the London Company, under the control of the liberal element, granted Virginia a colonial assembly. A little later both Plymouth and Massachusetts developed legislative assemblies. In the course of time all the colonies had assemblies with power to pass laws concerning the affairs of the colony. All such laws were subject to the authority of the government of Great Britain and could be disallowed, or declared not laws, by the Board which controlled the colonies. But these colonial laws usually dealt with things that the British at home knew or cared nothing about and very few were disallowed. But the practice caused the colonial governments to recognize the fact that in certain things they were controlled by a higher government.

Colonial courts were established to interpret and enforce the laws made by the colonial legislatures. These courts also applied the English common law to cases arising in the colonies. The British allowed appeals to be taken from these colonial courts to the superior British courts. Thus, in this way also, the colonies were made to understand that their colonial governments were subject to control by the British government.

Statehood. The final act of making the first states took place in the early part of the Revolutionary War. The colonial governments had always, in theory at least, received their authority to govern from the king. Colonial officials swore allegiance to the king just as all our officers take an oath to support the Constitution. All legal papers were in the name of the king. All charges of violation of law ended with the phrase "against the peace and dignity of the King."

When the representatives of the thirteen colonies declared themselves free and independent states, Congress advised the states to adopt written constitutions in place of their old charters. That was done by each of the states. In every case the people were declared to be sovereign. In one or two cases the state simply changed their charter to read "the people" instead of "the King." Everywhere indictments were made to read "against the peace and dignity of the state" instead of "against the peace and dignity of the King."

With the adoption of these new constitutions the making of the American state was complete. After the formation of the national government in 1789 new states were admitted but each new state was organized according to the general plan worked out in the original thirteen states.

The State Constitution. What is a state constitution? In answering this question we may say briefly that a state constitution is the fundamental law, sometimes called the organic law, of the state. The word fundamental means basic, original, a part of the foundation. Hence all laws not fundamental such as those made by the legislature, must be in agreement with the fundamental law. We may get a better idea of a constitution by answering the question, "What does a constitution do?" A state constitution does five things.

1. *It names or designates the people as the sovereign power in the state.* This is done in a short statement at the beginning called *the preamble*. The important clause in the preamble is "We, the people do ordain and establish this constitution for the state of _____." There may be modifying and explanatory phrases and clauses but the above words will be found somewhere in every preamble to a state constitution. It is these words that declare the people are the sovereign power in the state.

2. *It makes a declaration of the individual rights of the people.* This part of the constitution is called a *bill of rights*. It is simply a list of rights each person has and which neither the state government, nor any official of the government may take away. This list of rights includes freedom of speech, freedom of

press, trial by jury, freedom of worship, and security of life, liberty and property.

3. *It provides for the organization of the government.* In all the states this part of the constitution provides for three departments of government, the legislative, the executive, and the judicial. Each department is given its separate powers. This is for the purpose of preventing tyranny on the part of any officer or agency of government.

4. *It includes miscellaneous provisions.* Most state constitutions, especially our more recent ones, have a section devoted to these miscellaneous provisions. They include such matters as taxation, education, banking and corporations. In our long constitutions there are many of these miscellaneous provisions which go into great detail. In the older short constitutions and in the United States Constitution these miscellaneous provisions are omitted. That means they are left to the legislature of the proposed state government.

5. *It provides for its own amendment.* Every state constitution has such a provision. The first written constitution to provide for its own amendment was that prepared by William Penn for his colony of Pennsylvania.

The interpretation of the state constitution is a duty that belongs to every official in the state whether a state or local officer. Every officer, when he assumes the duties of his office, must take an oath to support the constitution and discharge faithfully the duties of his office. In doing that he must interpret the constitution as it may apply to his official acts. For example, it becomes the duty of a member of the legislature to vote against a law that he believes to be unconstitutional. To do otherwise would be to violate his oath to support the constitution.

Penn Receiving Charter from King Charles II

However, there may be differences of opinion as to the interpretation of the meaning of the constitution with respect to any act of an official or any particular provision of a law. If there is such difference of opinion the final interpretation must be made by a court when some specific case involving the act or law comes before the court. The court is the proper governmental agency to make such an interpretation for two reasons: first, the judges are required to be learned in the law, and therefore should be capable of interpreting all law, both legislative and constitutional, relating to a specific case; second, the court cannot decide a case properly without interpreting all law, both legislative and constitutional, relating to the case. The decision of cases and, therefore, the interpretation of law, are the business of the courts.

The Increased Work of State Government. Since the days of Thomas Jefferson there has been an amazing increase in the work of state governments. We now believe that the government which provides the best methods for co-operation, in doing the work that is of value to all citizens, is the best government. The theory of a century ago made only individual effort and independence important. The present theory makes co-operative effort and social service also important. Certainly both are important and neither should be neglected. The greatest possible development of the individual together with the best and most effective co-operation in all worth-while common tasks of society is the good to be sought by government.

The increase in the work of the state has developed in two ways: In the first place, all the fields of work done by the early state have been greatly expanded. For example, the police power of the state has been extended to include in the work of the state anything of importance to the health and safety of its people. Thus the work of the state is extended to sanitation and health, the prevention and control of disease, the prevention of accidents, the regulation of traffic, and the inspection of food, drugs, hotels, public carriers,[1] and eating houses.

Education is another field in which there has been a great increase in the work of the state. The early state was responsible for elementary education only. The modern state provides for elementary, high-school, college, and university education. Elementary and high-school education have been placed under local government but the state still keeps the control and gives aid for carrying on the work. Many states provide directly for free college and university education at great expense to the state.

Formerly the work of education was carried on by local government under a few general laws of state government. The local government paid practically all the expenses of the work not borne by the parents of the children, and had full control of the schools. In 1934 the state as a whole paid nearly one-fourth of the expense of elementary and high-school education, and all the expenses of state-supported college and university education. There were great differences, however, among the various states. In Delaware the state paid about ninety-two per cent of the total expense, while in Oregon and Iowa the states paid less than two per cent. In the majority of cases the states paid less than one-third of the cost of education. The relative proportion of the total funds contributed by the states has shifted back and forth during the past forty years. During recent years the states have assumed an in-

[1] **public carriers.** Railways and streetcars.

creasing share in public-school support. Through
methods of classification and inspection the states control practically all schools, they fix the qualifications
of all teachers, and they determine what shall be taught
and largely how it shall be taught by furnishing
courses of study. In many cases the state adopts the
textbooks used in the schools.

Modern inventions have so vastly increased our commerce and industry that there can be little comparison
made between the work of the early state and that of
the states of the present time. All our states have
created public service commissions to control and regulate railroads, electric power and lighting corporations,
streetcar companies, telephone companies, warehouses,
and other agencies engaged in industry and commerce.
Child-labor laws and workingmen's compensation laws
are part of the states' work in regulating commerce
and industry.

In the second place, there have been many kinds of
work assumed by the modern state that were not recognized as state work at all in our early history. Our
roads and highways are a good example of work that
has been largely transferred from local to state government. The surveying, locating, construction, and
maintenance of roads was formerly thought of as entirely the work of local government. However, with
the coming of the automobile and the construction of
hard surface highways to replace the graded dirt roads
of former days, the work of surveying, locating, constructing, and maintaining our highways has been
very largely transferred from local to state govern-

ment. (See page 294.) In our early history the entire
expense of roads was borne by local governments except where private parties were permitted to operate
toll bridges and roads. Now private toll roads and for

Courtesy Portland Cement Association

Modern Road Building Machinery

the most part private toll bridges have disappeared.
Great systems of state and national highways have
been constructed and are being maintained at state
expense plus some financial aid from the national
government.

State highway departments have been created in
every state. Thousands of men are continually em-

ployed in the construction and maintenance of the highways. State police forces have been organized whose special business is patrolling the highways. Many of the states have a great central highway office building, and a number of regional office buildings for housing the office force doing the bookkeeping, blue-printing, and other office work of the state department. Hundreds of great high-powered machines, such as graders and cement mixers are owned and kept continually at work by the states. Hundreds of millions of dollars' worth of state bonds have been issued and sold. Our total annual state expenditure for highways has reached the enormous sum of over a billion dollars.

The state has assumed responsibility and work in many fields where co-operation is necessary. The field of highway construction and maintenance illustrates what the state is doing in many other fields. In each of these fields where new work has been undertaken by the states, boards or commissions have been created to have charge of the work. Most of the states now have from one hundred to two hundred of these boards, or commissions, each having charge of some type of state work. This fact indicates the great increase in the work of modern state governments.

State governmental organization. The general form of organization which developed in our colonial period and which was incorporated in our first state constitutions has, along general lines, become permanent. All our state governments have the powers of government separated into legislative, executive, and judicial departments. However, the great increase in the responsibility of the modern state has added to this work and in some cases has caused changes in form in each of these departments. The work of the executive department has been so greatly expanded that there is a tendency to consider it in two sections: the executive and administrative. We shall follow that tendency and discuss the state government under the four divisions of legislative, executive, administrative, and judicial.

Legislative Department. The legislative power of the state is exercised (except in the case of direct legislation in some states) by a representative legislature elected by the people.

1. *Form and structure.* The official name of the legislature is different in the various states. In twenty-three states it is the *Legislature,* in twenty the *General Assembly,* and in two the *General Court.* In the beginning some of the states had one-house legislatures. But by 1836 all the states had the two-house legislature similar to our national Senate and House of Representatives. In the past few years, since the great increase in the responsibility of state governments, there has been increasing sentiment in favor of one-house state legislatures. It is urged that the two-house system is too slow, preventing needed action, that political control can be applied too easily, and that it is unnecessarily expensive. It is claimed that a small one-house legislature can and will give the modern business problems which make up so much of the work of the modern state, better and more intelligent consideration. Recently Nebraska has adopted this system.

In size the upper house, usually called the Senate, is smaller than the lower house. The range is from seventeen members in Delaware and Nevada to sixty-seven in Minnesota. Lower houses range in size from thirty-five members in Delaware to four hundred and twenty in New Hampshire.

Representation in most of the states is based on the county. Usually each county must have one representative in the lower house, but counties with large population have more representatives in proportion to their population. In some of the New England states, representation in the lower house is based on the town. Representation in the upper house is usually based upon districts which are generally composed of one or more counties depending on the population. In populous counties like Cook County, Illinois, there may be several senatorial districts in one county.

Terms, sessions, and compensation of members vary widely in the different states. In most states members of the lower houses are elected for two years and senators for four years.

The sessions of the legislature are held every two years in most of the states. They are limited in length in thirty-one states and unlimited in seventeen states. The limits range from forty days in two states to one hundred fifty days in one state. The usual limit of sixty days is found in twenty states.

In some states legislators are paid an annual salary and in others they are paid by the day. The salaries range from one hundred to twenty-five hundred dollars a year in different states. In states that pay by the day the range is from three to ten dollars. In some of these states the pay ceases or is reduced to one dollar a day at the end of a certain period, usually sixty to ninety days.

2. *Systems of lawmaking.* There are two systems of lawmaking. We may call one the English, or *committee of the whole* system, the other the American, or *committee system.*

In the first, the committee of the whole system, bills prepared by the government or executive department are given first consideration. These bills are considered in the committee of the whole; that is, the entire House becomes a committee for consideration of the bill. Discussion is freer than in the formal sessions of the House. When the committee has finished discussing and amending a bill it votes for or against the passing of the bill. The committee adjourns and the House is immediately called to order by the Speaker[2] and passes or votes against the bill. After all government bills have been acted upon, private bills may be introduced. However, in actual practice in England but few private bills are introduced.

This English system is after all the system of representative government that has developed through the experience of the ages. Representative government is centered around the budget and the taxes necessary to raise the money required by the budget. The executive department is the money-spending department of the government. It knows what the money has been spent

---

[2] **the Speaker.** The chairman of the lower house.

for and how much is needed to continue the same governmental activities or to increase them in case that seems desirable. The budget bill can be made up, either directly or indirectly, only by the executive department because it alone has the figures. The budget bill should provide for the money needed and state the purposes for which it is to be used. Then the representatives should meet as a committee of the whole, where every member can and should be present, and where any citizen may be in the galleries to hear the discussion. They should pass upon the budget item by item, grant what they think best, and deny what they think should be denied. That is real representative government. After the budget bill is disposed of there would not be much left for the legislature to do. If some new work should be undertaken, that had not been proposed in the budget, it could be brought up by a private bill after the government bills had been acted upon.

In the second, the committee system of legislation, the House organizes by electing a Speaker and subordinate officers. Then the House adjourns and usually the Speaker appoints the various committees that handle the bills that are to be introduced. There are usually about forty such committees, but in some states there are as many as sixty. The names of these standing committees will indicate the nature of the bills each committee considers. There are usually committees on banking, ways and means, appropriations, railroads, highways, education, health, agriculture, and many other subjects. Some of the important committees have as many as thirty to forty members. Every member serves on at least one committee and most of them on four or five. The House usually meets about noon leaving the mornings open for committee meetings.

After the committees are appointed and the House meets again, the introduction of bills is in order. Most members have at least one and some of them have a dozen bills ready to introduce. Literally hundreds of bills are introduced. The titles are read by a clerk and the Speaker refers each bill to the committee which he thinks is the proper one to consider it. In a single session of a state legislature there are usually from one thousand to three thousand bills introduced. Bills prepared by the executive officials of the government in theory have no right of way over other bills in the committee system.

This committee system is in general use in our state legislatures. There are many objections to the system. There is a great waste of time in considering many unwise bills. For example, many times bills are proposed the contents of which are already law. Many bills are proposed by members to get publicity, or to satisfy some little group of their constituents. Bills are introduced by request which even the member introducing them is unwilling to approve. Most of the private bills are not carefully prepared and take up the time of the committees unnecessarily. The real work of legislation is done in the committee rooms, and the committee meetings, except in the case of public hearings, are secret. This is the worst evil in the system. It gives the political boss his best chance to influence legislation. Members have to serve on so many committees that they have little time to consider any legislation except that which is prepared in their own committee rooms. This means that most members vote in the House in the way the committee reports without knowing much about the bill being voted on.

But with all the evils of the committee system we Americans hold on to it probably because we are unwilling to give government bills precedence and to do away with the privileges of members to introduce bills at will. The English committee of the whole system would do away with the consideration of thousands of useless bills; it would bring all legislation out in the open; and it would do away with much of the influence of lobbyists[3] and of the political boss, exercised in the secrecy of the committee room.

Each of the important committees is likely to receive many bills on the same subject. The committee studies these, selects one, or sometimes writes a new bill containing parts of several of the bills referred to it, and recommends its passing. Sometimes a committee will recommend the passing of no bills, or perhaps a committee simply keeps the bills referred to it and makes no report. This is called "pigeon-holing" a bill, and is the end of many of the thousands of bills which are introduced.

The bills reported favorably by the committees are placed in order on a list called the Calendar of the House. The House considers them in this order unless

---

[3] **lobbyists.** Interested persons who solicit legislators to influence their votes.

they are changed by order of the House, and then it may discuss them, amend them, and vote upon them. If a bill passes this vote it is printed as amended and placed on the calendar for third reading and final passage. It may be debated again but in most states it may not be amended at this time. If passed it is sent to the other house, where it goes through similar steps, and if passed there, it is sent to the governor for his signature, which makes it a law of the state. Usually a majority vote of the members present is sufficient to pass a bill on the first vote but in many states a majority vote of all the members elected is required to pass a measure on the final vote.

3. *Lobbyists.* Pressure group lobbyists and business lobbyists exercise much influence on legislation. By pressure groups we mean organizations of citizens whose prosperity seems necessary for the betterment of a large group of people. Some of these pressure groups are labor organizations, farmers' organizations, chambers of commerce, automobile associations, women's clubs, and professional associations like the State Bar Associations, State Medical Associations, and State Teachers' Associations. Such pressure groups are usually represented by secretaries, but sometimes by committees of members. They are legitimate and frequently have a large influence in lawmaking because they have specific knowledge and experience in some public work that is of importance to the whole country. Public health, public education, the needed reorganization of the courts, and the better enforcement of law and order illustrate these fields of interest.

Business lobbyists are the paid representatives of private business whose task is to prevent excessive taxation of their products. Sometimes these lobbyists try to obtain special privileges for the private interest they represent.

4. *Direct legislation.* Throughout most of our history all state laws were passed by state legislatures. But about the beginning of the present century some of the western states adopted in their constitutions a method of lawmaking known as the *initiative and referendum.* (See page 301.) By this method anyone could draft a law, and get a small percentage of the voters (usually from five to ten per cent) to sign a petition so as to have the law placed on the ballot at the next election for vote by the people. If it received the necessary favorable vote it became a law of the state. The first part of this process, that of framing the proposed law and of getting sufficient petitioners to place the proposal on the ballot, is known as the *initiative.* The voting on the law is the *referendum.* The referendum may be used to approve a law passed by the legislature. In that case there is a period of time, usually about three months, between the passage of the law and the date it will go into effect. During this period those opposed to the law may get petitions and file them with the Secretary of State. If sufficient petitions are filed, the law is suspended until after the next election when it is placed upon the ballot, and if there is a majority vote against it, it is disapproved. The initiative and referendum were adopted by nearly half the states, soon after they were introduced.

The Executive Department. When the colonial governments became state governments in 1776 the executive department of the government was not in favor with the people. The governors had, for the most part, been appointed by the king, and as appointees of the king they had opposed the elected legislatures in many of the issues drawn between the king and the colonies. Therefore, in the new state constitutions the powers and duties of the governor were reduced as much as possible. But since governors are now elected by the people and since there is an increasing necessity for the execution and administration of new laws, along with the increased responsibility of the state, the powers and duties of the office of the governor have also increased. The governors have, in general, obtained and deserved the confidence of the people. At the present time the governor is more powerful than he has ever been before in the history of the American state.

The *Governor* or chief executive is the only elected state official in whom the greater part of the voters have a personal interest. Many voters try to become acquainted with the qualifications and the records of the candidates for governor. This holds true both in the primaries, which nominate the candidates, and in the general elections at which the governor is elected. The governor, in half of the states, is elected for a two year term; in New Jersey he is elected for three years, and in the other states the term is four years. To be eligible a man or woman must be thirty years of age in most states. He must have been a citizen of the United

States for a certain period ranging from two to twenty years. In most states he must have been a resident of the state from one to ten years. The governor's salary is fixed by law (sometimes legislative, and sometimes constitutional) and ranges from three thousand to twenty-five thousand dollars.

The governor's powers and duties are many and varied. Chief of these is his duty to see that the laws are faithfully executed. But this is very difficult because the execution of one large group of state laws is in the hands of elected state officials over whom the governor has no control and who are responsible to no one, except in a general way to the people. The execution of another large group of laws is in the hands of local governments. The governor of course has no control over the mayors, sheriffs, and other local officials charged with the execution of such laws.

It is true the governor could call out the militia to enforce the law. But no governor would care to go to this extent except when the use of the militia is required for the most serious situations of law violation. The governor also makes many appointments, recommends new legislation, exercises the veto power,[4] and issues pardons.

The heads of the various state departments are usually elected by the people. But as there are so many of them and they are considered minor state officials, not many voters pay a great deal of attention to the qualifications and experience of candidates for these posi-

[4] **veto power.** The power of the executive to prevent the passing of measures approved by the legislature.

tions. Since they are all elected independently of the governor and of each other, there can be little effective organization of the executive work of the state government.

There is considerable patronage[5] attached to each of these departments. There is great temptation for the elected head of each department to try to organize a little personal machine that will support him for another term or for another office, frequently the governorship.

The following elected executive officers are usually found in the states:

The *Lieutenant Governor,* who serves when the governor is absent and is president of the Senate.

The *Secretary of State,* who keeps the official records of the state and has charge of state documents.

The *Treasurer,* who has charge of the state funds.

The *State Auditor* (called the comptroller in some states), who audits the accounts of the state and issues warrants upon the treasurer.

The *Attorney General* who is the chief law officer of the state and gives legal advice to the other executive officers.

The *State Superintendent of Schools,* who has general supervision over education of the state.

The Administrative Organization. In recent years, since the state governments have been assuming a continually increasing load of work, another type of organization called the administrative organization has developed. There has been some effort to distinguish

---

[5] **patronage.** The control of nomination and political office.

between executive and administrative work, but the distinction is difficult to make. However, the governor is far more powerful in this administrative organization than he is with the elective executives mentioned above. Most of the officials and members of the boards and commissions that have been added in recent years are appointed by the governor and are subject to removal by him.

The new work of this administrative organization, as well as the officials in charge of it, varies greatly in the different states. The titles of the officials and the names of the boards or commissions usually indicate the type of work performed. Among the most important are the following boards or commissions: agriculture, public works, social security, old-age pensions, pensions for the blind, immigration, public service, workingmen's compensation, engineering, highways, mine inspection, civil service, pure food, health, penal institutions, and various state schools and institutions. This list might be extended almost indefinitely, as the states usually have from one hundred to two hundred of these agencies, each in charge of some line of work which the modern state has undertaken. The national government has aided many of these new fields by grants of financial aid.

The responsibility for all this administrative organization through his appointees adds to the work of the governor and increases his power in the state. Thus with the increased responsibility of the states the governor is continually becoming more and more powerful.

The Judicial Department. We first described the legislative or lawmaking branch of state government because the first step in developing government is making the law. After a law is made it would be worthless if it were not enforced. Therefore, we next described the law enforcing or executive and administrative department of state government. But in the process of enforcing law there is likely to be some question as to its meaning. The officers of the executive department may think that it means one thing and the citizen who is affected may think it means something very different. In that case it is necessary to have some disinterested third party, capable of understanding the law, interpret it in any case that may come up. For that purpose every state has a judicial department to interpret the law.

The judicial department consists of a system of courts. It is difficult to describe them because there are likely to be differences in many states. In all the states some of the courts are local but the highest court is state wide in its jurisdiction.[6] To say that a court has state-wide jurisdiction simply means that the court has a right to consider cases from any part of the state. In general the system of courts is as follows:

1. The *Justices' Court* is the lowest court in the judicial system. It is a local court and usually has jurisdiction in the county in which the justice is located. There are usually one or two justices of the peace in each township in the county. In states where

[6] **jurisdiction.** Power to exercise judicial authority in civil or in criminal matters.

the county is not divided into townships there are a number of justices located throughout the county at convenient places. There are two kinds of cases, civil and criminal, and the justice of the peace has jurisdiction in both kinds of cases. In most states in civil cases the jurisdiction of the justice of the peace is limited to amounts which are seldom more than one hundred dollars. In criminal cases the justices' court is limited to petty or small offenses, usually known as misdemeanors. In most towns and cities there are also city courts of about the same level as justices' courts, generally known as municipal courts or police courts.

Justices of the peace are sometimes appointed but are usually elected. They need not be men learned in the law but should be honest, sensible citizens. Justices are paid fees instead of a salary. This is unfortunate because it tempts the justice to divide the fees with the lawyer who will bring him cases. Appeals may be taken from the justices' court to some higher court.

2. *County and Circuit Courts* are the great trial courts of the states. If the jurisdiction of the court is confined to one county it is usually called *county court*. If the judge serves two or more counties the court is called *circuit court* or *district court*. These courts may be appealed to from justices' courts but they have *original jurisdiction*[7] in the more important civil cases and the more serious criminal cases. These courts are courts of record; that is, there is provided a court stenographer who takes the testimony in the cases that

[7] **original jurisdiction.** Power to hear and decide a lawsuit in the first instance.

are tried. In the event of appeal of a case to a higher court, witnesses are not required to be present at the higher court. The copy of the testimony in the trial court is laid before the judges of the higher court and their decision is determined by the testimony originally given in the trial court.

3. The *District Appellate Courts* are, in many states, the next courts above the county or circuit courts. The appellate courts are for the purpose of hearing appeals in the less important and less serious cases appealed from the trial courts. They usually have from three to five judges and each court will have jurisdiction over a certain part of the state, perhaps a third or a half. These courts usually write out their opinions which are published in book form, called reports, and become a part of the great body of the common law. *Common law* is the name given to the opinions by the higher courts on the important cases which they decide. This common law has been accumulating in England and America for more than five hundred years, so that there are now thousands of volumes of these court reports.

4. The *Supreme Court* is the name usually given to the highest court in a state, although it is called the "Court of Appeals" in New York and New Jersey. This court consists of from three to nine judges. Most of these courts have original jurisdiction in some of the most important cases, but the greater part of the work of all of them is hearing cases appealed from the lower courts. The judges of the supreme court are appointed by the governor in six states, and they are

elected by the legislature or by the people in the remaining states. In three states the judges serve for life, but the great majority of their terms range from six to twelve years.

5. *Special Courts.* In addition to the regular courts described above many states have special courts which handle only certain types of cases. Probably the most common among these are the *Probate Courts.* These are courts for settling the estates of deceased persons, settling matters concerning wills, and protecting orphans in their rights.

Juvenile Courts have been created in many states and cities in recent years. These courts try children who have violated the law. The young offenders are not brought into the regular court where they may be associated with hardened criminals, nor are they treated as criminals, but as children who need special care. If the offense is so serious that the child must be punished severely he is not sent to jail or to the penitentiary but to a reform school or to an industrial school.

Small Claims Courts have been provided in some cities. In these courts cases involving a small sum, usually less than twenty dollars, may be brought with little or no cost. No one need employ a lawyer. They are sometimes called "the poor man's court."

There has been much criticism of our state courts. It is said (1) that there are too many delays, (2) that the courts do not convict many times when there is no doubt of the guilt of the accused parties, (3) that criminals escape justice because the courts are bound by old forms and legal points, (4) that we do not have sufficient numerical records of crime and criminals, (5) that courts are so expensive that ordinary disputes cannot be settled there, (6) that crime is on the increase because certainty and swiftness of punishment is practically unknown in our courts, (7) that procedure is slow and cumbersome, and (8) that a skillful attorney can delay a case until justice is defeated.

Many proposals for reform have been made. Those most practical and most likely to bring good results are the proposals of the American Bar Association and the various state bar associations. These proposed reforms, affecting some of these criticisms, include a reorganization of the entire court system of a state under the supervision of a judicial council. They give the judicial council power to make rules of procedure instead of leaving such power to the legislature, as is the case now in most of the states. Another reform which will add much to the efficiency of the courts is the strict enforcement of the rules of the bar and the suspension of lawyers guilty of violating these rules. Many state bar associations are doing excellent work in this field.

As a consequence, improvement in the courts has been very noticeable in recent years. Most judges are hardworking, public servants who know the law and work faithfully. While judges are usually elected, there is in most states an unwritten code of ethics that keeps judges from making political speeches in a campaign. More and more judges are by their rulings preventing delays and compelling attorneys to try cases when they are set for trial. Many of our courts now have their dockets[8] clear and force cases to trial with little delay. Capable, fearless prosecutors[9] are making great progress in punishing those higher up in organized crime. In these ways, many of the criticisms given are gradually being met and conditions are being improved.

Test and Study Exercises

Aids to Learning.

1. Note that the work of the state government has been greatly increased in the fields of sanitation and health, traffic and transportation, education, commerce, and industry.

2. Remember that the state is supreme in all powers not delegated to the national government and not prohibited to the states by the Constitution of the United States.

3. It is important to know the three-fold division of power in the state governments as in the national government—legislative, executive and administrative, and judicial.

4. Observe the tendency in recent years to employ direct legislation through the initiative and the referendum.

Test Exercises.

On a separate sheet of paper write the following sentences including the missing words.

1. The American state was complete with the adoption of their ____.

2. ____ said: "That government is best which governs least."

3. The state government is handled through the ____, ____, and ____ departments.

4. ____ is a state with a one-house legislature.

5. The worst evil of the committee system of legislature is that the real work of legislation is ____.

6. The most important power of the governor is the ____ of the laws.

7. The governor is continually becoming more ____.

---

[8] **dockets.** Records containing lists of cases to be tried.

[9] **prosecutors.** Attorneys who conduct proceedings in a court on behalf of the government.

8. Children who violate the law are tried in ____ ____.

9. The governmental attorney who conducts proceedings in a court is called the ____.

10. A chief criticism of our courts is that there are too many ____.

Suggested Activities.

1. Read in your United States history the story of the establishment of the different colonies. Be ready to report to the class those which were proprietary, royal, and charter colonies.

2. Read the Bill of Rights in the United States Constitution and compare it with that in your own state constitution. Where did it receive the name?

3. Find out the names and location of the State colleges or universities of all kinds in your own state. What part of the students in your state graduating from high school each year could be enrolled in these schools?

4. With an automobile road map of your state, see how many miles of hard surfaced roads there are in your own county. Compare this with neighboring counties.

5. Learn whether your state has the initiative and the referendum process of direct legislation.

6. *Class Activity:* The teacher may appoint a committee to write your Secretary of State at your state capital to inquire the following facts: the number of legislators in each house, the length of their term, their salary, the term of the governor, his salary.

CHAPTER XXII

YOUR NATIONAL GOVERNMENT

PREPARATORY NOTE: You have read about the growth of our nation from the original thirteen colonies to the present forty-eight states. The development of this union and the liberty resulting from it are traced in this chapter in the Legislative, Executive, and Judicial Departments of our national government. The future of our country depends upon millions of citizens who, thoughtfully and conscientiously, do their best to make our government a true democracy.

The Foundation of the National Government. The great orator and statesman, Daniel Webster, in his "Reply to Hayne" in 1830, closed what was probably the best and most effective speech he ever made with these words: "Liberty and Union, now and forever, one and inseparable." In that expression Webster combined the two great ideals of our national government. The development of each can be traced throughout colonial history, beginning two centuries before Webster, until both ideals were written into our national constitution at the time of the organization of our republic. These two great principles of Union and Liberty have furnished the issues around which the struggles of our development as a nation have taken place.

Union. The growth of the idea of the union of the colonies was slow and was brought about only by necessity of one kind or another. Usually it was the necessity for defense against some outside force. There are a number of instances of efforts to secure union among the colonies. These were important precedents for the development of a more perfect union. They are as follows:

1. *The New England Confederation* of 1643 was an organization of four New England colonies for the purpose of defense against the Indians.

2. *King James II's union* of eight distinct colonial governments, consisting of all New England, New York, and New Jersey, came under the rule of one governor in 1688. This union was a complete failure for two reasons. It abolished all colonial assemblies in the united colonies and it did not provide for a representative assembly. For these reasons the union failed through the destruction of liberty.

3. *The Congress of Albany* in 1754 made an attempt to unite the colonies. Seven colonies were represented. Benjamin Franklin wrote a constitution, which the congress adopted, providing for the union of the colonies. However, the constitution was rejected by the colonies because they thought it meant the loss of liberty, and by the British government because they thought it provided too much liberty.

4. *The Stamp Act Congress* of 1765 brought together representatives from nine colonies to protest against the new tax. The colonists thought this tax interfered with the liberty of the colonies.

A Group from the First Continental Congress
Henry, Adams Dickinson, Washington, Hancock (seated at right), Lee

5. *The First Continental Congress* met in 1774 and twelve of the thirteen colonies were represented. The purpose of the Congress was to protest against British interference with the liberties of the colonies, and to organize for resistance.

6. *The Second Continental Congress* (1775 to 1781) carried on the war in defense of the liberties of the colonies. Finally, in order to secure liberty, it declared the independence of the colonies and created a new nation, the United States of America.

7. *The Articles of Confederation* provided for a permanent union of the states in a confederation. It also included a Congress which became the national government from 1781 to 1789. This government failed because it was not able to protect the liberty and rights of individuals nor to preserve order. Without order there can be no liberty.

8. *The Constitution of the United States* and the government organized under it in 1789 marked the end of experimental unions and the beginning of the steady development and expansion of the union under our government. In the preamble to the Constitution the purpose is stated in these words: "We, the people of the United States, in order to form a more perfect union . . . . and secure the blessings of liberty to ourselves and our posterity, do ordain and establish this Constitution for the United States of America."

Liberty. The development of liberty in America, like that of union, was slow and only achieved by struggle and sacrifice. Some of the important steps in securing and preserving our liberty follow.

1. *The Charter of the London Company* which founded our first permanent colony, Virginia, contains a statement that the emigrants are entitled "to all liberties, franchises, and immunities of British subjects." While this statement may have been of little practical value to the colonists of that time it was valuable later as it established the theory that all colonists enjoyed all the "rights and liberties of Englishmen." That gave them all constitutional rights and liberties, including the rights expressed in the "Magna Charta," the English charter of liberties.

2. *Representative colonial assemblies* were established with power to make local laws. The first was the Virginia Assembly in 1619. This was followed within a decade by the organization of a representative assembly in Plymouth, and in the Massachusetts Bay colonies. Long before the Revolutionary War all the colonies had representative assemblies.

3. Penn's *Frame of Government* was a constitution which he granted the people of his colony. As proprietor in Pennsylvania, Penn had very large powers of government given him by the king. This frame of government was the first constitution ever written that provided for its own amendment by representatives of the people. (Compare page 310.) In this way the people, through the action of their representative assembly, could change the organization of their government and provide for such liberties as seemed best. It was a long step toward securing liberty.

4. *The Declaration of Independence* summarized the natural rights and liberties of man. This was prob-

ably the greatest single step in the development of our liberties. It was necessary to fight for the liberty set forth in this famous declaration, and this fact made the union and liberty inseparable during the Revolutionary War.

5. *The first ten amendments to the Constitution* became our national bill of rights. They were a great advance in making our liberties permanent. The framers of the Constitution promised in advance to make these amendments and in this way they were able to secure its ratification. Thus union and liberty proved to be inseparable at that time.

The Government as Organized in 1789. The federal government was very much like the state governments then in existence. There had been a very careful separation of all the powers of government between the national government and the state governments by the constitution. The general lines of this separation of powers were made by granting to the national government certain powers enumerated. Those not enumerated, unless specifically denied to the states, were reserved to the states. There was much discussion of the meaning and extent of certain of these grants of power in our early history.

The expansion of the United States began almost immediately after the organization of the government. Three states were admitted during Washington's administration. In 1803 the Jefferson administration more than doubled the area of the United States by the purchase of Louisiana from France. Other territory has been added to the United States by treaty, con-

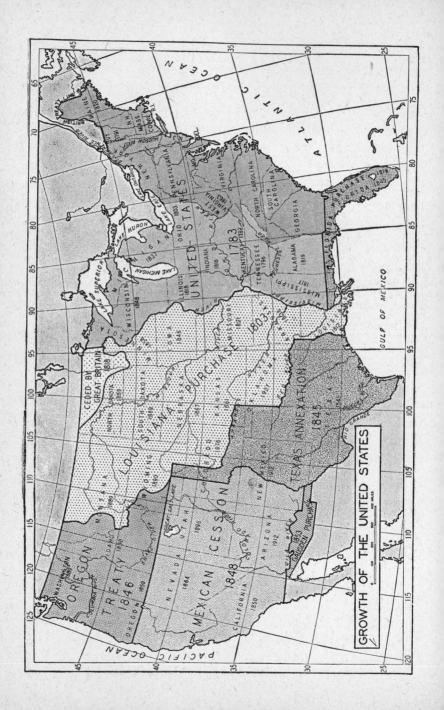

GROWTH OF THE UNITED STATES

quest, and purchase, as can be seen on the map showing the growth of our country. This territory has been
organized and admitted into the Union as states until
the United States now comprises forty-eight states
besides Alaska and some insular territories and possessions. So great has our expansion been that we
now have a total population of nearly one hundred
thirty million people and a total area of over three million square miles.

The Union has been greatly strengthened by this
expansion, and by the action of the national government in dealing with serious problems. These problems cover a range of topics extending from taxation
and banking during Washington's time to international relations and social security at the present time.
Probably the greatest single step in preserving the
Union was the solution of the question of the right of
a state to secede. The War between the States and
the constitutional changes introduced by the fourteenth amendment settled this question once and for
all time.

The states and the national government have co-
operated well in doing the increasing amount of governmental work required by modern conditions. Yet
it is very difficult to distinguish between co-operation
between the state and federal governments and the centralization of power in the hands of the national government. Sometimes the effort to solve some problem
or to carry out some plan begins with co-operation
and ends in centralization.

Our National Legislative Department. Most of the powers delegated to our national government by the constitution are given to the legislative department. This department is composed of a Congress consisting of the House of Representatives and the Senate. The

The United States Senate Chamber

illustrations show the chambers of the United States Senate and of the House of Representatives.

The House of Representatives now has four hundred and thirty-five members. That is about one representative for every three hundred thousand people. The Senate has ninety-six members. The constitution provides there shall be two senators from each state. Thus Nevada with less than a hundred thousand people has two senators while New York with more than twelve million people also has only two senators.

All the members of the House of Representatives and one-third of the Senators are elected every two years. The period of two years which the members of

© *Underwood & Underwood*

The Hall of the House of Representatives

the House serve is called a session of Congress. The different sessions of Congress are numbered from March 4, 1789, when the first Congress began. The seventy-sixth Congress convened January, 1939. Congress holds one regular session each year and may be called for extra sessions by the president.

Each House is judge of the qualifications and election of its own members. The Senate has a standing committee which investigates the use of money, fraud, and unfair practices in the election of its members. Several men elected to the Senate have been refused seats in that body because of fraud or the excessive use of money in the campaign. Each House elects its own officers, with the exception of the presiding officer of the Senate. The Constitution provides that the vice-president shall preside over the Senate. Each House makes and enforces its own rules. The way in which bills are presented to Congress is very much the same as that used in the various state legislatures. (See page 322.)

The chief work of Congress is to determine which taxes shall be levied and to what extent, and to appropriate the money necessary to carry on the government. As we have learned before (page 319), the executive department spends the money and is supposed to know how much money is required to carry on the work of the government. It is expected to make a budget showing the amount of money spent, what it was spent for during the last fiscal or financial year, and the amount needed for the next fiscal year. Congress makes the appropriations asked for in the budget if it approves the work for which the appropriation is asked. If any particular work is not approved by Congress no appropriation is made for that work. Congress has, for the most part throughout our history, made specific appropriations for specific work. The executive department must then use the money for the purpose for which it is appropriated. This is as it should be, because it is the only way Congress can control the expenditure of the people's money by the executive department. The control of governmental expenditures is the chief duty of Congress.

A second important duty of Congress is to determine the policies of the government. If it seems necessary that we enter into war, it is Congress that must determine the question. If there is a demand that the government take up some new kind of work it is Congress that passes upon the policy and provides the agency or agencies to do the work, upon the recommendation of the president. A little more than fifty years ago Congress decided to undertake the regulation of railroads. It created a new agency, the Interstate Commerce Commission, to do that work. Since that time a great many agencies have been created by Congress and added to the executive branch of the government, as we shall soon learn.

Many of these agencies created by Congress were undertaken as emergency work and thought to be temporary. However, when a government agency is created and develops an organization of thousands of employees it is difficult to bring it to an end. There are soon so many people interested in its continuance that public sentiment may be influenced to keep up work that was begun as emergency work. With such an increase of government work, there is likely to be a great increase in government employees and government expenses and taxes. As the policy-determining branch of the government, Congress has the responsibility for everything undertaken by the government.

Our National Executive Department. The executive department of our government was provided for in article two of the Constitution. The executive power was "vested in a President of the United States of America." He has more powers in total than most of the constitutional monarchs of the world. The most important ones are as follows:

1. He executes the laws of the nation and signs or vetoes bills which have been passed by Congress.

2. He appoints thousands of officers with the consent of the Senate—ambassadors, ministers, and consuls to foreign nations, members of his cabinet, judges, postmasters, and many others of lesser importance.

3. He may make treaties with the consent of two-thirds of the Senate.

4. He receives foreign ministers and has power to recognize such new governments as he chooses.

5. He is commander-in-chief of the army, the navy, and the various state militias when they are called into actual service. Although he cannot declare war, yet he can send the military forces of the nation into disputed territory so that conflict is almost necessary.

6. He may call special sessions of either or both Houses of Congress and he recommends to their consideration such measures as he considers necessary. He sends or reads an annual message to Congress.

The annual salary of the president is seventy-five thousand dollars and in addition there are payments for secretaries, clerks, traveling expenses, and his official dwelling. This beautiful home, called the White House, is shown in the accompanying photograph.

The execution of the laws is the part of the president's work that has continually expanded. The presi-

© *Underwood & Underwood*
Front View of the White House

dent is assisted in this work by ten departments each in charge of a head called a secretary. These ten secretaries are the president's official advisers and form his cabinet. These departments were created by Congress in the following order, which also serves as the order in which the departmental heads would succeed

to the presidency upon the death of both the president
and vice-president.

1. *The Department of State* has charge of our
foreign relations. It negotiates treaties, issues passports,[1] and handles negotiations with all our foreign
representatives. It also has charge of many domestic
relations and is the keeper of the laws of Congress
and of the great official seal of the United States.

2. *The Department of the Treasury* collects all
tariff duties, internal revenue, and income taxes. It
supervises the making of all our money and stamps.
It also has many non-financial duties such as control
of narcotics, the secret service, and the officers in
charge of quarantine[2] and scientific research.[3] The
offices of the department are in the building shown in
the following photograph.

3. *The Department of War* has charge of the military forces of the United States. It supervises the
militia, the Military Academy at West Point, and
training camps throughout the country. It also administers the Army War College in Washington and the
Panama Canal Zone.

4. *The Department of Justice* directs the work of
United States district attorneys and gives legal advice
to the president and his departmental heads.

5. *The Post Office Department* is the largest department of all and regularly employs three or four

[1] **passports.** Formal documents issued to citizens, permitting them to
travel abroad.

[2] **quarantine.** A period of time in which a ship entering a port is inspected
to prevent the spread of contagious diseases.

[3] **scientific research.** Careful examination, as in the fields of the various
sciences, for seeking facts or principles.

hundred thousand persons. It is a very highly specialized business which must be thoroughly organized. It
supervises the mail delivery, postal money orders,
postal savings banks, the proper safeguarding of the
uses of the mail, and the dead-letter office to which go
millions of pieces of undelivered mail each year.

The United States Treasury Building

6. *The Navy Department* has charge of our large
and growing navy and the Naval Academy at Annap-
olis where naval officers are trained. It administers
also the United States Marine Corps, and the Naval
War College at Newport, Rhode Island.

7. *The Department of the Interior* has charge of
many domestic responsibilities such as the surveying
and selling of public lands, the claims for pensions,

irrigation projects, geological surveys,[4] national parks, and Indian affairs; and also our islands. The National Reclamation Act placed the supervision of irrigation for sixteen states under this department. The largest of these projects is on the Salt River in Arizona. A section of this is shown in the photograph.

Courtesy A. T. & S. F. Ry. Co.

Irrigating Date Trees in Phoenix, Arizona

8. *The Department of Agriculture* investigates many types of work carried on by our farmers—fighting plant diseases, fertilizing soil, destroying insect pests, and surveys connected with plants and animals.

---

[4] **geological surveys.** Systematic examinations of an area for the purpose of determining its rock masses.

It also supervises the national forest service, the bureau of home economics, and the new Farm Credit Administration (F.C.A.).

9. *The Department of Commerce* handles the census of population every tenth year, the safeguarding of weights and measures, the granting of patents, and the supervision of steamboats and navigation.

10. *The Department of Labor* has charge of labor statistics, labor standards, the United States conciliation service, the children's bureau, and the women's bureau.

In addition to the work of government assigned to the ten regular executive departments there is an ever increasing amount of work assigned to administrative boards, commissions, and agencies of one kind or another. These agencies are not connected with or under the supervision of any of the ten regular departments. They are provided for by Congress. The members are appointed by the president and the agencies are under the general supervision of the president.

Beginning with the Smithsonian Institution (1846) some of the more important of the early agencies are the Government Printing Office (1860), the Civil Service Commission (1883), the Interstate Commerce Commission (1887), the Pan American Union (1890), the Federal Reserve System which has the supervision of the twelve Federal Reserve Banks (1913), the Federal Trade Commission (1914), the United States Tariff Commission (1916), and the Federal Power Commission (1920). The date when Congress established each of these independent administrative agencies shows that those mentioned as well as others were successful long before the economic crisis of 1929.

As a result of that crisis many new economic and social policies were established which are generally known as the *New Deal.* A great many new independent agencies were created to carry out the work in accordance with these policies.

On July 1, 1939, a reorganization was made in the Executive Department which reassigned many new agencies and old bureaus. As a result, three major groups were made of these new agencies.

During the Second World War, many more new agencies were established to deal with the emergency. Most of them gradually ceased to function when the war crisis was ended and their work completed.

The Federal Security Agency includes the following organizations: the *Food and Drug Administration,* formerly in the Department of Agriculture; the *Social Security Board* with jurisdiction over old-age insurance, unemployment compensation, and public assistance; the *Public Health Service,* formerly in the Department of the Treasury (See page 125); and the *Office of Education,* formerly in the Department of the Interior. (See page 155.)

The agency also cares for the following institutions: the *Columbia Institute for the Deaf;* the *American Printing House for the Blind; Freedmen's Hospital;* and *Saint Elizabeths Hospital.*

The Federal Works Agency includes the *Public Building Administration;* the *Public Roads Adminis-*

tration; the *Federal Fire Council;* the *Federal Real Estate Board* which makes recommendations in the case of communities suffering from the loss of tax revenue on Government-owned land, and consults with departments which wish to dispose of or acquire additional Federal-owned real property, and makes recommendations in regard to the disposition of surplus real property; and the *Bureau of Community Facilities* which is concerned with loans and grants to public and non-profit private agencies to finance construction of certain public works.

The Federal Loan Agency consists of the *Reconstruction Finance Corporation* (R.F.C.) which makes government loans; the *R.F.C. Mortgage Company;* the *Federal National Mortgage Association* which facilitates the construction and the financing of moderately priced housing projects and apartments; and the *War Damage Corporation* created during the Second World War to provide through insurance reasonable protection against loss or damage to property.

Other independent agencies help finance, industry, and agriculture. The *Federal Deposit Insurance Corporation* (F.D.I.C.) insures payments of certain deposits made in banks. The *Securities and Exchange Commission* (S.E.C.) protects investors in stocks, bonds, and other securities. The *Tennessee Valley Authority* (T.V.A.) generates and sells electric power, as the result of dam building and power control, promoting the welfare of the people of the Tennessee Valley. The *Agricultural Adjustment Administration* (A.A.A.) was created to restore to prewar levels the

prices of agricultural products. Another agency in
this group, the *National Recovery Administration*
(N.R.A.), was declared unconstitutional by the
Supreme Court. Regardless of the immediate outcome
of these New Deal legislations, these measures have
become so firmly entrenched that they will continue to
affect American citizens for many generations in the
future.

The reorganization of the administrative agencies
of the national government has been proposed by the
presidents from 1900 to the present. Some kind of
reorganization of these agencies has been especially
urged by Presidents Theodore Roosevelt, William
Howard Taft, Woodrow Wilson, and Franklin D.
Roosevelt. Under the present semi-independent status
of these agencies there is much duplication of work
and unnecessary publication of pamphlets and bul-
letins. The employees of each agency are anxious to
show that the work of their particular agency is important. If the public were not led to believe in the
importance of their agency it might be discontinued
and the employees would be out of work. This means
that the ever increasing government work is performed
by a thousand units. Each one has its attention centered on a small portion of the whole and is thought of
as independent of the great government of which it
is a part.

Naturally if these agencies and the executive departments were organized into a great working whole and
their efforts co-ordinated, the president would be the
proper official to head the new organization. This

would of course add greatly to the executive powers. There is and always has been jealousy between the legislative and executive branches of the national government. Therefore, Congress has been slow to authorize the effective organization of the departments and agencies of government it has created. However, the duplication of effort, the extravagance, and the waste in these agencies as they now exist will doubtless force Congress to do something about it.

The merit system of civil service in the executive and administrative work of the nation had a small beginning in 1883 when Congress created the *Civil Service Commission*. The merit system embodied the idea of appointing and promoting officials on the basis of ability only. The abuses of the spoils system[6] in official appointments had become very bad and notorious. Consequently a few reformers in the two major parties were able to force upon an unwilling Congress this small beginning of the merit system. Two presidents, Grover Cleveland and Theodore Roosevelt, were especially noted for their services in improving and extending the merit system, usually called civil service. In 1943 there were nearly three million people in the Executive branch of the government of the United States (as distinguished from military and naval service). Of these about sixteen thousand were appointed by the president and confirmed by the Senate. About 95% of the total employees were directly under the jurisdiction of the Civil Service Commission.

[6] **spoils system.** The practice of giving government positions to members of the political party in power, regardless of merit.

The power of the president to remove appointive federal officials is now well established. The constitution is silent on the subject. For about seventy-five years it was generally assumed that the president had such power. Then Congress in 1867 in the conflict with President Johnson passed the tenure of office[7] act over the president's veto. This act made it unlawful for the president to remove an official confirmed by the Senate without the consent of the Senate. Later the tenure of office act was repealed by Congress.

Court decisions in recent years have established the president's power of removal without the consent of the Senate. While this power of removal is seldom used it is an effective weapon in the hands of the president that enables him to control the official conduct of an appointee or dismiss him and appoint one whom he can control. It is difficult to see how the president could be held responsible for the execution of the law, as he is by the Constitution, unless he had the power to remove appointed officials.

Our National Judicial Department. The judicial department is provided for in article three of the Constitution. Its jurisdiction is defined, the system of courts is referred to, and the judges are made appointive for life. Congress was charged with the duty of organizing the judicial department as outlined in the Constitution.

A system of courts was necessary under the Constitution. Congress was empowered to create a body of federal laws dealing with a great many important

[7] **tenure of office.** Security in holding a position.

problems. If these laws were to function it was absolutely necessary to have courts to interpret them and
to make decisions in all disputes and controversies
that might arise in the execution of the federal law.

The Constitution prescribes the jurisdiction of the
United States system of courts. It extends to all cases
arising under the Constitution, the federal laws, and
treaties. The supreme court is given original jurisdiction "in all cases affecting ambassadors, other public
ministers and consuls, and those in which a state shall
be a party." In the other cases mentioned above the
supreme court has appellate[8] jurisdiction "with such
exceptions, and under such regulations as Congress
shall make."

The federal court system as provided by Congress
consists of three courts: the *District Court,* the *Circuit
Court of Appeals,* and the *Supreme Court.*

1. There are about ninety districts in the federal
court system, and about one hundred forty-five district
judges. Every district has at least one district judge
and several of them two or more who hold court
separately. Thus the district court is a one-judge
court. The district courts are the great trial courts of
the federal system. Almost any violation of federal
law may be brought before a district court. The court
is served by a United States district attorney and a
United States marshal. These officers are appointed
by the president for a term of years. They have about
the same duties in the federal courts as the prosecuting
attorney and the sheriff have in the state courts. The

[8] **appellate.** Referred from a lower court.

court appoints its own clerk and minor officers. Appeals may be taken from the district courts to the circuit court of appeals, or in important cases, to the supreme court.

2. The United States is divided into ten circuits and in each circuit from three to six judges of the circuit

The New Chambers of the Supreme Court

court of appeals are appointed. These courts have only appellate jurisdiction, and their decisions are final in most cases.

3. The supreme court is the head of the federal court system. It is the only court provided for by

name in the Constitution. It has certain original jurisdiction given it in the Constitution. In addition,
appeals can be made to it from the decisions of the
lower federal courts and also from state supreme
courts on questions which involve federal laws. The
new home of the supreme court is shown in the photograph on the foregoing page.

Congress has the power to increase or decrease the
number of judges of the supreme court, but a decrease
cannot become effective until a vacancy occurs. At
the present time there are nine judges, the chief
justice and eight associate judges. When the court
has heard and considered a case it makes the decision
by a vote. As there are nine judges there cannot be
a tie vote if all the judges are present. There may be
a vote of five to four. There have been a number of
such decisions of important cases. While they are just
as legal as a unanimous decision they have been made
the object of much public criticism. After the decision
has been made the chief justice appoints some judge
to write the opinion or he may write it himself. Most
chief justices have written their full share of opinions.
Any judge who has voted against the majority of the
court may write a dissenting opinion. The records of
the case, including a statement of the facts, sometimes
an outline of the arguments of the attorneys and the
opinion, or opinions, in the case are then published.
These reports fill about two hundred seventy-five volumes and include the records of more than thirty
thousand cases. They are a great source of information
in constitutional law.

Laws may be declared unconstitutional by the federal courts. This power of the courts to declare laws, that are in conflict with some provision of the written Constitution, null and void,[9] is the result of the historic development of the American colonies. This right and duty of courts to declare laws unconstitutional is called *judicial review*.

Judicial review rests upon a few principles that were generally accepted when the Constitution was written. Probably most of them are accepted at the present time. First, there are certain natural rights that cannot be transferred. Second, these rights are placed in written constitutions by the people who are sovereign. Third, the written constitution is the fundamental law of the land. Fourth, ordinary law passed by legislatures, usually called statutory or legislative law, is inferior to the constitutional law. Fifth, it is the business and duty of courts to interpret and apply all law which may apply to a case under consideration. Sixth, if statutory law is in conflict with the constitutional law bearing on the case, the statutory law is null and void. That is, it is not law at all because it is in conflict with the fundamental law.

Judicial review is never exercised by a court until a case is brought before it. The practice of the courts in judicial review has been much criticized. However, it is difficult to see how a written constitution can remain a fundamental law of the land without some such action by the courts.

[9] **null and void.** Of no legal binding force.

Test and Study Exercises

Aids to Learning.

1. Remember that the Constitution of the United States vests all legislative powers in Congress.

2. Note that the Supreme Court is the only court mentioned specifically in the Constitution of the United States.

3. Observe the increasing amount of work which has been assigned to administrative boards, commissions, and agencies by various presidents during the past fifty years or more.

4. Notice that the Constitution of the United States has become recognized as the supreme authority for the interpretation of national law.

Test Exercises.

On a separate sheet of paper write the numbers from one through twelve on the left margin. Then write *yes* or *no* after each number depending on your judgment as to the answer to the following:

1. Is social security legislation a desirable goal for all the people?

2. Is the control of governmental expenditures the chief duty of Congress?

3. Is Congress the policy-determining branch of the government?

4. Is the president required by the Constitution to appoint ten cabinet officers?

5. Is the president in supreme command of the army and navy?

6. May the president appoint heads of various administrative boards with the authority of Congress?

7. Does the Constitution give the president power to remove appointed federal officials?

8. Is the federal court system fully described in the Constitution?

9. Are violations of federal law brought before the district courts?

10. Must decisions of the supreme court be based upon a unanimous vote?

11. Does the Constitution authorize the supreme court to declare laws null and void?

12. Have there always been nine judges of the supreme court?

Suggested Activities.

1. Make a list of the administrative agencies created by Congress during the past ten years. What benefits have resulted from each of them?

2. Read a biography or account of President Cleveland or President Theodore Roosevelt to see what they did to extend the merit system.

3. Read magazine articles or some such book as Theodore Roosevelt's *Letters to His Children* to learn how a president is able to conduct his private life.

4. *Group Activity:* The teacher may ask several pupils to locate magazine articles describing the work of the supreme court during recent years.

5. *Group Activity:* The teacher may choose sides for a debate on the subject, Resolved: That decisions of the supreme court should be unanimous.

CHAPTER XXIII

YOUR HERITAGE AS AN AMERICAN CITIZEN

PREPARATORY NOTE. You may know persons who have received some inheritance. You may not expect an inheritance of property, but there is another kind of inheritance of far greater value. That is the inheritance of American citizenship.

Your Inheritance of Citizenship. You have now come to the end of your consideration of the *Fundamentals of Citizenship*. You have traced your growth as a citizen of this country: first, as an individual developing physically, mentally, morally, economically, and civically; second, as a citizen member of various groups—the home, the school, and the community; third, as a member of a community which concerns itself with public health, protection, education and recreation, dependents, city planning, industry, and immigrants; and fourth, as a citizen of three separate and yet co-operative forms of government—local, state, and national. Throughout all this discussion you have realized your importance and your personal growth as an individual.

Through your study you have learned what it means to be an American citizen and that the privileges of American citizenship are the outgrowth of centuries of struggle. You have seen how representative government originated and have learned that through the national and state constitutions the fundamental elements of liberty and representative government are secured.

Your government is a co-operative enterprise and if it is to be conducted in the interests of all the people, you should bear your part in an intelligent, honest and efficient manner.

Your Intellectual Inheritance. Chief among the treasures of your inheritance is the wisdom of all the ages. The learning of the Egyptians, the Greeks, and the Romans, the records of the monk in his monastery, the stories, poems, plays, and historical records by the wisest men of all times are here available.

Knowledge is acquired through trial and experience. In very early times the only way men could transmit knowledge was by the spoken word or by signs. The only way one generation could give knowledge to the next was to tell it to the children who remembered it so that they, in turn, could pass it on to their children. But after a long time, a system of writing was developed and knowledge could then be recorded and passed on more carefully. The Greeks studied and learned much. They wrote many poems, plays, histories, and works on philosophy. The Romans through nearly a thousand years had a great government, and wrote many laws.

Much of this written knowledge was kept in libraries and monasteries. For a thousand years after the great Roman state ceased to exist the scholars of Europe were keeping records and writing books. A short time before Columbus discovered America, the printing press was invented. Books became cheaper and many more people could have them. For the past four hundred years the experiences of the human race have been written in books—and your government through its development of schools and libraries, and its guaranty of freedom of the press has placed this accumulation of the world's knowledge within your reach. While you may choose only a part of this great wealth of learning, it is here for you to have and to enjoy if you will.

Your Religious Inheritance. Religion has been important in the progress of civilization. Many kinds of religion have been developed by the human race. The countries, from which your ancestors came, once had state churches established by the government; all were required to belong to the same state church. Many came to America so that they could worship God as they pleased. In the Constitution of the United States you find the guaranty of religious freedom. Thus America has become the refuge for those persecuted because of religious beliefs. The American idea, that all should be allowed to worship as they choose, is now found in nearly every civilized country. America had an important part in bringing about this religious freedom. This is one of the most valuable parts of your heritage.

Your Material Heritage. You also have a share in the great natural resources of the American continent. Its rich soil, its great forests, its immense beds of coal, its precious metals, its useful minerals, its wells of oil, its waterways, and its abundant supply of building materials give the people of America the greatest opportunity ever offered in the world's history to build great cities, to establish large industries, to make attractive homes, and to become a contented, happy people.

Your Political Inheritance. Government in America has preserved and developed the best in civilization. You hold the key that unlocks the door to its enjoyment—American citizenship. The Declaration of Independence made possible the heritage of the American citizen; the Constitution of the United States has long safeguarded this treasure and stands as a guaranty of its security. The constitutional amendments and the state constitutions have made this inheritance even safer.

The principles for which our leaders have stood have become a vital part of our national spirit. Courage in the face of difficulties, loyalty to truth, sympathy, honor, and generosity, interwoven with a love of country and a spirit of service have been protected again and again.

Looking Forward. These inheritances are not to be hoarded; rather the door should be opened wide that those less fortunate may share. They will gain a richer meaning if the wealth of this nation is poured into the hands of coming generations. Development of air routes and waterways, extension of railroads, the education of all the people, the conservation of natural resources and of human life can have only one result— a richer, happier land.

As unselfish service throughout the ages has created these treasures and kept them secure, so must you, through a life of active, unselfish service to your community and to your nation, have a share in keeping these treasures safe for the America that is yet to be.

Test and Study Exercises

Aids to Learning.

1. Note that you have inherited citizenship in the greatest co-operative government in the world, which citizenship carries with it a great intellectual, religious, and material inheritance.

2. Remember that a good citizen does not hoard these inheritances, but through his active, intelligent service enriches them and thereby makes his community a more wholesome place in which to live.

Test Exercises.

1. What are your various kinds of inheritances as a citizen of this country?

2. How has the learning of past ages been handed down to the present generation?

3. When was the printing press invented?

4. Where do you find a guaranty of religious freedom?

5. What is your material inheritance?

6. What safeguards your political inheritance?

Suggested Activities.

1. Study the following quotations and be prepared to tell in your own words what they mean to you.

"Citizens, by birth or choice, of a common country, that country has a right to concentrate your affections. The name of American, which belongs to you in your national capacity, must always exalt the just pride of patriotism. Respect for the authority of this government, compliance with its laws, acquiescence in its measures, are duties enjoined by the fundamental maxims of true liberty."

—*George Washington*

"Let every American, every lover of liberty, every well-wisher to his posterity swear by the blood of the Revolution never to violate in the least particular the laws of the country, and never to tolerate their violation by others. As the 'patriots of seventy-six' did to the support of the Declaration of Independence, so to the support of the Constitution and laws let every American pledge his life, his liberty, and his sacred honor."

—*Abraham Lincoln*

2. The teacher will appoint three speakers on each side to debate this question: Resolved, That our intellectual inheritance is more valuable than our material inheritance.

4. When a number of flags are grouped and displayed from staffs, the Flag of the United States should be in the center or at the highest point of the group.

5. When flags of states or cities or pennants of societies are flown on the same halyard with the Flag of the United States, the National Flag should always be at the peak. When flown from adjacent staffs, the Flag of the United States should be hoisted first and lowered last. No flag or pennant should be placed above or to the right of the Flag of the United States.

6. When flags of two or more nations are displayed, they should be flown from separate staffs of the same height and the flags should be of approximately equal size. (International usage forbids the display of the flag of one nation above that of another nation in time of peace.)

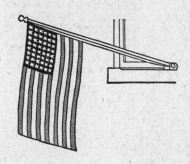

7. When the Flag is displayed from a staff projecting horizontally or at an angle from the window sill, balcony, or front of building, the union of the Flag should go clear to the head of the staff unless the Flag is at half-mast.

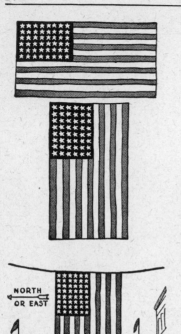

8. When the Flag of the United States is displayed in a manner other than by being flown from a staff, it should be displayed flat, whether indoors or out. When displayed either horizontally or vertically against a wall, the union should be uppermost and to the Flag's own right, i.e., to the observer's left. When displayed in a window it should be displayed the same way, i.e., with the union or blue field to the left of the observer in the street. When festoons, rosettes, or drapings of blue, white, and red are desired, bunting should be used, but never the flag.

9. When displayed over the middle of the street, as between buildings, the Flag of the United States should be suspended vertically with the union to the north in an east-and-west street or to the east in a north-and-south street.

10. When used on a speaker's platform, the Flag should be displayed above and behind the speaker. It should never be used to cover the speaker's desk nor to drape over the front of the platform. If flown from a staff it should be on the speaker's right.

11. When used in unveiling a statue or monument, the Flag should not be allowed to fall to the ground but should be carried aloft to wave out, forming a distinctive feature during the remainder of the ceremony.

12. When flown at half-mast, the Flag is first hoisted to the peak and then lowered to the half-staff position, but before lowering the Flag for the day it is raised again to the peak. On Memorial Day the Flag is displayed at half-staff from sunrise until noon and at full staff from noon until sunset, for the Nation lives and the Flag is the symbol of the living Nation.

13. When used to cover a casket, the Flag should be placed so that the union is at the head and over the left shoulder. The Flag should not be lowered into the grave nor allowed to touch the ground. The casket should be carried foot first.

14. When the Flag is displayed in church, it should be from a staff placed on the congregation's right as they face the clergyman. The service flag, the state flag, or other flag should be at the left of the congregation. If in the chancel, the Flag of the United States should be placed on the clergyman's right as he faces the congregation, and other flags on his left.

15. When the Flag is in such a condition that it is no longer a fitting emblem for display is should not be cast aside or used in any way that might be viewed as disrespectful to the national

colors, but should be destroyed as a whole, privately, preferably
by burning or by some other method in harmony with the rever-
ence and respect we owe to the emblem representing our country.

How to Respect the Flag. 1. Do not permit disrespect to be
shown to the Flag of the United States.

2. Do not dip the Flag of the United States to any person or
any thing. The regimental color, state flag, organization or insti-
tutional flag will render this honor.

3. Do not display the Flag of the United States with the union
down except as a signal of distress.

4. Do not place any other flag or pennant above or to the right
of the Flag of the United States.

5. Do not let the Flag of the United States touch the ground
or trail in the water.

6. Do not place any object or emblem of any kind on or above
the Flag of the United States.

7. Do not use the Flag as drapery in any form whatever. Use
bunting of blue, white, and red.

8. Do not fasten the Flag in such manner as will permit it to
be easily torn.

9. Do not drape the Flag over the hood, top, sides, or back of
a vehicle, or of a railroad train, or boat. When the Flag is displayed on a motor car, the staff should be affixed firmly to the
chassis or clamped to the radiator cap.

10. Do not display the Flag on a float in a parade except from
a staff.

11. Do not use the Flag as a covering for a ceiling.

12. Do not use the Flag as a portion of a costume or of an
athletic uniform.

13. Do not put lettering of any kind upon the Flag.

14. Do not use the Flag in any form of advertising nor fasten
an advertising sign to a pole from which the Flag of the United
States is flying.

15. Do not display, use, or store the Flag in such a manner
as will permit it to be easily soiled or damaged.

Use of Bunting. Bunting of the national colors should be used for a speaker's desk, for the front of a platform, or for general decoration. It should have the blue above, the white in the middle, and the red below.

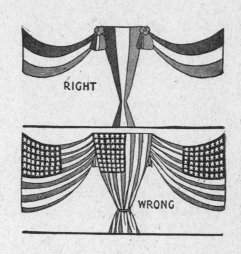

How to Salute the Flag. During the ceremony of hoisting or lowering the Flag or when the Flag is passing in a review, all persons present should face the Flag, stand at attention, and salute. Those present in uniform should render the military salute. When not in uniform, men should remove the headdress with the right hand and hold it at the left shoulder, the hand being over the heart. Men without hats should salute in the same manner. Aliens should stand at attention. Women should salute by placing the right hand over the heart. The salute to the Flag in the moving column should be rendered at the moment the Flag passes.

Salute When Giving the Pledge to the Flag. In pledging allegiance to the Flag of the United States of America, the approved practice in schools, suitable also for civilian adults, is as follows:

"I pledge allegiance to the Flag of the United States of America, and to the Republic for which it stands, one Nation indivisible, with liberty and justice for all."

The right hand should be placed over the heart. Civilians always show full respect to the Flag, when the pledge is given, by merely standing at attention, men removing the headdress. Persons in uniform render the military salute.

When the national anthem is played and the Flag is not displayed, all should stand at attention, facing the music.

DECLARATION OF INDEPENDENCE

A Declaration by the Representatives of the United States of America, in Congress Assembled July 4, 1776

When, in the course of human events, it becomes necessary for one people to dissolve the political bands which have connected them with another, and to assume, among the powers of the earth, the separate and equal station to which the laws of nature and nature's God entitle them, a decent respect to the opinions of mankind requires that they should declare the causes which impel them to the separation.

We hold these truths to be self-evident: That all men are created equal; that they are endowed by their Creator with certain unalienable rights; that among these are life, liberty, and the pursuit of happiness. That, to secure these rights, governments are instituted among men, deriving their just powers from the consent of the governed; that, whenever any form of government becomes destructive of these ends, it is the right of the people to alter or to abolish it, and to institute a new government, laying its foundation on such principles, and organizing its powers in such form, as to them shall seem most likely to effect their safety and happiness. Prudence, indeed, will dictate that governments long established should not be changed for light and transient causes; and accordingly all experience hath shown that mankind are more disposed to suffer, while evils are sufferable, than to right themselves by abolishing the forms to which they are accustomed. But when a long train of abuses and usurpations, pursuing invariably the same object, evinces a design to reduce them under absolute despotism, it is their right, it is their duty, to throw off such government, and to provide new guards for their future security. Such has been the patient sufferance of these colonies; and such is now the necessity which constrains them to alter their former systems of government. The history of the present King of Great Britain is a history of repeated injuries and usurpations, all having in direct object the establishment of an absolute tyranny over these states. To prove this, let facts be submitted to a candid world.

He has refused his assent to laws the most wholesome and necessary for the public good.

He has forbidden his governors to pass laws of immediate and pressing importance, unless suspended in their operation till his assent should be obtained; and, when so suspended, he has utterly neglected to attend to them.

He has refused to pass other laws for the accommodation of large districts of people, unless those people would relinquish the right of representation in the legislature,—a right inestimable to them, and formidable to tyrants only.

He has called together legislative bodies at places unusual, uncomfortable, and distant from the depository of their public records, for the sole purpose of fatiguing them into compliance with his measure.

He has dissolved representative houses repeatedly, for opposing, with manly firmness, his invasions on the rights of the people.

He has refused, for a long time after such dissolutions, to cause others to be elected, whereby the legislative powers, incapable of annihilation, have returned to the people at large for their exercise; the state remaining, in the meantime, exposed to all the dangers of invasions from without and convulsions within.

He has endeavored to prevent the population of these states; for that purpose obstructing the laws for the naturalization of foreigners, refusing to pass others to encourage their migration hither, and raising the conditions of new appropriations of lands.

He has obstructed the administration of justice, by refusing his assent to laws for establishing judiciary powers.

He has made judges dependent on his will alone for the tenure of their offices, and the amount and payment of their salaries.

He has erected a multitude of new offices and sent hither swarms of officers to harass our people and eat out their substance.

He has kept among us in times of peace, standing armies, without the consent of our legislatures.

He has affected to render the military independent of, and superior to, the civil power.

He has combined with others to subject us to a jurisdiction foreign to our constitutions and unacknowledged by our laws, giving his assent to their acts of pretended legislation:

For quartering large bodies of armed troops among us;

For protecting them, by a mock trial, from punishment for any murders which they should commit on the inhabitants of these states;

For cutting off our trade with all parts of the world;

For imposing taxes on us without our consent;

For depriving us, in many cases, of the benefits of trial by jury;

For transporting us beyond seas, to be tried for pretended offenses;

For abolishing the free system of English laws in a neighboring province, establishing therein an arbitrary government, and enlarging its boundaries, so as to render it at once an example and fit instrument for introducing the same absolute rule into these colonies;

For taking away our charters, abolishing our most valuable laws, and altering, fundamentally, the forms of our governments;

For suspending our own legislatures, and declaring themselves invested with power to legislate for us in all cases whatsoever.

He has abdicated government here, by declaring us out of his protection and waging war against us.

He has plundered our seas, ravaged our coasts, burned our towns, and destroyed the lives of our people.

He is at this time transporting large armies of foreign mercenaries to complete the works of death, desolation, and tyranny already begun with circumstances of cruelty and perfidy scarcely paralleled in the most barbarous ages, and totally unworthy the head of a civilized nation.

He has constrained our fellow-citizens, taken captive on the high seas, to bear arms against their country, to become the executioners of their friends and brethren, or to fall themselves by their hands.

He has excited domestic insurrection among us, and has endeavored to bring on the inhabitants of our frontiers the merciless Indian savages, whose known rule of warfare is an undistinguished destruction of all ages, sexes, and conditions.

In every stage of these oppressions we have petitioned for redress in the most humble terms; our repeated petitions have been answered only by repeated injury. A prince whose character is thus marked by every act which may define a tyrant is unfit to be the ruler of a free people.

Nor have we been wanting in our attentions to our British brethren. We have warned them, from time to time, of attempts by their legislature to extend an unwarrantable jurisdiction over us. We have reminded them of the circumstances of our emigration and settlement here. We have appealed to their native justice and magnanimity; and we have conjured them, by the ties of our common kindred, to disavow these usurpations, which would inevitably interrupt our connections and correspondence. They, too, have been deaf to the voice of justice and consanguinity. We must, therefore, acquiesce in the necessity which denounces our separation, and hold them, as we hold the rest of mankind, enemies in war, in peace, friends.

We, therefore, the representatives of the United States of America, in General Congress assembled, appealing to the Supreme Judge of the world for the rectitude of our intentions, do, in the name and by the authority of the good people of these colonies, solemnly publish and declare, That these united colonies are, and of right ought to be, free and independent states; that they are absolved from all allegiance to the British crown, and that all political connection between them and the state of Great Britain is, and ought to be, totally dissolved; and that, as free and independent states, they have full power to levy war, conclude peace, contract alliances, establish commerce, and do all other acts and things which independent states may of right do. And, for the support of this declaration with a firm reliance on the protection of Divine Providence, we mutually pledge to each other our lives, our fortunes, and our sacred honor.

CONSTITUTION OF THE UNITED STATES

PREAMBLE

We, the people of the United States, in order to form a more perfect union, establish justice, insure domestic tranquility, provide for the common defense, promote the general welfare, and secure the blessings of liberty to ourselves and our posterity, do ordain and establish this Constitution for the United States of America.

ARTICLE I

Sec. I. All legislative powers herein granted shall be vested in a Congress of the United States, which shall consist of a Senate and House of Representatives.

Sec. II. 1. The House of Representatives shall be composed of members chosen every second year by the people of the several states; and the electors in each state shall have the qualifications requisite for electors of the most numerous branch of the state legislature.

2. No person shall be a Representative who shall not have attained to the age of twenty-five years, and been seven years a citizen of the United States, and who shall not, when elected, be an inhabitant of that state in which he shall be chosen.

3. Representatives and direct taxes shall be apportioned among the several states which may be included within this Union, according to their respective numbers, which shall be determined by adding to the whole number of free persons, including those bound to service for a term of

years, and excluding Indians not taxed, three-fifths of all other persons. The actual enumeration shall be made within three years after the first meeting of the Congress of the United States, and within every subsequent term of ten years, in such manner as they shall by law direct. The number of Representatives shall not exceed one for every thirty thousand, but each state shall have at least one Representative; and until such enumeration shall be made, the state of New Hampshire shall be entitled to choose three; Massachusetts, eight; Rhode Island and Providence Plantations, one; Connecticut, five; New York, six; New Jersey, four; Pennsylvania, eight; Delaware, one; Maryland, six; Virginia, ten; North Carolina, five; South Carolina, five; Georgia, three.

4. When vacancies happen in the representation from any state, the executive authority thereof shall issue writs of election to fill such vacancies.

5. The House of Representatives shall choose their Speaker and other officers, and shall have the sole power of impeachment.

Sec. III. 1. The Senate of the United States shall be composed of two Senators from each state, chosen by the legislature thereof, for six years; and each Senator shall have one vote.

2. Immediately after they shall be assembled in consequence of the first election, they shall be divided, as equally as may be, into three classes. The seats of the Senators of the first class shall be vacated at the expiration of the second year, of the second class at the expiration of the fourth year, and the third class at the expiration of the sixth year, so that one-third may be chosen every second year; and if vacancies happen by resignation or otherwise, during the

recess of the legislature of any state, the executive thereof may make temporary appointments until the next meeting of the legislature, which shall then fill such vacancies.

3. No person shall be a Senator who shall not have attained to the age of thirty years, and been nine years a citizen of the United States, and who shall not, when elected, be an inhabitant of that State for which he shall be chosen.

4. The Vice-President of the United States shall be President of the Senate, but shall have no vote, unless they be equally divided.

5. The Senate shall choose their other officers, and also a President "pro tempore," in the absence of the Vice-President, or when he shall exercise the office of President of the United States.

6. The Senate shall have the sole power to try all impeachments. When sitting for that purpose, they shall be on oath or affirmation. When the President of the United States is tried, the Chief Justice shall preside; and no person shall be convicted without the concurrence of two-thirds of the members present.

7. Judgment, in cases of impeachment, shall not extend further than to removal from office, and disqualification to hold and enjoy any office of honor, trust, or profit under the United States; but the party convicted shall, nevertheless, be liable and subject to indictment, trial, judgment, and punishment, according to law.

Sec. IV. 1. The times, places, and manner of holding elections for Senators and Representatives shall be prescribed in each state by the legislature thereof; but the Congress may, at any time, by law, make or alter such regulations, except as to the places of choosing Senators.

2. The Congress shall assemble at least once in every year; and such meeting shall be on the first Monday in December, unless they shall by law appoint a different day.

Sec. V. 1. Each house shall be judge of the elections, returns, and qualifications of its own members; and a majority of each shall constitute a quorum to do business; but a smaller number may adjourn from day to day, and may be authorized to compel the attendance of absent members, in such manner and under such penalties as each house may provide.

2. Each house may determine the rules of its proceedings, punish its members for disorderly behavior, and, with the concurrence of two-thirds, expel a member.

3. Each house shall keep a journal of its proceedings, and from time to time publish the same, excepting such parts as may, in their judgment, require secrecy; and the yeas and nays of the members of either house on any question shall, at the desire of one-fifth of those present, be entered on the journal.

4. Neither house, during the session of Congress, shall, without the consent of the other, adjourn for more than three days, nor to any other place than that in which the two houses shall be sitting.

Sec. VI. 1. The Senators and Representatives shall receive a compensation for their services, to be ascertained by law, and paid out of the Treasury of the United States. They shall, in all cases, except treason, felony, and breach of the peace, be privileged from arrest during their attendance at the session of their respective houses, and in going to and returning from the same; and for any speech or debate in either house they shall not be questioned in any other place.

2. No Senator or Representative shall, during the time for which he was elected, be appointed to any civil office under the authority of the United States, which shall have been created, or the emoluments whereof shall have been increased, during such time; and no person holding any office under the United States shall be a member of either house during his continuance in office.

Sec. VII. 1. All bills for raising revenue shall originate in the House of Representatives; but the Senate may propose or concur with amendments, as on other bills.

2. Every bill which shall have passed the House of Representatives and the Senate shall, before it becomes a law, be presented to the President of the United States; if he approve, he shall sign it; but if not, he shall return it, with his objections, to that house in which it shall have originated, who shall enter the objections at large on their journal, and proceed to reconsider it. If, after such reconsideration, two-thirds of that house shall agree to pass the bill, it shall be sent, together with the objections, to the other house, by which it shall likewise be reconsidered, and, if approved by two-thirds of that house, it shall become a law. But in all such cases the votes of both houses shall be determined by yeas and nays; and the names of the persons voting for and against the bill shall be entered on the journal of each house respectively. If any bill shall not be returned by the President within ten days (Sundays excepted) after it shall have been presented to him, the same shall be a law, in like manner as if he had signed it, unless Congress, by their adjournment, prevent its return; in which case it shall not be a law.

3. Every order, resolution, or vote, to which the concurrence of the Senate and House of Representatives may be

necessary (except on a question of adjournment) shall be presented to the President of the United States, and, before the same shall take effect, shall be approved by him, or, being disapproved by him, shall be repassed by two-thirds of the Senate and House of Representatives, according to the rules and limitations prescribed in the case of a bill.

Sec. VIII. The Congress shall have power—

1. To lay and collect taxes, duties, imposts, and excises; to pay the debts and provide for the common defense and general welfare of the United States; but all duties, imposts, and excises shall be uniform throughout the United States:

2. To borrow money on the credit of the United States:

3. To regulate commerce with foreign nations, and among the several states, and with the Indian tribes:

4. To establish a uniform rule of naturalization, and uniform laws on the subject of bankruptcies throughout the United States:

5. To coin money, regulate the value thereof, and of foreign coin, and fix the standard of weights and measures:

6. To provide for the punishment of counterfeiting the securities and current coin of the United States:

7. To establish post offices and post roads:

8. To promote the progress of science and useful arts, by securing, for limited times, to authors and inventors the exclusive right to their respective writings and discoveries:

9. To constitute tribunals inferior to the Supreme Court:

10. To define and punish piracies and felonies committed on the high seas, and offenses against the law of nations:

11. To declare war, grant letters of marque and reprisal, and make rules concerning captures on land and water:

12. To raise and support armies; but no appropriation of money to that use shall be for a longer term than two years:

13. To provide and maintain a navy:

14. To make rules for the government and regulation of the land and naval forces:

15. To provide for calling forth the militia to execute the laws of the Union, suppress insurrections, and repel invasions:

16. To provide for organizing, arming, and disciplining the militia, and for governing such part of them as may be employed in the service of the United States, reserving to the states respectively, the appointment of the officers, and the authority of training the militia according to the discipline prescribed by Congress:

17. To exercise exclusive legislation, in all cases whatsoever, over such district (not exceeding ten miles square) as may, by cession of particular states, and the acceptance of Congress, become the seat of government of the United States, and to exercise like authority over all places purchased by the consent of the legislature of the state in which the same shall be, for the erection of forts, magazines, arsenals, dock-yards, and other needful buildings: And,

18. To make all laws which shall be necessary and proper for carrying into execution the foregoing powers, and all other powers vested by this Constitution in the government of the United States, or in any department or office thereof.

Sec. IX. 1. The migration or importation of such persons as any of the states now existing shall think proper to admit, shall not be prohibited by the Congress prior to the year one thousand eight hundred and eight; but a tax or duty may be imposed on such importation, not exceeding ten dollars for each person.

2. The privilege of the writ of "habeas corpus" shall not be suspended, unless when, in cases of rebellion or invasion, the public safety may require it.

3. No bill of attainder, or "ex post facto" law, shall be passed.

4. No capitation or other direct tax shall be laid, unless in proportion to the census or enumeration hereinbefore directed to be taken.

5. No tax or duty shall be laid on articles exported from any state.

6. No preference shall be given, by any regulation of commerce or revenue, to the ports of one state over those of another; nor shall vessels bound to or from one state be obliged to enter, clear, or pay duties in another.

7. No money shall be drawn from the Treasury, but in consequence of appropriations made by law; and a regular statement and account of the receipts and expenditures of all public money shall be published from time to time.

8. No title of nobility shall be granted by the United States; and no person holding any office of profit or trust under them shall, without the consent of the Congress, accept of any present, emolument, office, or title of any kind whatever, from any king, prince, or foreign state.

Sec. X. 1. No state shall enter into any treaty, alliance, or confederation; grant letters of marque and reprisal; coin money; emit bills of credit; make anything but gold and silver coin a tender in payment of debts; pass any bill of attainder, ex post facto law, or law impairing the obligation of contracts; or grant any title of nobility.

2. No state shall, without the consent of the Congress,

lay any imposts or duties on imports or exports, except what may be absolutely necessary for executing its inspection laws, and the net produce of all duties and imposts laid by any state on imports or exports, shall be for the use of the Treasury of the United States; and all such laws shall be subject to the revision and control of the Congress.

3. No state shall, without the consent of Congress, lay any duty of tonnage, keep troops or ships of war in time of peace, enter into any agreement or compact with another state or with a foreign power, or engage in war, unless actually invaded, or in such imminent danger as will not admit of delay.

ARTICLE II

Sec. I. 1. The executive power shall be vested in a President of the United States of America. He shall hold his office during the term of four years, and, together with the Vice-President, chosen for the same term, be elected as follows:

2. Each state shall appoint, in such manner as the legislature thereof may direct, a number of electors equal to the whole number of Senators and Representatives to which the state may be entitled in the Congress; but no Senator or Representative, or person holding an office of trust or profit under the United States, shall be appointed an elector.

3. [Annulled. See Amendments, Art. 12.]

4. The Congress may determine the time of choosing the electors, and the day on which they shall give their votes, which day shall be the same throughout the United States.

5. No person except a natural-born citizen, or a citizen of the United States at the time of the adoption of this Constitution, shall be eligible to the office of President;

neither shall any person be eligible to that office who shall not have attained to the age of thirty-five years, and been fourteen years a resident within the United States.

6. In case of the removal of the President from office, or of his death, resignation, or inability to discharge the powers and duties of the said office, the same shall devolve on the Vice-President; and the Congress may by law provide for the case of removal, death, resignation, or inability, both of the President and Vice-President, declaring what officer shall then act as President, and such officer shall act accordingly, until the disability be removed, or a President shall be elected.

7. The President shall, at stated times, receive for his services a compensation which shall neither be increased nor diminished during the period for which he shall have been elected; and he shall not receive, within that period, any other emolument from the United States, or any of them.

8. Before he enter on the execution of his office, he shall take the following oath or affirmation:—

"I do solemnly swear (or affirm) that I will faithfully execute the office of President of the United States, and will, to the best of my ability, preserve, protect, and defend the Constitution of the United States."

Sec. II. 1. The President shall be commander-in-chief of the army and navy of the United States, and of the militia of the several states, when called into the actual service of the United States; he may require the opinion, in writing, of the principal officer in each of the executive departments, upon any subject relating to the duties of their respective offices; and he shall have power to grant reprieves and pardons for offenses against the United States, except in cases of impeachment.

2. He shall have power, by and with the advice and consent of the Senate, to make treaties, provided two-thirds of the Senators present concur; and he shall nominate, and, by and with the advice and consent of the Senate, shall appoint ambassadors, other public ministers, and consuls, judges of the Supreme Court, and all other officers of the United States whose appointments are not herein otherwise provided for, and which shall be established by law. But the Congress may, by law, vest the appointment of such inferior officers as they think proper in the President alone, in the courts of law, or in the heads of departments.

3. The President shall have power to fill up all vacancies that may happen during the recess of the Senate, by granting commissions which shall expire at the end of their next session.

Sec. III. He shall, from time to time, give to the Congress information of the state of the Union, and recommend to their consideration such measures as he shall judge necessary and expedient; he may, on extraordinary occasions, convene both houses, or either of them, and, in case of disagreement between them with respect to the time of adjournment, he may adjourn them to such time as he shall think proper; he shall receive ambassadors and other public ministers; he shall take care that the laws be faithfully executed; and shall commission all the officers of the United States.

Sec. IV. The President, Vice-President, and all civil officers of the United States, shall be removed from office on impeachment for, and conviction of, treason, bribery, or other high crimes and misdemeanors.

ARTICLE III

Sec. I.   The judicial power of the United States shall be vested in one Supreme Court, and in such inferior courts as the Congress may, from time to time, ordain and establish. The judges, both of the Supreme and inferior courts, shall hold their offices during good behavior, and shall, at stated times, receive for their services a compensation which shall not be diminished during their continuance in office.

Sec. II.   1.   The judicial power shall extend to all cases in law and equity arising under this Constitution, the laws of the United States, and treaties made, or which shall be made, under their authority; to all cases affecting ambassadors, and other public ministers, and consuls; to all cases of admiralty and maritime jurisdiction; to controversies to which the United States shall be a party; to controversies between two or more states; between a state and citizens of another state; between citizens of different states; between citizens of the same state, claiming lands under grants of different states, and between a state, or the citizens thereof, and foreign states, citizens, or subjects.

2.   In all cases affecting ambassadors, other public ministers, and consuls, and those in which a state shall be a party, the Supreme Court shall have original jurisdiction. In all other cases beforementioned, the Supreme Court shall have appellate jurisdiction, both as to law and fact, with such exceptions, and under such regulations, as the Congress shall make.

3.   The trial of all crimes, except in cases of impeachment shall be by jury; and such trial shall be held in the state where the said crimes shall have been committed; but when not committed within any state, the trial shall be at

such place or places as the Congress may by law have directed.

Sec. III. 1. Treason against the United States shall consist only in levying war against them, or in adhering to their enemies, giving them aid and comfort. No person shall be convicted of treason unless on the testimony of two witnesses to the same overt act, or on confession in open court.

2. The Congress shall have power to declare the punishment of treason; but no attainder of treason shall work corruption of blood, or forfeiture, except during the life of the person attained.

ARTICLE IV

Sec. I. Full faith and credit shall be given in each state to the public acts, records, and judicial proceedings of every other state. And the Congress may, by general laws, prescribe the manner in which such acts, records, and proceedings shall be proved, and the effect thereof.

Sec. II. 1. The citizens of each state shall be entitled to all privileges and immunities of citizens in the several states.

2. A person charged in any state with treason, felony, or other crime, who shall flee from justice, and be found in another state, shall, on demand of the executive authority of the state from which he fled, be delivered up to be removed to the state having jurisdiction of the crime.

3. No person held to service or labor in one state, under the laws thereof, escaping into another, shall, in consequence of any law or regulation therein, be discharged from such service or labor, but shall be delivered up on claim of the party to whom such service or labor may be due.

Sec. III. 1. New states may be admitted by the Congress into this Union, but no new state shall be formed or erected within the jurisdiction of any other state; nor any state be formed by the junction of two or more states, or parts of states, without the consent of the legislatures of the states concerned, as well as of the Congress.

2. The Congress shall have power to dispose of and make all needful rules and regulations respecting the territory or other property belonging to the United States; and nothing in this Constitution shall be so construed as to prejudice any claims of the United States, or of any particular state.

Sec. IV. The United States shall guarantee to every state in this Union a republican form of government, and shall protect each of them against invasion, and, on application of the legislature, or of the executive (when the legislature cannot be convened), against domestic violence.

ARTICLE V

The Congress, whenever two-thirds of both houses shall deem it necessary, shall propose amendments to this Constitution, or, on the application of the legislatures of two-thirds of the several states, shall call a convention for proposing amendments, which, in either case, shall be valid to all intents and purposes, as part of this Constitution, when ratified by the legislatures of three-fourths of the several states, or by conventions in three-fourths thereof, as the one or the other mode of ratification may be proposed by the Congress; provided that no amendment which may be made prior to the year one thousand eight hundred and eight shall in any manner affect the first and fourth clauses in the Ninth Section of the First Article; and that no state, without its consent, shall be deprived of its equal suffrage in the Senate.

ARTICLE VI

1. All debts contracted, and engagements entered into, before the adoption of this Constitution, shall be as valid against the United States under this Constitution as under the Confederation.

2. This Constitution, and the laws of the United States which shall be made in pursuance thereof, and all treaties made, or which shall be made, under the authority of the United States, shall be the supreme law of the land; and the judges in every state shall be bound thereby, anything in the Constitution or laws of any state to the contrary notwithstanding.

3. The Senators and Representatives beforementioned, and the members of the several state legislatures, and all executive and judicial officers, both of the United States and of the several states, shall be bound by oath or affirmation to support this Constitution; but no religious test shall ever be required as a qualification to any office or public trust under the United States.

ARTICLE VII

The ratification of the conventions of nine states shall be sufficient for the establishment of this Constitution between the states so ratifying the same.

AMENDMENTS TO THE CONSTITUTION

Art. I. Congress shall make no law respecting an establishment of religion, or prohibiting the free exercise thereof;

or abridging the freedom of speech, or of the press; or the right of the people peaceably to assemble and to petition the government for a redress of grievances.

Art. II.   A well-regulated militia being necessary to the security of a free state, the right of the people to keep and bear arms shall not be infringed.

Art. III.   No soldier shall, in time of peace, be quartered in any house, without the consent of the owner, nor in time of war, but in a manner to be prescribed by law.

Art. IV.   The right of the people to be secure in their persons, houses, papers, and effects, against unreasonable searches and seizures, shall not be violated; and no warrants shall issue but upon probable cause, supported by oath or affirmation, and particularly describing the place to be searched, and the persons or things to be seized.

Art. V.   No person shall be held to answer for a capital, or otherwise infamous crime, unless on a presentment or indictment of a grand jury, except in cases arising in the land or naval forces, or in the militia, when in actual service in time of war or public danger; nor shall any person be subject for the same offense to be twice put in jeopardy of life or limb; nor shall be compelled, in any criminal case, to be witness against himself, nor be deprived of life, liberty, or property, without due process of law; nor shall private property be taken for public use without just compensation.

Art. VI.   In all criminal prosecutions, the accused shall enjoy the right to a speedy and public trial by an impartial jury of the state and district wherein the crime shall have been committed, which district shall have been previously ascertained by law, and to be informed of the nature and cause of the accusation; to be confronted with the witnesses against him; to have compulsory process for obtaining witnesses in his favor; and to have the assistance of counsel for his defense.

Art. VII.   In suits at common law, where the value in controversy shall exceed twenty dollars, the rights of trial by jury shall be preserved; and no fact, tried by a jury, shall be otherwise re-examined in any court of the United States, than according to the rules of the common law.

Art. VIII.   Excessive bail shall not be required, nor excessive fines imposed, nor cruel and unusual punishment inflicted.

Art. IX.   The enumeration in the Constitution of certain rights shall not be construed to deny or disparage others retained by the people.

Art. X.   The powers not delegated to the United States by the Constitution, nor prohibited by it to the states, are reserved to the states respectively, or to the people.

Art. XI.   The judicial power of the United States shall not be construed to extend to any suit in law or equity, commenced or prosecuted against one of the United States by citizens of another state, or by citizens or subjects of any foreign state.

Art. XII.   1.   The electors shall meet in their respective states, and vote by ballot for President and Vice-President, one of whom, at least, shall not be an inhabitant of the same state with themselves; they shall name in their ballots the person voted for as President, and in distinct ballots the person voted for as Vice-President; and they shall make distinct lists of all persons voted for as President, and of all

persons voted for as Vice-President, and of the number of
votes for each; which lists they shall sign and certify, and
transmit, sealed, to the seat of the government of the United States, directed to the President of the Senate. The
President of the Senate shall, in the presence of the Senate
and House of Representatives, open all the certificates, and
the votes shall then be counted; the person having the
greatest number of votes for President shall be the President, if such number be a majority of the whole number
of electors appointed; and if no person have such majority,
then from the persons having the highest numbers, not
exceeding three, on the list of those voted for as President,
the House of Representatives shall choose immediately, by
ballot, the President. But, in choosing the President, the
votes shall be taken by states, the representation from each
state having one vote; a quorum for this purpose shall consist of a member or members from two-thirds of the states,
and a majority of all the states shall be necessary to a
choice. And if the House of Representatives shall not
choose a President, whenever the right of choice shall devolve upon them, before the fourth day of March next
following, then the Vice-President shall act as President,
as in the case of the death or other constitutional disability
of the President.

2. The person having the greatest number of votes as
Vice-President shall be the Vice-President, if such number
be a majority of the whole number of electors appointed;
and if no person have a majority, then from the two highest
numbers on the list the Senate shall choose the Vice-President; a quorum for the purpose shall consist of two-thirds
of the whole number of Senators, and a majority of the
whole number shall be necessary to a choice.

3. But no person constitutionally ineligible to the office

of President shall be eligible to that of Vice-President of the United States.

Art. XIII. 1. Neither slavery nor involuntary servitude, except as a punishment for crime, whereof the party shall have been duly convicted, shall exist within the United States, or any place subject to their jurisdiction.

2. Congress shall have power to enforce this article by appropriate legislation.

Art. XIV. 1. All persons born or naturalized in the United States, and subject to the jurisdiction thereof, are citizens of the United States and of the state wherein they reside. No state shall make or enforce any law which shall abridge the privileges or immunities of citizens of the United States; nor shall any state deprive any person of life, liberty, or property, without due process of law, nor deny to any person within its jurisdiction the equal protection of the laws.

2. Representatives shall be apportioned among the several states according to their respective numbers, counting the whole number of persons in each state, excluding Indians not taxed. But when the right to vote at any election, for the choice of electors for President and Vice-President of the United States, Representatives in Congress, the executive and judicial officers of a state, or the members of the legislature thereof, is denied to any of the male inhabitants of such state, being twenty-one years of age, and citizens of the United States, or in any way abridged, except for participation in rebellion or other crime, the basis of representation therein shall be reduced in the proportion which the number of such male citizens shall bear to the whole number of male citizens twenty-one years of age in such state.

3. No person shall be a Senator or Representative in Congress, or elector of President and Vice-President, or hold any office, civil or military, under the United States, or under any state, who, having previously taken an oath as a member of Congress, or as an officer of the United States, or as a member of any state legislature, or as an executive or judicial officer of any state, to support the Constitution of the United States, shall have engaged in insurrection or rebellion against the same, or given aid or comfort to the enemies thereof. But Congress may, by a vote of two-thirds of each house, remove such disability.

4. The validity of the public debt of the United States, authorized by law, including debts incurred for payment of pensions and bounties for services in suppressing insurrection or rebellion, shall not be questioned. But neither the United States nor any state shall assume or pay any debt or obligation incurred in aid of insurrection or rebellion against the United States, or any claim for the loss or emancipation of any slave; but all such debts, obligations, and claims shall be held illegal and void.

5. Congress shall have power to enforce, by appropriate legislation, the provisions of this article.

Art. XV. 1. The right of citizens of the United States to vote shall not be denied or abridged by the United States, or by any state, on account of race, color, or previous condition of servitude.

2. The Congress shall have power to enforce this article by appropriate legislation.

Art. XVI. The Congress shall have power to lay and collect taxes on incomes, from whatever source derived, without apportionment among the several states, and without regard to any census or enumeration.

Art. XVII. The Senate of the United States shall be composed of two Senators from each state, elected by the people thereof, for six years; and each Senator shall have one vote. The electors in each state shall have the qualifications requisite for electors of the most numerous branch of the state legislatures.

When vacancies happen in the representation of any state in the Senate, the executive authority of such state shall issue writs of election to fill such vacancies. Provided, that the legislature of any state may empower the executive thereof to make temporary appointment until the people fill the vacancies by election as the legislature may direct.

This amendment shall not be so construed as to effect the election or term of any Senator chosen before it becomes valid as part of the Constitution.

Art. XVIII. Sec. 1. After one year from the ratification of this article, the manufacture, sale, or transportation of intoxicating liquors within, the importation thereof into, or the exportation thereof from the United States and all territory subject to the jurisdiction thereof, for beverage purposes, is hereby prohibited.

Sec. 2. The Congress and the several states shall have concurrent power to enforce this article by appropriate legislation.

Sec. 3. This article shall be inoperative unless it shall have been ratified as an amendment to the Constitution by the legislatures of the several states, as provided in the Constitution, within seven years from the date of the submission hereof to the states by the Congress.

Art. XIX. 1. The right of citizens of the United States

to vote shall not be denied or abridged by the United States or by any state on account of sex.

2. Congress shall have power to enforce this article by appropriate legislation.

Art. XX. Sec. 1. The terms of the President and Vice-President shall end at noon on the twentieth day of January, and the terms of Senators and Representatives at noon on the third day of January, of the years in which such terms would have ended if this article had not been ratified; and the terms of their successors shall then begin.

Sec. 2. The Congress shall assemble at least once in every year, and such meetings shall begin at noon on the third day of January, unless they shall by law appoint a different day.

Sec. 3. If, at the time fixed for the beginning of the term of the President, the President-elect shall have died, the Vice-President-elect shall become President. If a President shall not have been chosen before the time fixed for the beginning of his term, or if the President-elect shall have failed to qualify, then the Vice-President-elect shall act as President until a President shall have qualified; and the Congress may by law provide for the case wherein neither a President-elect nor a Vice-President-elect shall have qualified, declaring who shall then act as President, or the manner in which one who is to act shall be selected, and such person shall act accordingly until a President or Vice-President shall have qualified.

Sec. 4. The Congress may by law provide for the case of the death of any of the persons from whom the House of Representatives may choose a President whenever the right of choice shall have devolved upon them, and for the case of the death of any of the persons from whom the Senate may choose a Vice-President whenever the right of choice shall have devolved upon them.

Sec. 5.   Sections 1 and 2 shall take effect upon the fifteenth day of October following the ratification of this article.

Sec. 6.   This article shall be inoperative unless it shall have been ratified as an amendment to the Constitution by the legislatures of three-fourths of the several States within seven years from the date of its submission.

Art. XXI.   Sec. 1.   The eighteenth amendment to the Constitution of the United States is hereby repealed.

Sec. 2.   The transportation or importation into any State, Territory, or possession of the United States for delivery or use therein of intoxicating liquors, in violation of the laws thereof, is hereby prohibited.

Sec. 3.   This article shall be inoperative unless it shall have been ratified as an amendment to the Constitution by conventions in the several States, as provided in the Constitution, within seven years from the date of the submission hereof to the States by the Congress.

COMPENDIUM OF CIVIC INFORMATION

TERRITORIES AND DEPENDENCIES OF THE UNITED STATES

Territories are those regions too sparsely settled or which for some other reason are not yet ready to be made states. Their type of government is that which is designed to prepare them to become states; however, it is not likely that the territories listed below will become states very soon. Dependencies are given whatever government best suits their needs.

Name	Date of Acquisition	Area Sq. Mi.	Population 1940	Territory or Dependency
Alaska...	Purchased from Russia in March, 1867......	586,400	72,524	Territory
Hawaii...	Annexed to U. S. July 7, 1898..............	6,407*	423,330	Territory
Guam....	Ceded to U. S. by Spain, December 10, 1898..	206	22,290	Dependency
Philippine Islands.	Ceded to U. S. by Spain, December 10, 1898..	114,400	16,356,000	Commonwealth**
Puerto Rico...	Ceded to U. S. by Spain, December 10, 1898..	3,435	1,869,255	Dependency
American Samoa.	Acquired by U. S. December 2, 1899......	76	12,908	Dependency
Panama Canal Zone...	Acquired by U. S. May 4, 1904............	554	51,827	Dependency
Virgin Islands.	Purchased from Denmark, March 3, 1917.	133	24,889	Dependency

*Includes Midway Islands.
**In 1934 the Philippine Islands were granted independence, which took place in 1946. Until then our government was represented there by a high commissioner.

UNITED STATES GOVERNMENT
Executive Department

The President. Harry S. Truman. Salary $75.000

Vice-President. (Vacancy) Salary $15,000

The Executive Office of the President

The White House Office; Liaison Office for Personnel Management; Bureau of the Budget.

Federal Security Agency; Watson B. Miller, Administrator

Activities: Social Security Board; Public Health Service; United States Office of Education; Office of Vocational Rehabilitation; Food and Drug Administration.

Federal Works Agency; Maj. Gen. Philip B. Fleming, Administrator

Activities: Public Buildings Administration; Public Roads Administration; Federal Fire Council; Federal Real Estate Board; Bureau of Community Facilities.

Federal Loan Agency; Charles B. Henderson, Acting Administrator

Activities: Reconstruction Finance Corporation; Federal National Mortgage Association; RFC Mortgage Company; War Damage Corporation.

The Cabinet. The salary of each cabinet member is $15,000

Department of State; George C. Marshall, Secretary

Activities: Formulation of Policy toward Other Countries; Treaties and Other International Agreements; International Trade Policy; Recognition of States, Governments, and Belligerency; Policy Relative to International Organization and Security; Foreign Service of the United States; Foreign Diplomatic and Consular Offices; Registration of Agents of Foreign Principals; Passports and Visas; Extradition Procedure; International Transport and Communications; Informational and Cultural Aspects of Policy; Domestic Functions; Publications.

Department of the Treasury; John W. Snyder, Secretary

Activities: Bureau of Comptroller of Currency; Bureau of Customs; Bureau of Engraving and Printing; Bureau of Internal Revenue; Bureau of the Mint; Bureau of Narcotics; Division of Monetary Research; Division of Research and Statistics; Division of Tax Research; Legal Division; Fiscal Service; War Finance Division; Foreign Fund Control; Procurement Division; U. S. Secret Service; Office of Tax Legislative Counsel.

War Department; Robert P. Patterson, Secretary

Activities: War Department General Staff; Special Staff; Army Service Forces; Army Ground Forces; Army Air Forces; Joint Army-Navy Boards; Panama Canal; Army War College; Arlington Memorial Amphitheater Commission.

Department of Justice; Tom C. Clark, Attorney General

Activities: General Government Legal Representation, Advice, and Opinions; Representation in U. S. Supreme Court; Antitrust Division; Tax Division; Claims Division; Lands Division; Criminal Division; Customs Division; Federal Bureau of Investigation; Bureau of Prisons; Board of Parole; Immigration and Naturalization Service; Board of Immigration Appeals.

Post Office Department; Robert E. Hannegan, Postmaster General

Activities: Care, Maintenance, and Operation of Federal Postal Service; Postal Treaties with Foreign Governments, subject to Approval of President; Award and Execution of Mail Contracts and Management of Foreign Mail Service; Management of Postal Savings, Money-Order, and Registered Mail Services; Supervision of Air and Railway Mail Service; Disposition of Dead Letters and Parcel Post.

Department of the Navy; James Forrestal, Secretary

Activities: Office of Commander in Chief, United States Fleet, and Chief of Naval Operations; Bureau of Aeronautics; Bureau of Medicine and Surgery; Bureau of Ordnance; Bureau of Ships; Bureau of Supplies and Accounts; Bureau of Yards and Docks; Headquarters United States Marine Corps; United States Coast Guard; Joint Army-Navy Boards.

Department of the Interior; Julius A. Krug, Secretary

Activities: General Land Office; Bureau of Reclamation; Geological Survey; Bureau of Mines; Office of Indian Affairs; National Park Service; Fish and Wildlife Service; Petroleum Conservation Division; Solid Fuels Administration for War; Division of Power; Division of Territories and Island Possessions; Puerto Rico Reconstruction Administration; Office of Land Utilization; Grazing Service; National Power Policy Committee.

Department of Agriculture; Clinton P. Anderson, Secretary

Activities: Agricultural Research Administration; Bureau of Agricultural and Industrial Chemistry; Bureau of Dairy Industry; Bureau of Animal Industry; Bureau of Etomology and Plant Quarantine; Bureau of Human Nutrition; Bureau of Plant Industry; Experiment Stations; Extension Service; Farm Credit Administration; Farm Security Administration; Forest Service; Rural Electrification Administration; Production and Marketing Administration; Commodity Credit Corporation; Federal Crop Insurance Corporation; Soil Conservation; Bureau of Agricultural Economics; Foreign Agricultural Relations.

Department of Commerce; W. Averell Harriman, Secretary

Activities: Business Advisory Council; Bureau of the Census; Coast and Geodetic Survey; Bureau of Foreign and Domestic Commerce; Inland Waterways Corporation; National Bureau of Standards; Patent Office; Weather Bureau; Office of Surplus Property; Civil Aeronautics Authority; Civil Aeronautics Administration; Civil Aeronautics Board.

Department of Labor; Lewis B. Schwellenbach, Secretary

Activities: United States Conciliation Service; Bureau of Labor Standards; Wage, Hour, and Public Contracts Division; Bureau of Labor Statistics; Children's Bureau; Women's Bureau.

JUDICIAL DEPARTMENT

Supreme Court of the United States.

Chief Justice Fred M. Vinson, appointed 1946. Salary $20,500.

*Associate Justices

Hugo L. Black, appointed 1937.

Stanley F. Reed, appointed 1938.

Felix Frankfurter, appointed 1939.

William O. Douglas, appointed 1939.

Frank Murphy, appointed 1940.

Robert H. Jackson, appointed 1941.

Wiley B. Rutledge, Jr., appointed 1943.

Harold H. Burton, appointed 1945.

*Salary of each, $20,000 yearly.

Court of Customs and Patent Appeals

MEMBERS	SALARY
Presiding Judge	$12,500
4 Associate Judges, each	12,500

Court of Claims

MEMBERS	SALARY
Chief Justice	$12,500
4 Associate Judges, each	12,500

United States Customs Court

MEMBERS	SALARY
Presiding Judge	$10,000
8 Associate Judges, each	10,000

Federal Circuit Courts

DISTRICT	JUDICIAL CIRCUIT	*No. of JUDGES
First	Me., Mass., N. H., R. I., Puerto Rico	3
Second	Conn., N. Y., Vt.	6
Third	Del., N. J., Pa.	5
Fourth	Md., N. C., S. C., Va., W. Va.	3
Fifth	Ala., Fla., Ga., La., Miss., Tex., Canal Zone	5
Sixth	Ky., Mich., Ohio, Tenn.	6

Federal Circuit Courts
(Continued)

DISTRICT	JUDICIAL CIRCUIT	*No. of JUDGES
Seventh	Ill., Ind., Wis.	5
Eighth	Ark., Iowa, Minn., Mo., Nebr., N. Dak., S. Dak.	7
Ninth	Ariz., Calif., Idaho, Mont., Nev., Oreg., Wash., Alaska, Hawaii	7
Tenth	Colo., Wyo., Utah, Kan., Okla., N. Mex.	4

*Salary of each, $12,500 yearly.

United States District Courts

There are one or more United States District Courts in each state.

Circuit Court of Appeals

Each of the Circuit Courts of Appeals includes the District and Circuit judges in its particular circuit. They meet in the following cities of the respective Districts.

DISTRICT	CITY	DISTRICT	CITY
First	Boston, and when necessary, San Juan, P. R.	Seventh	Chicago
Second	New York	Eighth	St. Louis, Kansas City, Omaha, and St. Paul
Third	Philadelphia	Ninth	San Francisco, and two other places designated by judges of this District
Fourth	Richmond and Asheville, N. C.		
Fifth	New Orleans, Atlanta, Ft. Worth, and Montgomery	Tenth	Denver, Wichita, and Oklahoma City
Sixth	Cincinnati		

LEGISLATIVE DEPARTMENT

The Congress

	TERM	SALARY	QUALIFICATIONS
Senate			
Vice - President, presiding officer	4 yrs.	$15,000	Must be a natural-born citizen; 35 yrs. old; and a resident in U. S. 14 yrs.
2 Senators from each state	6 yrs.	$10,000	Must be 30 yrs. old; a U. S. citizen for 9 yrs.; an inhabitant of the state electing him.
House of Representatives No. of Representatives depends on population of states and apportionment determined by Congress. The presiding officer is called the Speaker.	2 yrs.	$10,000	Must be 25 yrs. old; a U. S. citizen for 7 yrs.; an inhabitant of the state electing him.

THREE WAYS IN WHICH A BILL MAY BECOME A LAW

1. A bill becomes a law when it is passed by both houses of Congress and signed by the President.

2. A bill becomes a law when it is vetoed by the President and passed by a two-thirds vote of both houses over his veto.

3. A bill becomes a law when it is passed by both houses of Congress and the President holds it for ten days without signing it. It is then enacted without his signature.

THE UNITED STATES CENSUS BUREAU

The Constitution requires that a population census of the United States be taken decennially. The first census was taken in 1790, and the most recent, the sixteenth, in 1940. The Census Bureau was made a permanent organization in 1902 and since 1913 has been a branch of the Department of Commerce. In 1927 the Bureau took, for the first time, a census of distribution of trade in some of the principal cities. One important feature of the Census Bureau's work is the monthly publication of the *Survey of Current Business,* which gives data regarding the movement of prices, stocks on hand, production, etc., for various lines of trade and industry, together with such other available data as may throw light upon the business situation.

The scope of the decennial census, which at first was little more than a simple count of the population by family groups and by sex and color, has been extended from time to time until in 1930 it covered in detail population, including occupations; agriculture, including irrigation and drainage; manufactures; mines, quarries, and oil and gas wells; distribution (wholesale and retail trade); and unemployment.

The Director of the Census is appointed by the President. The permanent organization includes seven chief statisticians; namely, for Population, for Manufactures, for statistics of States and Cities, for Agriculture, for Vital Statistics, for Distribution, and for Cotton and Vegetable Oils. The regular force of the Bureau at Washington during intercensal periods comprises about 800 persons, and in addition approximately 750 special agents are employed intermittently in the South for the collection of data in regard to cotton and cottonseed. During a decennial census period the office force in Washington reaches a maximum of about 6,000 employees, and nearly 100,000 enumerators. These, together with a large number of supervisors, clerks, and other employees, are engaged in the task of collecting data, compiling statistics, and preparing reports for publication.

A decennial census of the United States is the most extensive investigation of its character undertaken by any governmental or other agency in any country; and the Bureau of Census is the largest statistical organization in the world.

STEPS AN ALIEN TAKES TO BECOME A CITIZEN

1. He may file his intention of naturalization as soon after his arrival in this country as he wishes if he is eighteen years of age or over. He should fill out application form N-300 and send it to the naturalization officer, accompanied by two signed photographs of himself. The fee for the declaration is $3.00 payable to the clerk of the court.

2. Two years later and after five years of continuous residence in this country, he may file his petition for citizenship. This must be done not more

than seven years after filing his first papers of intention. He must have at least two citizens as witnesses who have personal knowledge of his continuous residence in this country. They must also furnish witness to his good moral character. He must be able to speak English unless physically unable to do so. The fee for petition is $8.00.

3. Not less than thirty days later he is notified to appear for final action before the court to renounce allegiance to the foreign government of which he is a subject or citizen and to take the oath of allegiance to the United States. In most Federal and many State courts the witnesses are needed only at the time of filing the petition and need not appear for this final hearing. If the court finds the petitioner qualified for citizenship, he administers the oath and the applicant is given the certificate of citizenship.

LIBRARY OF CONGRESS

The Library of Congress was established in 1800 in Washington, D. C. It was destroyed by the burning of the Capitol in 1814 and in 1851 lost 35,000 volumes in another fire. The present library building, which cost $6,347,000, exclusive of land and subsequent additions, was opened to the public in November, 1897. It is located but a short distance from the Capitol and is the largest and finest building of its kind in the world.

The library contains approximately 5,000,000 books and pamphlets, over 1,000,000 maps, another million volumes and pieces of music, and some 500,000 prints. This collection has been built up through appropriations by Congress, by deposits under the Copyright Law, by gifts and exchanges, and by special additions. The material available is rich in history, political science, in official documents, national, state, and foreign, and in literary, historical, or other matters relating to America, including important files of American newspapers and original manuscripts. The manuscript collections are especially noteworthy for material on American history, some of the most distinguished of which have been received by transfer from the executive departments, the library now being regarded as the main custodian of the historical archive material in the possession of the government. Copies are also being made of documents concerning American history which are a part of foreign archive offices or other institutions. The library already has a large body of transcripts from such sources. This policy of transcribing and copying, where necessary by facsimile, is applied also to maps and to music.

The library is also the custodian of the originals of the Declaration of Independence and of the Constitution of the United States.

The Copyright Department is a distinct division of the Library of Congress. It is under the immediate charge of the Register of Copyrights, who acts directly under the supervision of the Librarian of Congress.

The Library is maintained by Congress through annual appropriations for various purposes.

SMITHSONIAN INSTITUTION

The Smithsonian Institution at Washington, D. C., was created by act of Congress in 1846, under the terms of the will of James Smithson, an Englishman, who bequeathed his fortune in 1826 to the United States to found an institution for the "increase and diffusion of knowledge among men." From the income of the fund a building, known as the Smithsonian Building, was erected on land given by the United States. The Institution's original endowment of $541,000 has been increased by gifts and accumulation of interest.

The Institution is legally an organization, having as its members the President of the United States, the Vice-President, the Chief Justice, and the President's Cabinet. It is governed by a Board of Regents consisting of the Vice-President, the Chief Justice, three members of the Senate, three members of the House of Representatives, and six citizens of the United States appointed by joint resolution of Congress. The secretary of Smithsonian Institution is its executive officer and the director of its activities.

Throughout its history, the Institution has conducted and encouraged important scientific researches and investigations through aiding investigators by making grants for research and exploration, providing for lectures, initiating scientific projects, and publishing scientific papers. It also maintains a library of 700,000 volumes which consist mainly of the proceedings of learned societies and scientific periodicals. While the body of the library is deposited in the Library of Congress and accessible to all its readers, a working library is maintained at the Institution.

It has administrative charge of the National Museum, the National Gallery of Art, including the Freer Gallery of Art; the International Exchange Service, the Bureau of American Ethnology, the National Zoological Park, the Astrophysical Observatory, and the United States Regional Bureau for the International Catalogue of Scientific Literature.

UNITED STATES BUREAU OF ENGRAVING AND PRINTING

The Bureau of Engraving and Printing of the Treasury Department manufactures all the paper money of the government; all stamps, including revenue stamps; all official checks, drafts, warrants, commissions, certificates, transportation requests, passports, and liquor permits. Its appropriation for the fiscal year ending June 30, 1936, aggregated $9,658,545, an increase of 10.25% over the previous year.

The major task of the Bureau of Engraving and Printing is the production of paper money. It is all printed from steel engraved plates. Since steel engravings are now little used except in printing money, practically all of the steel engravers in the country work here. The engravings are transferred to flat plates which print twelve notes at an impression. Paper specially made for the government is used. The method of printing is such as is employed almost nowhere else. Infinite care is taken that every note shall be perfect and that none of the distinctive paper is lost in the process of manufacture. Each note is subjected to a score of examinations.

The total weight of paper currency manufactured during 1936 was about 940 tons. It would have loaded 24 forty-ton freight cars. Over half of these notes were one-dollar bills.

Of bonds, notes, and certificates, there were delivered 17,601,254 sheets. Postage and other stamps accounted for 269,806,292 additional sheets. During the year 2,500 tons of stamps were manufactured, about 60 carloads of them. Other miscellaneous forms manufactured at this plant consumed about 36,277,721 sheets, weighing about 600 tons, and making about 15 carloads.

COINAGE MINTS

Location	Established
Philadelphia	1792
San Francisco	1852
Denver	1862

ASSAY OFFICES

New York	Helena, Mont.
Carson City, Nev.	Seattle
Denver	Salt Lake City
Boise, Idaho	

FEDERAL RESERVE CITIES

Dist.	City	Dist.	City	Dist.	City
1	Boston	5	Richmond	9	Minneapolis
2	New York	6	Atlanta	10	Kansas City
3	Philadelphia	7	Chicago	11	Dallas
4	Cleveland	8	St. Louis	12	San Francisco

GOVERNMENT OF DISTRICT OF COLUMBIA

The District of Columbia is the seat of the Federal Government of the United States. Almost its entire activity is governmental, there being about 65,000 civil service employees in the city. The distinctive feature of the District is the fact that the legislative department is carried on by Congress directly, and the executive department is under an Executive Commission named by the President and confirmed by the Senate. Each house of the Congress has a committee on District of Columbia. Taxation, current and for improvements, is borne chiefly by the taxpayers of the District. The residents have no vote in municipal matters in the District, but retain their state residence and vote at home on all occasions.

AREA OF NATIONAL FORESTS IN THE UNITED STATES

United States Department of Agriculture
June 30, 1938

STATE	ACRES	STATE	ACRES	STATE	ACRES
Ala.	570,054	Mich.	1,774,454	Pa.	432,308
Alaska	21,348,215	Minn.	2,384,877	Puerto Rico.	34,903
Ariz.	11,400,859	Miss.	938,624	S. C.	519,853
Ark.	2,024,310	Mo.	1,088,647	S. Dak.	1,079,543
Calif.	19,452,635	Mont.	16,218,341	Tenn.	529,577
Colo.	13,629,532	Nebr.	206,026	Tex.	639,452
Fla.	1,317,015	Nev.	4,988,080	Utah	7,661,764
Ga.	566,295	N. H.	663,254	Vt.	160,539
Idaho	19,884,456	N. Mex.	8,558,286	Va.	1,291,036
Ill.	172,361	N. C.	911,971	Wash.	9,003,395
Ind.	34,209	N. Dak.	480	W. Va.	891,091
Iowa	100	Ohio	34,234	Wis.	1,320,413
Ky.	392,771	Okla.	150,923	Wyo.	8,644,163
Mass.	1,651	Oreg.	13,788,802	Total	175,238,168

NATIONAL PARKS IN THE UNITED STATES

Under supervision of the Secretary of the Interior.

NAME	LOCATION	YEAR CREATED	ACRES
Abraham Lincoln*	Kentucky	1916	108
Acadia	Maine	1919	12,160
Antietam*	Maryland	1890	40
Bryce Canyon	Utah	1928	35,200
Carlsbad Caverns	New Mexico	1930	10,240
Chickamauga & Chattanooga*	Georgia & Tennessee	1890	5,733
Crater Lake	Oregon	1902	160,640
Fort Donelson*	Tennessee	1928	108
Fredericksburg*	Virginia	1927	
General Grant	California	1890	2,560
Gettysburg*	Pennsylvania	1895	2,530

NATIONAL PARKS IN THE UNITED STATES *(Continued)*

Under supervision of the Secretary of the Interior

NAME	LOCATION	YEAR CREATED	ACRES
Glacier	Montana	1910	981,760
Grand Canyon	Arizona	1919	645,760
Grand Teton	Wyoming	1929	96,000
Great Smoky Mountains	North Carolina and Tennessee	1930	297,600
Guilford Courthouse*	North Carolina	1917	110
Hawaii	Hawaii	1916	156,800
Hot Springs	Arkansas	1921	960
Kings Mountain*	South Carolina	1931	......
Lassen Volcanic	California	1916	104,320
Mesa Verde	Colorado	1906	51,200
Moores Creek*	North Carolina	1926	30
Morristown	New Jersey	1933	853
Mount McKinley	Alaska	1917	1,939,200
Mount Rainier	Washington	1899	241,920
Petersburg*	Virginia	1926	185
Platt	Oklahoma	1902	853
Rocky Mountain	Colorado	1915	259,200
Sequoia	California	1890	386,560
Shiloh*	Tennessee	1894	3,583
Stones River*	Tennessee	1927	345
Sully's Hill	North Dakota	1904	780
Vicksburg*	Mississippi	1899	1,322
Wind Cave	South Dakota	1903	11,520
Yellowstone	Wyoming, Montana, and Idaho	1872	2,200,320
Yosemite	California	1890	752,640
Zion	Utah	1919	94,720

*In charge of Secretary of War.

THE INTERNATIONAL COURT OF JUSTICE

The Permanent Court of International Justice, established after the First World War, held its inaugural session at The Hague, Holland, in February, 1922. Although the United States was not a member of the Court, four American judges served on it. After the Second World War the Statute of the Court was revised and annexed to the United Nations Charter. The

United States became a member of this revised International Court of Justice from the outset. In February, 1946, the new judges were elected and the Court began its work at The Hague. The membership of the Court at that time was as follows:

Alejandro Alvarez ....Chile
J. Philadelpho de Barros Azevedo...............Brazil
Jules Basdevant ....France
J. Gustavo Guerrero ....El Salvador
Arnold D. McNair...............................Great Britain
I. Fabela Alfaro ....Mexico
Green H. Hackworth.............................United States
Helge Klaestad ....Norway
Sergei B. Krylov...............................U.S.S.R.
Charles de Visscher ....Belgium
Abdel Hamid Badawi.............................Egypt
Hsu Mo ....China
John E. Read...................................Canada
Bohdan Winiarski ....Poland
Milovan Zoricic ....Yugoslavia

STATE STATISTICS

STATE	NO. OF REPRESENTA- TIVES	TOTAL POPULATION 1940	URBAN PERCENTAGE 1940	SCHOOL ENROLL- MENT 1941-1942
Alabama	9	2,832,961	30.2	666,738
Arizona	2	499,261	34.8	116,430
Arkansas	7	1,949,387	22.2	441,106
California	23	6,907,387	71.0	1,225,850
Colorado	4	1,123,296	52.6	214,022
Connecticut	6	1,709,242	67.8	266,808
Delaware	1	266,505	52.3	42,505
Dist. of Columbia	..	663,091	100.0	96,520
Florida	6	1,897,414	55.1	369,036
Georgia	10	3,123,723	34.4	713,094
Idaho	2	524,873	33.7	118,821
Illinois	26	7,897,241	73.6	1,196,770
Indiana	11	3,427,796	55.1	669,148
Iowa	8	2,538,268	42.7	490,934
Kansas	6	1,801,028	41.9	362,812
Kentucky	9	2,845,627	29.8	575,107
Louisiana	8	2,363,880	41.5	461,835

STATE STATISTICS (*Continued*)

STATE	No. of REPRESENTA- TIVES	TOTAL POPULATION 1940	URBAN PERCENTAGE 1940	SCHOOL ENROLL- MENT 1941-1942
Maine	3	847,226	40.5	158,061
Maryland	6	1,821,244	59.3	286,974
Massachusetts	14	4,316,721	89.4	656,974
Michigan	17	5,256,106	65.7	914,205
Minnesota	9	2,792,300	49.8	497,026
Mississippi	7	2,183,796	19.8	593,428
Missouri	13	3,784,664	51.8	694,779
Montana	2	559,456	37.8	102,906
Nebraska	4	1,315,834	39.1	257,194
Nevada	1	110,247	39.3	23,993
New Hampshire	2	491,524	57.6	72,515
New Jersey	14	4,160,165	81.6	678,628
New Mexico .'........	2	531,818	33.2	131,347
New York	45	13,479,142	82.8	2,126,193
North Carolina	12	3,571,623	27.3	871,765
North Dakota	2	641,935	20.6	133,203
Ohio	23	6,907,612	66.8	1,164,160
Oklahoma	8	2,336,434	37.6	510,264
Oregon	4	1,089,684	48.8	189,466
Pennsylvania	33	9,900,180	66.5	1,734,842
Rhode Island	2	713,346	91.6	105,946
South Carolina	6	1,899,804	24.5	475,210
South Dakota	2	642,961	24.6	129,680
Tennessee	9	2,915,841	35.2	635,736
Texas	21	6,414,824	45.4	1,303,323
Utah	2	550,310	55.5	134,632
Vermont	1	359,231	34.3	60,511
Virginia	9	2,677,773	35.3	556,377
Washington	6	1,736,191	53.1	343,121
West Virginia	6	1,901,974	28.1	443,337
Wisconsin	10	3,137,587	53.5	493,430
Wyoming	1	250,742	37.3	55,711
United States	435	131,669,275	56.5	24,562,473

STATE STATISTICS (*Continued*)

STATE	ENTERED UNION	AREA SQ. MI.	TERM OF GOVERNOR'S OFFICE YEARS	GOVERNOR'S SALARY
Alabama	1819	51,998	4	$ 6,000
Arizona	1912	113,956	2	7,500
Arkansas	1836	53,335	2	6,000
California	1850	158,297	4	10,000
Colorado	1876	103,948	2	5,000
Connecticut	1788	4,965	2	12,000
Delaware	1787	2,370	4	7,500
Dist. of Columbia	....	70	.	......
Florida	1845	58,666	4	7,500
Georgia	1788	59,265	2	7,500
Idaho	1890	83,888	2	5,000
Illinois	1818	56,665	4	12,000
Indiana	1816	36,354	4	8,000
Iowa	1846	56,147	2	7,500
Kansas	1861	82,158	2	5,000
Kentucky	1792	40,598	4	10,000
Louisiana	1812	48,506	4	12,000
Maine	1820	33,040	2	5,000
Maryland	1788	12,327	4	4,500
Massachusetts	1788	8,266	2	10,000
Michigan	1837	57,980	2	5,000
Minnesota	1858	84,682	2	7,000
Mississippi	1817	46,865	4	7,500
Missouri	1821	69,420	4	5,000
Montana	1889	146,997	4	7,500
Nebraska	1867	77,520	2	7,500
Nevada	1864	110,690	4	7,000
New Hampshire	1788	9,341	2	5,000
New Jersey	1787	8,224	3	20,000
New Mexico	1912	122,634	2	5,000
New York	1788	49,204	4	25,000
North Carolina	1789	52,426	4	10,500
North Dakota	1889	70,837	2	4,000
Ohio	1803	41,040	2	10,000
Oklahoma	1907	70,057	4	6,500
Oregon	1859	96,699	4	7,500

STATE STATISTICS (*Continued*)

STATE	ENTERED UNION	AREA SQ. MI.	TERM OF GOVERNOR'S OFFICE YEARS	GOVERNOR'S SALARY
Pennsylvania	1787	45,126	4	$18,000
Rhode Island	1790	1,248	2	8,000
South Carolina	1788	30,989	4	7,500
South Dakota	1889	77,615	2	3,000
Tennessee	1796	42,022	2	4,000
Texas	1845	265,896	2	12,000
Utah	1896	84,990	4	6,000
Vermont	1791	9,564	2	5,000
Virginia	1788	42,627	4	10,000
Washington	1889	69,127	4	6,000
West Virginia	1863	24,170	4	10,000
Wisconsin	1848	56,066	2	6,000
Wyoming	1890	97,914	4	8,000

The number of Electoral Votes for each state equals the sum of the number of its Representatives and the number of its Senators; or, in each case, 2 more than the number of Representatives listed above. A majority of Electoral Votes is necessary for a Presidential election.

STATE QUALIFICATIONS FOR VOTING

STATES AND REQUIRE-MENTS FOR VOTERS (Other than Citizenship)	PREVIOUS RESIDENCE REQUIRED				PERSONS EXCLUDED (Other than felons, idiots, and the insane)
	State	County	City	Precinct	
ALABAMA–Good character and understanding; poll tax receipt; registration.	2 y	1 y	3 m	3 m	Traitors; embezzlers of public funds; those guilty of corrupt election practices.
ARIZONA–Registration.	1 y	30 d	30 d	30 d	Those under guardianship; those convicted of treason.
ARKANSAS – Good understanding; poll tax receipt.	1 y	6 m	30 d	30 d	Convicts, until pardoned.
CALIFORNIA–Naturalization for 90 days, or treaty of Queretaro; registration.	1 y	90 d	......	40 d	Bribers; Chinese; malfeasants.
COLORADO – Registration.	1 y	90 d	30 d	10 d	Those under guardianship; those convicted of an infamous crime, unless pardoned or having served term.
CONNECTICUT–Good character; ability to read English; registration.	1 y	......	6 m	......	Those convicted of felony or other infamous crime, unless pardoned; inmates of state institutions.
DELAWARE–Registration; ability to read Constitution in English, and to write name.	1 y	3 m	......	30 d	Paupers.

STATE QUALIFICATIONS FOR VOTING (*Continued*)

STATES AND REQUIREMENTS FOR VOTERS (Other than Citizenship)	PREVIOUS RESIDENCE REQUIRED				PERSONS EXCLUDED (Other than felons, idiots, and the insane)
	State	County	City	Precinct	
FLORIDA–Registration.	1 y	6 m	......	30 d	....
GEORGIA–Registration; payment of poll tax.	1 y	6 m	......	......	....
IDAHO–Registration...	6 m	30 d	......	......	Those under guardianship; those convicted of treason or embezzling public funds; those guilty of corrupt election practices, unless pardoned.
ILLINOIS–Registration.	1 y	90 d	......	30 d	Convicts, unless pardoned.
INDIANA............	6 m	60 d*	......	30 d	Persons disqualified by judgment of a court; U. S. soldiers, marines, and sailors.
IOWA–Registration....	6 m	60 d	......	10 d	....
KANSAS–Registration in cities of first and second class.	6 m	......	30 d	30 d	Bribers; those under guardianship; dishonorably discharged U. S. officials; defrauders of the government; those who have borne arms against the government.
KENTUCKY–Registration.	1 y	6 m	......	60 d	Traitors; bribers.

*Township.

STATE QUALIFICATIONS FOR VOTING (*Continued*)

States and Requirements for Voters (Other than Citizenship)	Previous Residence Required				Persons Excluded (Other than felons, idiots, and the insane)
	State	County	City	Precinct	
LOUISIANA – Good character; ability to understand the Constitution; registration.	2 y	1 y	......	3 m	....
MAINE–Registration; ability to read constitution of state in English.	6 m	6 m	6 m	......	Paupers; persons under guardianship; Indians not taxed.
MARYLAND–Ability to read; registration.	1 y	6 m	6 m	......	Those convicted of larceny or other infamous crime, unless pardoned; those guilty of corrupt election practices; those under guardianship.
MASSACHUSETTS – Ability to read and write English; registration.	1 y	......	6 m	......	Those under guardianship; paupers (except U. S. soldiers); those guilty of corrupt election practices.
MICHIGAN–Registration.	6 m	20 d*	20 d	......	....
MINNESOTA–Registration in first, second, and third class cities; citizenship for three months.	6 m	30 d	30 d	30 d	Traitors unless restored to civil rights; those under guardianship.
MISSISSIPPI–Ability to read or understand the state constitution; registration.	2 y	1 y	1 y	1 y	Delinquent taxpayers.

*Township.

STATE QUALIFICATIONS FOR VOTING (*Continued*)

STATES AND REQUIREMENTS FOR VOTERS (Other than Citizenship)	PREVIOUS RESIDENCE REQUIRED				PERSONS EXCLUDED (Other than felons, idiots, and the insane)
	State	County	City	Precinct	
MISSOURI–Registration in counties of 100,000 or more, and cities of 10,000 or more.	1 y	60 d	60 d	......	Paupers; those convicted of felony or other infamous crime or misdemeanor or violating right of suffrage, unless pardoned; disfranchised by second conviction.
MONTANA–Registration.	1 y	30 d	30 d	30 d	....
NEBRASKA–Registration in all cities.	6 m	40 d	10 d	10 d	U. S. soldiers and sailors; traitors, unless pardoned.
NEVADA–Registration.	6 m	30 d	30 d	10 d	Traitors; Chinese and Indians; unamnestied confederates against U. S.
NEW HAMPSHIRE–Registration.	6 m	6 m	6 m	6 m	Paupers (except honorably discharged soldiers); non-taxpayers.
NEW JERSEY – Registration.	1 y	5 m	15-30 d	......	Paupers; convicts unless pardoned.
NEW MEXICO–Registration.	1 y	90 d	......	30 d	Indians not taxed.

STATE QUALIFICATIONS FOR VOTING (*Continued*)

STATES AND REQUIREMENTS FOR VOTERS (Other than Citizenship)	PREVIOUS RESIDENCE REQUIRED				PERSONS EXCLUDED (Other than felons, idiots, and the insane)
	State	County	City	Precinct	
NEW YORK–Citizenship 90 days; if acquired by marriage must be resident of U. S. for 5 years plus 90 days; ability to read and write English if never having voted before January 1, 1922; registration.	1 y	4 m	......	30 d	Those convicted of bribery or any infamous crime, unless pardoned; bettors on elections; those guilty of corrupt election practices.
NORTH CAROLINA–Ability to read; registration.	1 y	......	......	4 m	Those convicted of infamous crime; atheists.
NORTH DAKOTA –Registration in some cities.	1 y	90 d	......	30 d	Convicts, unless pardoned.
OHIO–Registration.....	1 y	30 d	20 d	20 d	U. S. soldiers and sailors.
OKLAHOMA.........	1 y	6 m	......	30 d	Paupers (except ex-soldiers and sailors).
OREGON–Registration 30 days before election; ability to read and write English; in drainage and irrigation districts must own land.	6 m	......	......	......	Non-resident U. S. soldiers and sailors.
PENNSYLVANIA–Citizenship for at least 1 mo.; registration; residence only 6 mo. if native.	1 y	......	......	2 m	Those guilty of corrupt election practices cannot vote for 4 years.

STATE QUALIFICATIONS FOR VOTING (*Continued*)

STATES AND REQUIRE-MENTS FOR VOTERS (Other than Citizenship)	PREVIOUS RESIDENCE REQUIRED				PERSONS EXCLUDED (Other than felons, idiots, and the insane)
	State	County	City	Precinct	
RHODE ISLAND– Registration for taxpayers once; non-taxpayers biennially.	2 y	......	6 m	6 m	Bribers; paupers; persons under guardianship; Narragansett Indians; persons living on land ceded to the United States.
SOUTH CAROLINA – Ability to read; registration.	2 y	1 y	4 m	4 m	Those convicted of treason, dueling, or other infamous crime; paupers.
SOUTH DAKOTA....	1 y	90 d	......	30 d	Those under guardianship; traitors, unless pardoned.
TENNESSEE–Poll tax receipt; registration in all counties of 50,000 or more and cities of 2,500 or more.	1 y	6 m	......	60 d	Those convicted of bribery or other infamous crime.
TEXAS–Registration by means of payment of poll tax.	1 y	6 m	6 m	6 m	Paupers; U. S. soldiers and sailors.
UTAH–Citizenship for 90 days; registration.	1 y	4 m	......	60 d	Those convicted of treason or crime against election law unless restored to civil right.
VERMONT–Registration; freeman's oath.	1 y	3 m	3 m	3m*	Convicts unless pardoned; those guilty of corrupt election practices.

*Town.

STATE QUALIFICATIONS FOR VOTING *(Continued)*

STATES AND REQUIREMENTS FOR VOTERS (Other than Citizenship)	PREVIOUS RESIDENCE REQUIRED				PERSONS EXCLUDED (Other than felons, idiots, and the insane)
	State	County	City	Precinct	
VIRGINIA–Payment of poll tax three years; registration; passing of literacy test.	1 y	6 m	6 m	30 d	Convicts unless pardoned; paupers, traitors; embezzlers, duelists and their abettors.
WASHINGTON–Ability to read and speak English.	1 y	90 d	30 d	30 d	Indians not taxed.
WEST VIRGINIA – Registration.	1 y	60 d	60 d	......	Paupers; bribers; traitors; U. S. soldiers and sailors.
WISCONSIN–Registration in cities of 5,000 population or over.	1 y	10 d	10 d	10 d	Those under guardianship; convicts, unless pardoned.
WYOMING–Registration.	1 y	60 d	10 d	10 d	Those unable to read state constitution.

EXPLANATION OF TERMS

Administrative Departments. The departments which carry on the actual work of the government in accordance with the law.

Allegiance. The tie of obligation or devotion to one's government.

Amendment. A change made in a law or constitution.

Anesthetic. A drug used for removing the feeling of pain.

Appellate Jurisdiction. The legal right of a court to hear a case appealed from a lower court.

Assessment. An official valuation of property for the purpose of taxation.

Auditor. An official who examines the public accounts.

Bill of Attainder. A legislative act which inflicts punishment without a judicial trial.

Bill of Rights. (1) A "charter of English liberty" which William the Third agreed to when he became King in 1689. (2) A summary of the rights and privileges guaranteed to the people of the United States by the Constitution, found in the first ten amendments and in a few sections of Article I.

Bond Issue. An interest-bearing certificate authorized by a public or private body for the purpose of borrowing money.

Borough. A form of municipal corporation, used in several states, corresponding to the incorporated town or village.

Boycott. An agreement to prevent dealings with a group opposed to your interests.

Bubonic Plague. A dangerous disease which is accompanied by fever and chills, and which is spread by rats.

Buddhism. The religion of the Hindu prince Buddha, of the fifth century before Christ.

Budget. An estimate of receipts and expenditures made before money has been spent.

Caucus. A meeting of the leaders of a political party or faction to decide on their policies or on their candidates for office.

Cerebral Hemorrhage. The bursting of a blood vessel in the brain.

Charter. A written document granted by a final authority which gives certain rights and privileges to a people, city, or colony.

City Commission. A form of government usually consisting of three to seven commissioners who are elected by the people of the city and who divide the work of governing among their members.

City Council. The legislative body of a city which passes the laws (usually called ordinances) for the government of the city.

City Manager. A person hired by the city council, to conduct the business of the city.

Civil Case. A case tried in court as the result of a dispute concerning property rights. The decision does not concern the guilt or innocence, but merely the obligations of the disagreeing parties. The parties are known as the plaintiff and the defendant.

Civil Service. Appointment to public office; the groups of public office holders appointed by competitive examination.

Code. A body of laws, compiled and arranged to form a system of laws.

Collective Bargaining. The system under which the officers of a labor organization carry on negotiations with the employer for improved working conditions.

Commission. Group of experts organized to study or control specific activities of the government.

Common Law. The body of decisions handed down by the courts. Common law is used in arriving at a decision when there is no regularly enacted law covering the case.

Confucianism. The moral system of Confucius, a Chinese philosopher of the fifth century before Christ.

Congressional District. A section within a state from which a representative to Congress is elected.

Constitution. Fundamental law or laws of government. The laws passed by the legislative body must not disagree with the constitution or fundamental law.

Contagious Disease. Any disease which may be transmitted from one person to another by contact, either direct or indirect.

Coroner. An official who inquires into accidental deaths.

Council-Manager Type of Government. Form of city government in which a few elective officers exercise all legislative powers. The manager corresponds to the general manager of a business firm.

Court of Record. A court in which all testimony of witnesses, motions of attorneys, and rulings of the judge are taken in shorthand, and later written out and kept as a record of the procedure of the court.

Criminal Case. A case tried in court in which the violation of a law is asserted. The party accused is called the defendant and if the violation of law is proven, he is said to be guilty.

Customs. Taxes collected upon the goods brought into this country.

Declaration of Intention. A solemn statement made in writing before a court, declaring one's intention to become a citizen of the country.

Democracy. A system of government in which the final power rests with the people as a whole, and is exercised by the people directly through votes, by their elected agents, or by the appointees of the elected agents.

Dictator. One who is given, or who takes, absolute authority to rule a country.

Direct Primary. A system of nominating candidates for office by direct vote of the members of a political party instead of by a delegate convention.

Direct Taxes. Taxes paid by the person owning the property upon which they are levied, such as a tax on land.

District or Circuit Court. A court which is held at various places in a district.

Division of Powers. The division of governmental powers, which are not prohibited by the Constitution, between the national government and the state government. Also the division of the national or state government into legislative, executive, and judicial powers.

Dockets. Records containing lists of cases to be tried.

Electoral College. A term applied to the entire body of presidential electors. This entire body never meets but the electors of each state meet at the state capital and cast their vote, and the results are sent to Washington, where the votes are counted and the results announced.

Epidemic. A disease that affects many in a community at the same time.

Excise. A duty or indirect tax levied upon certain specified articles grown or manufactured within the United States.

Ex Officio. A phrase meaning because of office. An *ex officio* member of a governing board is one who holds his position because he occupies a related office.

Ex Post Facto Law. A law providing punishment for acts committed before the law existed.

Federal Courts. The courts of the judicial system of the United States — the Supreme Court, Circuit Courts, and District Courts.

Federal Government. A government in which the powers are assigned by a number of member governments, such as the government at Washington.

Fees. Compulsory payments which cover the cost or a part of the cost of an official act which benefits the person making the payment.

Felony. A serious crime punishable by death or imprisonment in the penitentiary, such as murder, burglary, and forgery.

Franchise. An agreement between an individual or corporation and a government (usually city or state) by which the person or company agrees to render public service to the citizens of the government in return for certain rights which the government gives; also the right of a citizen to vote.

Freedom of Assembly. The constitutional right which citizens have to meet together in an orderly manner in groups of any number for any purpose which is not criminal.

Freedom of Petition. The constitutional right which citizens of the United States have of presenting to governmental officials or others, a written request asking the person or persons addressed to do something.

Freedom of Press. The constitutional right which citizens of the United States have of printing any fact or opinion without fear of interference by governmental authority.

Freedom of Speech. The constitutional right which citizens of the United States have of stating any fact or opinion without fear of interference by governmental authority.

Germicide. A drug that kills germs.

Geological Survey. Systematic examinations of an area for the purpose of determining its rock masses.

Grand Jury. A jury of not less than seven, nor more than twenty-three qualified adults whose duty is to examine charges of crime in secret session and to demand the trial of those persons against whom there is sufficient evidence.

Hinduism. The ancient beliefs of the people of India, based on the caste system.

Illiteracy. Inability to read and write any language. The amount of illiteracy in a country is usually reckoned in the percentage of people over ten years of age not able to read or write.

Impeachment. The process provided by most constitutions for removing from office those officials who have been guilty of a high crime or misdemeanor.

Incinerator. A furnace for burning waste and garbage.

Income Tax. A percentage of one's income paid for the support of the government, state or federal.

Industrial Revolution. The changes brought about by the use of power-driven machinery in manufacturing. These changes came in England between 1775 and 1825.

Inheritance Tax. A special kind of property tax levied upon property at the death of the owner and paid by the heirs receiving the inheritance.

Initiative and Referendum. Initiative—a plan of lawmaking in which it is possible for any person or group of persons to propose laws to be voted upon and adopted or defeated at an election. Referendum—the right to approve or reject a law by popular vote, either when passed by a legislature or proposed by initiative petition.

Injunction. A court decree commanding some one to do or not to do a certain act, or not to cease performing an act. An injunction might compel a power company to continue furnishing electricity for the people of a city, or it might compel it to lower the rate.

Inoculation. The scientific prevention of a severe disease by causing it to occur in a mild form.

Internal Revenue. All the revenue of a country except that collected from import duties.

Jurisdiction. Power to exercise judicial authority in civil or in criminal matters.

Libel. A publication without just cause or excuse, tending to expose another to public contempt or ridicule. It may be in print, writing, picture, or effigy.

Lobbyists. Interested persons who solicit legislators to influence their votes.

Magna Charta. A famous document which enumerated many of the rights of Englishmen, and which was signed by King John at Runnymede in 1215.

Mayor. The principal officer of a municipality; the chief magistrate of a city.

Meningitis. A very severe disease of the membranes of the brain and the spinal chord.

Merit System. The plan of appointing officers because of superior qualifications, allowing them to hold office as long as their work is satisfactory, and recognizing unusual excellence of service if promotions are made.

Misdemeanor. Any crime less than a felony. In the case of misdemeanor, punishment provided by law is less than imprisonment in the penitentiary.

Mohammedanism. The religion of Mohammed, the Arabian prophet of the seventh century.

Naturalization. The act of receiving an alien into the country, and investing him with the rights and privileges of a natural subject or citizen.

Null and Void. A phrase meaning of no legal or binding force.

Original Jurisdiction. Power to hear and decide the first trial of a lawsuit.

Parliament. The English representative body, consisting of the House of Lords and the House of Commons.

Paroled. Released on good behavior.

Party Platform. A declaration of principles and policies made by a political party in a national or state convention.

Passports. Formal documents issued by the federal government to citizens, permitting them to travel abroad.

Patriotism. Love of one's country. The passion which causes a person to serve his country, either in defending it from invasion or in protecting its rights and maintaining its laws and institutions.

Patronage. The control of nomination and political office.

Petit Jury. A jury of six or twelve qualified adults summoned to try a case in court. So called in distinction from the grand jury.

Picketing. The act of persuading labor not to work during a strike.

Pictograph. A chart presenting facts by the use of picture symbols.

Pneumonia. A disease which is characterized by inflammation of the lungs.

Political Party. A voluntary organization of citizens of a government organized for the purpose of promoting certain policies, and nominating and attempting to elect candidates for office who will put the policies of the organization into effect.

Political Rights. The privilege of sharing and having a voice in policies and practices of government.

Poll Tax. A uniform tax of a given amount for each person over a given age, frequently demanded as a qualification for voting.

Preamble. The introductory part of a constitution, which states the reasons for adopting it.

Primaries. Preliminary elections to select candidates for final elections.

Prosecutors. Attorneys who conduct proceedings in a court on behalf of the government.

Protective Tariffs. Duties on imports which protect the development of industries in our own country.

Public Carriers. Railways, street cars, and buses.

Public Utilities. Such undertakings as telephone companies, water systems, and electric power and light systems, whose services the public must have.

Quarantine. A period of time in which a ship entering a port is inspected to prevent the spread of contagious diseases.

Racketeer. One who engages in a dishonest scheme by which innocent victims are forced through fear to pay money or suffer damage to their property or persons.

Raw Materials. Natural products not yet prepared for use.

Recall. The right of voters to remove unsatisfactory officials.

Recorder. An official who keeps the official copy of transactions.

Registration. The listing of all legal voters in a precinct or district by name and residence; required in practically all cities to prevent voters from voting in more than one precinct.

Rehabilitation. The act of restoring to a former condition; training the handicapped for new vocations.

Scientific Research. Careful examination, as in the fields of the various sciences, for seeking facts or principles.

Serums. Blood fluids used for inoculation for the prevention of certain diseases.

Septic Tanks. Tanks in which sewage is kept to decompose.

Shoddy. A cloth of inferior quality.

Slander. A report circulated with malice, tending to injure the reputation of another.

Soil Erosion Labor. Work to prevent the wearing away of soil due to the effect of water or wind.

Sovereign. Supreme power, not subject to any other. A state is called a sovereign state when this supreme power resides within itself, whether it be exercised by a single individual, by a small group, or by the whole people.

Speaker. The chairman of the lower house.

Spoils System. The practice of giving government positions to members of the political party in power, regardless of merit.

Suffrage. The right to vote.

Sureties. Bonds or guaranties for the performance of some act.

Tenement House. A dwelling house found in large cities, divided for the use of many poor families.

Tenure of Office. Security in holding a position.

Toll. The charges made for the public privilege of using canals, roads, or bridges.

Tuberculosis. A disease of the lungs, intestines, bones, or other parts of the body, characterized by small swellings in the tissues.

Unwritten Constitution. The body of customs which have taken definite form and are fundamental in the organization of our government, and yet have not been reduced to formal constitutional law.

Veto Power. The power of the executive to prevent the passing of measures approved by the legislature.

Vocational Education. Education which is intended to give knowledge or skill in some trade or occupation.

Warrants. Orders which authorize the payment of money.

Writ of Habeas Corpus. A court order requiring that a person be brought immediately before a court to learn the reason for his imprisonment or detention.

INDEX

Accidents, prevention of, 57, 130, 131, 140-142, 203, 207.

Addams, Jane, 90, 94.

Administrative organization; national, 346-350, 353-358, 407, 408; state, 327, 328.

Agricultural Adjustment Administration (A. A. A.), 355, 356.

Agriculture, department of, 117.

Aids to Learning, 19, 28, 36, 54, 62, 72, 85, 93, 107, 126, 142, 164, 181, 195, 211, 224, 247, 262, 279, 304, 334, 363, 369.

Air transportation, 188, 194.

Amendments: national, 237, 241, 250, 341, 343, 397-405; state, 310.

American Bar Association, 333.

American Federation of Labor, 207, 208.

American's creed, 265.

Antifederalists, 236, 242.

Antin, Mary, 220, 224, 225.

Antitoxins, 119, 124.

Appellate courts, 331.

Army, 132, 133.

Articles of Confederation, 232-235, 339.

Assessor, 289, 293.

Attorney, district: county, 289; federal, 359; state, 334.

Attorney General: federal, 350; state, 327.

Auditor: county, 289; state, 327.

Australian Ballot, 246, 247.

Ballot, 246, 247, 302, 324.

Banks: explanation of, 200; Federal Reserve, 200, 353, 414; national, 200; regulation of, 210; savings, 49, 201, 209.

Bargaining, collective or group, 208, 210.

Bill: of Attainder, 238, 240; of Rights, 309, 341.

Bills, procedure for, 319-323, 410.

Blind, 121, 166-169.

Board: of Education, 154, 155; of Health, 123-125; of Review, 61.

Bok, Edward, 12, 224, 225.

Bonds, 50, 51, 253, 316.

Books, other interesting, 19, 28, 36, 73, 94, 108, 182, 196, 220, 225, 364.

Boston, city planning, 191.

Boycotts, 208.

Boy Scouts, 34, 35, 160.

Bryce, James, 239.

Buddhism, 87.

Budget: family and personal, 41-43, 72; government, 261, 262, 319, 320, 346, 347; time schedule, 26-28, 37, 44.

Building and loan associations, 50, 51.

Building code, 184, 185.

Bureau of Engraving and Printing, 200, 413, 414.

Business: and government, 208-210, 229, 230; management, 201, 203, 209, 210.

Cabinet, presidential, 242, 349-353.

Camp Fire Girls, 160.

Capital, defined, 203.

Capitol: national, 162; state, 240.

Career, planning a, 37-41, 81-83.

Catholics, 88.

Caucus, 293.

Census, 411.

Character, development of, 21, 30-35, 69, 80, 81, 136, 158, 159.

Charters, 209, 306-308, 340.

438

Pardons, *see* Parole.

Parks: city, 159, 192; national, 162, 415, 416; state, 160-162.

Parole system, 179, 180.

Parties, political: development of, 227, 242, 243; organization and work of, 241-246.

Partnership, defined, 201.

Pasteur, Louis, 121, 122.

Patrols, schoolboy, 56, 57, 130, 131.

Penn, William, 310, 340.

Pensions: government employees, 174; old-age, 173.

Personality, development of, 17, 20-25, 31, 56, 68, 69, 79.

Picketing, 208.

Pilgrims, 213, 214, 282.

Playgrounds, *see* Parks.

Pledge, to the flag, 264, 267, 377.

Police: local, 128-130, 140, 174, 303; national, 132-134; protection, 291; state, 131, 132, 312, 316.

Policemen, 128, 129, 258, 270, 303.

Policewomen, 129.

Political parties, *see* Parties.

Poor, *see* Community Dependents.

Possessions, United States, 341, 343, 406.

Postal Savings, 49.

Post Office, department of, 350, 351.

Preamble to the Constitution, 339, 383.

Precincts, 299.

President: cabinet of, 242, 349-353; as Commander-in-Chief of the Army and Navy, 132; powers and work of, 347-349, 353, 357, 358; salary of, 259, 348.

Primaries, 301, 325.

Prison, 179-181.

Probate court, 332.

Production, defined, 202.

Profits, defined, 203.

Property, 252.

Property tax, 150, 251, 252.

Proprietorship, defined, 201.

Protective tariffs, 209.

Public Health Service, 125, 230.

Public Safety, department of, 140.

Public Works Administration (P. W. A.), 354.

Pupin, Michael, 220, 224, 225.

Pure food laws, 116, 117, 125.

Quarantine, 119, 124, 125, 302.

Radio, 157.

Railroads, regulation of: national, 347; state, 314.

Real estate, 50, 200, 251.

Recall of commissioners, 301.

Reconstruction Finance Corporation (R. F. C.), 355.

Recorder, county, 289.

Recreation, 17, 21, 81, 157-164, 207, 259.

Red Cross, 91.

Referendum, 301, 324.

Religious: education, 89, 90; freedom, 269, 271, 367; influence, 33, 34, 86-90, 92, 93.

Rent, defined, 202.

Representation: in national government, 236, 344, 345; in state government, 319, 320.

Republican party, 244.

Roads, 189, 190, 257, 294, 314-316.

Roosevelt, Franklin D., 356, 407.

Roosevelt, Theodore, 14, 15, 19, 177, 356, 357.

Royal Canadian Mounted Police, 131.

Safety, 56, 57, 140.

Sales tax, 251, 252.

Salvation Army, 218.

Savings: economic efficiency, 40-43, 45, 46, 48, 49; investing wisely, 49-53.

School: boards and management, 154, 155, 293; cost of, 53, 76, 150, 151, 278; development of, 147-150; early American, 90, 282; free education, 144, 147, 151, 152, 156, 313; for the handicapped, 167, 168, 170-